D1394433

The Treatment of Horses by Homoeopathy

by

G. MacLeod

MRCVS, DVSM, Vet FF Hom

Index by Lyn Greenwood

THE C. W. DANIEL CO. LTD.
1 CHURCH PATH,
SAFFRON WALDEN,
ESSEX CB10 1JP, UNITED KINGDOM

2nd impression 1983
3rd impression 1984
4th impression 1986
5th impression 1988
6th impression 1990
7th impression (in paperback format) 1991
Revised edition 1993
9th impression 1995
10th impression 1997

ISBN 0 85207 249 X

Typeset by MS Typesetting, Castle Camps, Cambridge
Printed in Great Britain by
Hillman Printers (Frome) Ltd, Frome, Somerset

Contents

Introduction

In the years which have passed since the first edition of this book was published, new viruses and patterns of disease have appeared which, together with an appreciation of new remedies gained in the treatment of various conditions, suggests that a new edition of the work is overdue.

These questions hopefully have been addressed in some small way in this new edition, and a more complete Materia Medica has also been added. This should provide a background of information in relation to the remedies discussed. Not every remedy which may be applicable to any particular condition is included – only the common ones. For a detailed description of any particular remedy reference should be made to a standard Materia Medica.

WHAT IS HOMOEOPATHY?

For readers who have little or no knowledge of homoeopathic medicine a brief description of its essentials is necessary to the proper understanding of the role of the remedies in treatment.

Homoeopathy is a branch of medicine which states that any substance which can cause symptoms of illness in man or animal can also be used in the treatment of any condition showing similar symptoms. The principle of likeness between disease condition and remedy is emphasised. If we imagine the illness and the provings of the remedy representing two clinical pictures we should endeavour as far as possible when treating to match one picture against the other. The closer the approximation of the two pictures (the likeness) the more likely we are to achieve satisfactory results in treatment. This is much easier to achieve in human than in veterinary medicine as subjective (mental) symptoms known only to the patient are difficult if not impossible to elicit in animals. Mental symptoms are extremely important in the treatment by homoeopathy in the human patient. Observation of an animal's behaviour and how it reacts to any given situation, to other animals or people, to noise, to climatic variations etc. will in some measure compensate for the lack of communication by speech. It is here that the pathological approach to prescribing has a part to play; in other words prescribing a remedy which has an elective affinity to one or other particular organ or body system.

One of our greatest homoeopaths, Dr Compton Burnett, described this concept in the following words – "I understand by an organ remedy not a drug which is topically applied to a suffering organ for its physical or chemical effect but a remedy that has an elective affinity for such organ by reason of which it will find the organ itself through the blood."

NATURE OF HOMOEOPATHIC REMEDIES

Homoeopathic remedies are obtained from all natural sources, e.g. plant and animal kingdoms and also minerals and their compounds. Homoeopathy is frequently referred to as herbal medicine – quite erroneously as the previous remarks will show. While herbal medicine employs many plants successfully it is unable to exploit the intrinsic merits of plants in the way that homoeopathic medicine is able to do, e.g. poisonous plants such as Aconite or Belladonna could not possibly be used as herbal remedies.

PREPARATION OF REMEDIES

Preparation of homoeopathic remedies is a scientific procedure which is best left to a qualified pharmacist trained in the particular techniques. Homoeopathy is too important for remedies to be prepared in any way but the best obtainable. Briefly the system is based on a series of dilutions and successions (of which more later) which is capable of rendering even a poisonous substance safe to use.

To prepare a potentised remedy a measured drop of a solution called mother tincture (Ø) derived from plant or biological material is added to 99 drops of a water/alcohol mixture and the resultant dilution subjected to a mechanical shock which is called succussion. This process which is essential to the preparation imparts energy to the medium which is rendered stable. One drop to 99 parts water/alcohol.

SELECTION OF POTENCIES

Once the simillimum or 'most likely' remedy has been selected the question of which potency to use arises. As a general rule in the author's experience the higher potencies which are more energised than the lower should be employed in acute infections or conditions while the lower should be reserved for chronic conditions with or without pathological changes being present. It will be found occasionally that there are exceptions to this point of view and indeed many practitioners especially on the continent rely mostly on lower potencies for general use.

The potencies mentioned under each remedy in the text covering the various diseases are a guide only. Higher potencies than those mentioned will necessitate professional advice.

ADMINISTRATION OF REMEDIES

Remedies are marketed as medicated tablets and powders and also as tincture and water dilutions. Owners must determine which system is the best for the particular animal being treated. Horses readily accept the remedy in powder form incorporated in a small piece of apple or carrot. When large numbers are involved as in some racing stables a useful method is to dissolve the remedy in sterile water and empty it under the lips by means of a small syringe. It is also legitimate to add the remedy to bran mash but it is preferable to administer the remedy as above.

CARE OF REMEDIES

The delicate nature of the remedies which is inherent in the preparation renders them subject to contamination by strong-smelling substances, e.g. camphor, disinfectants etc. and also by strong sunlight. It is essential therefore that they be kept away from such influences and stored in a cool dry place away from strong light. The use of amber glass bottles is helpful in this connection for storage of tablets.

NOSODES AND ORAL VACCINES

It will be noticed in the text under treatment of various specific conditions that reference is made to the term nosode, and it is necessary to explain fully to what this term refers.

A nosode (from the Greek NOSOS meaning disease) is a disease product obtained from any part of the system in a case of illness and thereafter potentised e.g. equine flu nosode prepared from respiratory secretions of affected horses. In specific, i.e. bacterial, viral and protozoal disease the causative organism may or may not be present in the material and the efficacy of the nosode in no way depends on the organism being present. The response of the tissues to invasion by bacteria or viruses results in the formation of substances which are in effect the basis of the nosode.

An oral vaccine is prepared from the actual organism which causes a disease and may derive from filtrates containing only the exotoxins of the bacteria or from emulsions containing both bacteria and their toxins. These filtrates and emulsions are then potentised and become oral vaccines.

There are two different ways of employing nosodes and oral vaccines.

1. Therapeutically and 2. Prophylactically

When we employ nosodes therapeutically we may use them for the condition from which the nosode was derived, e.g. cat flu nosode in the treatment of a viral rhinotracheitis. This may be termed isopathic, i.e. treatment with a substance taken from an animal suffering from the same disease: or we may employ the nosode in any condition, the symptoms of which resemble the symptom-complex of the particular nosode e.g. the use of the nosode *Psorinum* in the treatment of the particular form of skin disease which appears in the provings of that nosode. This method may be termed homoeopathic, i.e. treatment with a substance taken from an animal suffering from a similar disease. In this connection it must be remembered that many nosodes have been proved in their own right, i.e. each has its own particular drug picture. Many veterinary nosodes have been developed but no provings exist for them and they are used almost entirely in the treatment or prevention of the associated diseases.

Autonosodes. This particular type of nosode is prepared from material provided by the patient alone, e.g. pus from a chronic sinus or fistula and after potentisation used for the treatment of the same patient. Many examples of this could be quoted but I think it is sufficient to explain the theory. Autonosodes are usually employed in refractory cases where well indicated remedies have failed to produce the desired response and frequently they produce striking results.

Oral Vaccines. As with nosodes, oral vaccines may be used both therapeutically and prophylactically. If the condition is caused wholly by bacterial or viral invasion the use of the oral vaccine is frequently attended by spectacular success but this is less likely when there is an underlying chronic condition complicating an acute infection. Here we may need the help of constitutional and other remedies.

Bowel Nosodes. The bowel nosodes are usually included under the heading of oral vaccines as the potentised vaccines are prepared from cultures of the organisms themselves. As a preliminary introduction to the study of the bowel nosodes let us consider the role of the E. coli organism. In the normal healthy animal the function of the E. coli bacteria is beneficial rendering complex materials resulting from the digestive process into simpler substances. If however, the patient is subjected to any change, e.g. stress, which affects the intestinal mucosa, the balance between normal health and illness will be upset and the E. coli organisms may then be said to have become pathogenic. This change in the patient need not be a detrimental one, as the administration of potentised homoeopathic remedies can bring it about. The illness therefore may originate in the patient which causes the bacterial to change their behaviour.

In laboratory tests it has been noticed that from a patient who had previously yielded only E. coli there suddenly appeared a large percentage of non-lactose fermenting bacilli of a type associated with the pathogenic group of typhoid and paratyphoid disease. Since the non-lactose fermenting bacilli had appeared after a latent period of 10–14 days following the administration of the remedy it would seem that the homoeopathic potentised remedy had changed the bowel flora. The pathogenic germ in this case was the result of vital stimulation set up in the patient by the potentised remedy; the germ was not the *cause* of any change. Each germ or bacillus is associated with its own peculiar symptom-picture and certain conclusions may be made from clinical and laboratory observation. These may be summarised as follows:

a) The specific organism is related to the disease.
b) The specific organism is related to the homoeopathic remedy.
c) The homoeopathic remedy is related to the disease.

The bowel nosodes which concern us in veterinary practice are as follows: 1. Morgan-Bach; 2. Proteus-Bach; 3. Gaertner-Bach; 4. Dys Co-Bach; 5. Sycotic Co-Paterson.

Morgan-Bach. Clinical observations have revealed the symptom-picture of the bacillus Morgan to cover in general digestive and respiratory systems with an action also on fibrous tissues and skin.

Proteus-Bach. The central and peripheral nervous systems figure prominently in the provings of this nosode, e.g. convulsions and seizures together with spasm of the peripheral circulation: cramping of the muscles is a common feature; angio-neurotic oedema frequently occurs and there is marked sensitivity to ultra-violet light. Associated remedies are Cuprum Metallicum, and Natrium Muriaticum.

Gaertner-Bach. Marked emaciation or malnutrition is associated with this nosode. Chronic gastro-enteritis occurs and there is a tendency for the animal to become infested with worms. There is an inability to digest fat. Associated remedies are Mercurius, Phosphorus and Silicea.

Sycotic Co-Paterson. The keynote of this nosode is sub-acute or chronic inflammation of mucous membranes especially those of the intestinal tract where a chronic catarrhal enteritis occurs. Chronic bronchitis and nasal catarrh are met with.

Associated remedies are Mercurius Corrosivus, Nitricum Acidum and Hydrastis.

MAIN INDICATIONS FOR THE USE OF THE BOWEL NOSODES

When a case is presented showing one or two leading symptoms which suggest a particular remedy, we should employ that remedy, if necessary in varying potencies, before abandoning it and resorting to another if unsatisfactory results ensue. In chronic disease there may be conflicting symptoms which suggest several competing remedies and it is here that the bowel nosodes may be used with advantage. A study of the associated remedies will usually lead us to the particular nosode to be employed. The question of potency and repetition of dosage assumes special importance when considering the use of bowel nosodes. The mental and emotional symptoms which are frequently present in illness in the human being are not available to a veterinary surgeon and he therefore concerns himself with objective signs and pathological change. The low to medium potencies, e.g. 6c.–30c. are more suitable for this purpose than the higher ones and can be safely administered daily for a few days. Bowel nosodes are deep-acting remedies and should not be repeated until a few months have elapsed since the first prescription.

I acknowledge the pamphlet written by the late Dr John Paterson.

I General Pathological Conditions

1. Inflammation. This is the process by which nature brings about healing of any damaged part, and can result from mechanical or bacterial cause, the latter being the more serious.

SYMPTOMS
There are four cardinal signs generally described as heat, swelling, redness and pain. The third, of course, is seldom recognisable in the horse. Swelling varies according to the location of the inflammation, e.g. it is more obvious in tissues which are plentifully supplied with blood. Pain is dependent on the amount of damage to nerve endings. A chronic form of inflammation can arise as a result of repeated irritation of a part and in this case the four signs mentioned above will be absent. Chronic inflammation leads to the formation of fibrous tissue during the healing process. The inflammatory process may resolve under treatment, but if neglected can lead to septic involvement or possibly death of tissue.

TREATMENT
Aconitum napellus 6c In all cases, give early. Dose: two hourly for four doses.
Belladonna 1M Pronounced heat, with smooth skin, possibly dilated pupils and full pulse. Dose: two hourly for four doses.
Ferrum phosphoricum 6x Local inflammation of vascular parts leading to congestion. Dose: three hourly for three doses.
Cantharis 6c Blistery or vesicular inflammation where the guiding symptom is excessive pain and burning heat, sometimes associated with strangury. Dose: two hourly for four doses.
Rhus toxicodendron 1M Vesicular type inflammatory rash leading to severe pruritis. Dose: once daily for seven days.

Arnica 30c   Superficial inflammation resulting from injury. Dose: two doses two hours apart.

Silicea 200c   In chronic inflammation, this remedy will help reabsorb fibrous tissue. Dose: once daily for seven days.

Hepar sulphuris 200c   In neglected cases, suppuration may occur. Dose: night and morning for four days.

Note:– Specific inflammations are considered in their appropriate chapters.

2. Abscesses. An abscess arises when the skin is broken, allowing entrance to the wound of pyogenic bacteria. Abscesses also occur as a result of generalised pyaemic states. They may be either hot (acute) or cold, and yield pus of varying character according to the type of infection. In slow forming abscesses it is not uncommon for the pus to become insipissated when it appears as a cheese-like mass.

SYMPTOMS

Acute inflammation accompanies the formation of a superficial abscess and appears as a rounded firm swelling which becomes more tense as the condition progresses and the abscess matures. Systemic symptoms are uncommon in this type. Deep abscesses involve subcutaneous and deeper tissues and may be accompanied by febrile disturbances such as rapid pulse and shallow respiration. This type of abscess occurs in the course of pyogenic infections such as joint-ill, brucellosis, etc.

TREATMENT

Hepar sulphuris 30c   Acute abscesses, when area is sensitive to touch and pain severe. Dose: two hourly for four doses.

Mercurius corrosivus 200c   Abscess yields greenish pus streaked with blood. Necrotic ulcers remaining after abscess has ruptured. Dose: three times daily for two days.

Kali bichromicum 30c   Yellowish stringy pus, difficult to expel. Dose: three times daily for three days.

Silicea 200c   Chronic or cold abscess, pus thin and creamy. Dose: once daily for seven days.

Sulphur iodatum 6c   Multiple small abscesses in various parts. Dose: night and morning for five days.

Anthracinum 30c Abscess surrounded by hard ring and bluish-black discolouration of the adjacent skin. Dose: once daily for four days.

Tarentula cubensis 30c General septic state leading to burning abscesses with a purplish colour, with threatened death of tissue. Dose: two hourly for four doses.

Externally, once the abscess has opened, an application once or twice daily of combined *Calendula* and *Hypericum* lotion will assist healing.

Note:– Nosodes such as *Streptococcus*, *Staphylococcus* and *Brucella abortus* will be useful, subject to the identification of the organism concerned.

3. Ulcers. The term ulcer implies a wound which involves any destruction of tissue, superficial or deep, and shows little tendency to heal. Ulceration may arise as a result of the presence in the wound of dead tissue resulting from deprivation of nerve supply. Weakness of blood supply may also contribute to the formation of an ulcer, which may be seen in the course of many specific diseases.

SYMPTOMS

The ulcer usually takes the form of a rounded area, either superficial or deep and may be raised above the level of the surrounding skin or level with it. There is usually an accompanying discharge which is at first serous but soon becomes purulent as a result of secondary infection.

TREATMENT

Mercurius sol. 30c Main ulcer is surrounded by small pimples. Ulcer yields a blood-streaked greenish pus and is usually irregular in shape rather than rounded. Dose: three times daily for four days.

Calcarea sulphurica 6c Ulcer has yellowish crust, discharging creamy pus. Dose: three times daily for four days.

Anthracinum 30c Severe burning heat round ulcer. Skin blackish and hard. Discharge of foul material. Dose: once daily for four days.

Echinacea 3x Tends to return after healing. Associated lymphatic glands enlarged. Dose: three times daily for three days.

Fluoric acid 6c Ulcers with red edges surrounded by vesicles. Pruritis is common. Strong-smelling perspiration. Dose: three times daily for four days.

Lachesis 30c Ulcers associated with a purplish or bluish discolouration of skin. Ulceration round veins. Dose: three hourly for four doses.

Nitric acid 200c Superficial ulcers which blood easily. Sensitive and have indefinite edges. Dose: once daily for one week.

Hepar sulphuris 200c Excessive sensitivity to touch. Foul-smelling pus and in acute cases may contain blood. Older ulcers slow to heal and are accompanied by severe pruritis. Dose: two hourly for four doses.

Silicea 200c Chronic ulcer showing tendency to burrow deeply and form fistulae. Dose: once daily for seven days.

Externally, a lotion of *Calendula* will aid materially in the healing process.

4. Sinus and Fistula. The term sinus implies an indolent tract of tissue which discharges purulent material. Fistula implies a tract which opens on the surface of the skin from a deeper tissue. The two names, however, have become almost synonymous. A sinus or blind fistula arises as a result of a deep wound or abscess discharging its material on the surface of the skin. Necrotic tissue deep in the wound can contribute to it, along with poor drainage from the deeper tissues. Sinuses and fistulae may be associated with specific conditions such as Poll Evil, Fistulous Withers and other diseases.

SYMPTOMS

The opening of the fistula or sinus varies in size and the surrounding tissues may show granulations or fibrosis according to the age of the lesion. Secondary fistulae may appear and connect with the main one. The purulent discharge may heal and then break out again once new deep-seated abscesses mature. The pus which is discharged may be blood-stained and is invariably foul-smelling.

TREATMENT

Hepar sulphuris 200c Inflammatory symptoms accompany sinus. Tissues extremely sensitive to touch. Dose: two hourly for four doses.

Mercurius sol. 30c Sinus discharges greenish thin pus streaked with blood. Surrounding tissues show small pimples or vesicles. Dose: three times daily for three days.

Kali bichromicum 30c Pus is tough and stringy, yellow, expressed with difficulty. Dose: three times daily for four days.

Silicea 200c Chronic involvement, pus thin and greyish, fibrous tissue forming. Dose: once daily for seven days. Useful in recurrent outbreaks. Dose: night and morning for seven days.

Calcarea fluorica 30c Sinus opening surrounded by hard elevated edges, with swelling of skin. Pus is thick and yellow. Dose: night and morning for seven days.

Externally the sinus tract should be irrigated with a solution of *Calendula* and *Hypericum*.

5. Wounds. Wounds may be open or external, or closed or internal. Open wounds are usually due to some form of external damage and take the form of incised, contused, lacerated or punctured.

SYMPTOMS
Primary signs include pain and possible haemorrhage, while secondary involvement shows in the form of repair, which may take various forms, including suppuration. There may be febrile involvement if the wound is extensive or is deep and punctured.

TREATMENT
Arnica 30c Give always as a routine remedy, especially in contused wounds. Dose: two doses two hours apart.

Hypericum 1M Lacerated wounds where nerve endings have been damaged and pain is obvious. Dose: two hourly for four doses.

Ledum 6c Deep punctured wounds. Surrounding skin cold and bluish. Dose: two hourly for four doses.

Calendula 6c This remedy will assist healing of tissues. Dose: three times daily for one day.

Externally a lotion made up of equal parts of *Calendula* and *Hypericum* will be of great assistance in promoting healing.

Note:– The combination of *Ledum* and *Hypericum* internally will be helpful in the prevention of tetanus and should always be given when a wound is likely to become infected.

6. Burns and Scalds. Various lesions result from burns, depending on the area of the skin involved and the depth of penetration. Burns which affect a large area are more serious than smaller deep burns.

TREATMENT

Aconitum napellus 6c The use of this remedy will obviate the effects of shock and will allay fear. Dose: every two hours for four doses.

Arnica 30c A useful routine remedy which should be given as soon as possible. Dose: two doses two hours apart.

Cantharis 6c Blisters, severe pain, skin hot and swollen. Dose: two hourly for four doses.

Urtica urens 6c   Mild burns showing watery blisters with tendency to itch. Dose: three hourly for four doses.

Apis 6c Oedema of subcutaneous tissues remaining after initial symptoms have subsides. Dose: two hourly for four doses.

Externally the application of a burn ointment containing *Cantharis*, *Urtica urens* and *Apis* will be most helpful. A compress of *Calendula* lotion will also be of considerable value.

II Affections of the Eye

1. Contusion of the Eyeball. This may arise from any blow inflicted by a blunt object.

SYMPTOMS
Small purpura-like haemorrhages are seen underneath the conjunctiva. Larger extravasations of blood accumulate in the anterior chamber of the eye. Severe injury may result in rupture of the sclera or cornea.

TREATMENT
Arnica 30c This should be given as soon as possible after occurrence of the injury. Dose: two doses three hours apart.
Hypericum 1M Intense pain associated with injury to nerves and soft structures. Dose: three times daily for two days.
Externally a lotion made up of *Calendula* and *Hypericum* will be of benefit, aiding the action of internal remedies. The dilution should be one in ten, and applied two or three times daily until improvements set in.

2. Open Wounds of the Eyeball. Such wounds, caused by any sharp pointed instrument may be either penetrating or non-penetrating. The former involve the iris and other surfaces as deep as the retina, while the latter involve the outer parts such as cornea and conjunctiva.

TREATMENT
A lotion made of *Calendula*, *Arnica* and *Hypericum* should be used to irrigate the eye two or three times daily. Use ten drops to a half-pint of warm water. Internally, the following remedies should be considered:–

Arnica 30c This remedy should always be given in an injury to combat shock and hasten recovery. Dose: one dose three hourly for two doses should suffice.

Hypericum 1M Pain caused by laceration of and injury to nerves and also helps to control haemorrhage. Dose: one dose two hourly for four doses.

Ledum 6c Penetrating, deep wounds. It can profitably be combined with *Hypericum* to relieve pain and prevent complications. Dose: one dose two hourly for four doses.

Hepar sulphuris 6c In this low potency, the remedy will help promote healing and discharge of pus, if secondary infection leads to purulent involvement. Dose: one dose three hourly for four doses.

3. Conjunctivitis. This term implies inflammation of the conjunctiva, the membrane covering the eye or the under-surface of the eyelid. It may arise from injuries or irritation from some extraneous matter.

SYMPTOMS

The eyelids become swollen and lachrymation occurs. Photophobia is intense and the eyelids remain closed in severe cases. Dullness of the cornea is evident. Acute cases are accompanied by febrile symptoms such as rapid pulse and respiration. Muco-purulent material gathers in the corners of the eye as the condition progresses. The cornea shows increased vascularity.

TREATMENT

Aconitum napellus 6c Early stages showing febrile symptoms. Dose: every hour for four doses.

Belladonna 1M Animal excitable showing rapid pulse and dilated pupils. The skin is hot and shiny, patchy sweating occurs. Dose: two hourly for four doses.

Euphrasia 6c Profuse lachrymation and photophobia. Dose: three times daily for two days.

Mercurius sol 30c Discharge becomes purulent and has greenish tinge. Salivation and slimy diarrhoea may be present. Dose: three times daily for two days.

Nux vomica 6c Digestive upsets accompany condition. Dose: three times daily for two days.

Arnica 30c   When condition has its origin in any form of injury. Dose: two doses, three hours apart.

Hypericum 1M   Signs of intense pain. Conjunctival blood-vessels become congested and prominent. Dose: two hourly for four doses.

Externally, a lotion of *Hypericum* and *Calendula* will be found beneficial in relieving pain and clearing the eye of discharge. It quickly promotes healing when used in a strength of one in ten.

4.   Keratitis – Inflammation of the Cornea.   This condition is commonly associated with conjunctivitis and has the same basic etiology. There are various forms recognised – suppurative and spotted. In the vascular form small blood vessels are prominent, while the suppurative form results in the formation of ulcers or abscesses in the cornea. The spotted form is more commonly associated with a simple corneal opacity.

SYMPTOMS

Pain is a constant feature, associated with lachrymation, closure of eyelids and photophobia. Blood vessels are prominent in the vascular form extending inwards from the conjunctiva.

TREATMENT

Aurum metallicum 30c   Vascular keratitis, along with extreme aversion to light. Dose: night and morning for one week.

Kali bichromicum 6c   Ulceration occurs, leading to a ropy, stringy yellow discharge. Signs of pain are slight. Dose: night and morning for five days.

Conium 30c   Corneal ulceration with signs of pain. Associated paralysis of ocular muscles. Dose: night and morning for one week.

Silicea 200c   Neglected cases. This remedy will heal ulceration and help to absorb scar tissue. It will also help to clear any remaining opacity. Dose: once daily for one week.

5.   Corneal Opacity.   This is a frequent accompaniment to keratitis. It may also arise as a sequel to ophthalmia or from injury of various kinds.

SYMPTOMS

There is a general haziness of the cornea, or it may assume a mottled appearance due to irregular distribution or opaque material. When injury is the cause the resulting opacity is sharply defined and intensely white.

TREATMENT

Silicea 200c   Helps to promote absorption of opaque material. Dose: one dose per week for four weeks.

Arnica 30c   Condition resulting from injury. Dose: one dose per day for three days.

Calcarea carbonica 200c   Accompanying ulceration and a mottled cornea. Dose: once daily for one week.

Calcarea fluorica 30c   Accompanying conjunctivitis and involvement of corneal blood vessels, making the cornea reddish and muddy. Dose: night and morning for one week.

Causticum 30c Accompanying blepharitis and tendency to cataract. Dose: night and morning for one week.

Cannabis sativa 6c   Respiratory distress, with strangury. Mucus and pus in urine. Dose: three times daily for three days.

Externally the daily application of *Cineraria* lotion will be extremely helpful.

6. Iritis.   Inflammation of the iris may affect the choroid and ciliary body. It is usually the result of toxins circulating in the blood as a result of bacterial disease, e.g. influenza. It is also a common sequel to periodic ophthalmia.

SYMPTOMS

Discolouration of the iris is a prominent sign, the structure assuming a dark, yellow appearance. It is accompanied by inflammation of the whole eye. Opacity of the aqueous humour occurs. Adhesions occur between the iris and the lens. Like periodic ophthalmia the condition tends to recur.

TREATMENT

Cinnabaris 6c   Redness pervades the whole eye after initial inflammation. There may be redness of mouth and throat with ulceration. Dose: night and morning for five days.

Euphrasia 6c   This good general remedy relieves pain, clears the eye of mucus or discharge. Lachrymation is acrid, thick and creamy. Dose: three times daily for five days.

Mercurius corrosivus 6c Severe pain, worse at night. There may be slimy blood-stained diarrhoea and the eye discharge is thin, acrid and greenish. Dose: three times daily for three days.

Rhus toxicodendron 30c Eyelids prominently swollen with surrounding cellulitis. Useful when condition results from exposure to damp for long periods. Dose: three times daily for five days.

7. Cataract. This consists of opacity of the crystalline lens or its capsule or the two together. It more frequently attacks the lens. The opacity may be complete or partial. Capsular cataract is usually dependent on injury and comes on quickly. Lenticular cataract is progressive and seen more frequently in older animals. It is also more resistant to treatment.

SYMPTOMS

An opaque body of whitish grey colour appears behind the pupil and is best seen when the pupil is dilated.

TREATMENT

Silicea 200c Fibrous or scar tissue, which this remedy will help to absorb. Especially useful when there is accompanying corneal ulceration. Dose: once a week for four weeks.

Argentum nitricum 30c When condition results from acute ophthalmia. Dose: once daily for two weeks.

Natrum muriaticum 200c Slowly developing cases associated with wasting and thirst consequent on a chronic nephritis. Dose: once daily for two weeks.

Naphthaline 6c Retinitis and corneal opacity. Dose: night and morning for one week.

Phosphorus 200c Very white opacity and periorbital oedema. Symptoms of liver disturbance may be present. Dose: once daily for one week.

Externally an application of *Cineraria* lotion will help, but it has to be continued for some considerable time.

8. Ophthalmia. This term implies inflammation of all the structures within the eye. It usually takes the form of a suppurative process.

SYMPTOMS

There is a discharge of purulent material from one or both eyes, associated with signs of toxaemia. There may be head shaking and aversion to light. Febrile symptoms invariably present.

TREATMENT

Aconite 6c   Early febrile stage. Dose: hourly for four doses.

Belladonna 200c   Symptoms of central nervous system involvement, such as head shaking, excitement and nervousness. Pulse full and bounding, skin hot and shiny. Dose: two hourly for four doses.

Kali hydriodicum 200c   Lachrymation and discharge. This remedy, given in time, often prevents the disease process becoming established. Dose: night and morning for four days.

Silicea 200c   Corneal opacity. Suppurative states. Dose: once daily for one week.

Mercurius corrosivus 200c   Eye assumes a reddish brown appearance. There may be a purulent discharge of a greenish colour and a slimy diarrhoea. Dose: night and morning for one week.

Argentum nitricum 30c   Profuse purulent discharge with corneal opacity and ulceration. The associated ciliary muscles are weak. Dose: night and morning for one week.

Rhus toxicodendron 1M   Orbital cellulitis and skin irritation. Muscular stiffness and erythematous sore throat may be present. Dose: once daily for one week.

Pulsatilla 30c   Purulent discharge is thick, acrid, creamy. Agglutination of eyelids. Engorgement of eye veins. Dose: night and morning for one week.

Hepar sulphuris 200c   Excess of purulent discharge. Lower potencies will hasten this, while the higher will hasten resolution. Dose: night and morning for a week.

9. Periodic Ophthalmia.   This is a specific form of ophthalmia, so called because of its recurrent or relapsing nature. It is more frequent in male than female animals and in the young subject rather than the old.

SYMPTOMS

Early signs include slight lachrymation and a gradual involvement, or more sudden appearances with profuse discharge. Extreme sensitivity to light accompanies these symptoms. The conjunctiva is red and swollen and there are febrile symptoms. The cornea gradually becomes whitish or opaque. The main peculiarity of this condition is that favourable cases show relapse and lead to a repetition of the symptoms. The disease may spread from one eye to the other and each attack leaves the eyes more damaged.

TREATMENT

The animal should immediately be placed in a darkened stall or loose-box, to avoid exposure to light.

Aconitum napellus 6x and Belladonna 200c These two remedies should be given at hourly intervals in alternation with each other, for four doses each.

Kali bichromicum 200c Discharge tough and stringy and is a deep yellow colour. Dose: night and morning for one week.

Conium 30c Excessive photophobia and lachrymation. Paralysis or weakness of eye muscles. Dose: night and morning for one week.

Graphites 6c Intolerance of light, especially artificial light. Eyelids red and fissured, with sticky discharge. Dose: three times daily for one week.

Silicea 200c This remedy will hasten resolution of scar tissue which may remain after damage by inflammation and ulceration. Dose: once daily for one week, followed by one dose weekly of potency 1M for four weeks.

10. Hydrophthalmia. This term is used to denote a general dilation of the structures of the eye, causing an increase in volume. It is seen occasionally in the horse.

SYMPTOMS

The entire eye increases markedly in size and there is excessive tension on palpitation. This leads to dilation of blood vessels, especially veins leading to oedema.

TREATMENT

Apis 6c This remedy will hasten resorption of fluid and reduces tension in the eyeball. Dose: three times daily for four days.

Osmium 6c Increase in intraocular tension. Pain and lachrymation. Dose: three times daily for five days.

Physostigma 6c   Profuse lachrymation accompanies a paresis of ciliary muscles. Contraction of pupils and photophobia. Dose: night and morning for one week.

Gelsemium 200c   Heaviness of eyelids, with twitching of orbital muscles. There is a generalised inflammation of the serous structures of the eye. Dose: once daily for one week.

Phosphorus 200c   Accompanying retinitis and periorbital oedema. Dose: night and morning for one week.

11.   Dacryocystitis – Inflammation of the Lachrymal Sac. This condition may be acute or chronic. It may be associated with a conjunctivitis or catarrhal condition of the nasal passages. It may follow an attack of strangles.

SYMPTOMS

Profuse lachrymation is an early sign, followed by a prominent swelling in the inner canthus of the eye, caused by distension of the sac. A lachrymal fistula may arise if the sac ruptures.

TREATMENT

Iodium 6c   Acute cases with dilation of pupils. Eyeballs are in constant motion. The animal may have a weathered appearance of the skin. Profuse lachrymation. Dose: night and morning for one week.

Silicea 200c   Swelling of the sac is accompanied by a similar condition of the duct. There may be an associated ulceration of cornea. Dose: once daily for five days.

Fluoric acid 30c   Associated lachrymal fistula. Dose: one night and morning for two weeks.

Natrum muriaticum 200c   Tendency to stricture of the lachrymal duct. Dose: once daily for ten days.

III   Affections of the Ear

1. Pus in the Guttural Pouch. This may arise from an accompanying inflammation of the pharynx, or as a result of spread from a neighbouring abscess. It is sometimes seen as a sequel to strangles. If not treated adequately in the acute stage, the condition becomes chronic.

SYMPTOMS
A nasal discharge first appears, seen especially when the head is lowered during grazing. The character of the discharge is thin and liquid, yellowish-white in colour. There is an accompanying swelling of the submaxillary and parotid glands which become firm and tender. There is difficulty in swallowing and respiration may be interfered with in severe cases.

TREATMENT
Hepar sulphuris 6x–200c   When used in the lower potencies, this remedy will hasten discharge of purulent material, while in higher potency it will help to resorb the condition. Dose: three times daily for two days of lower potencies. One dose night and morning for four days of the higher potency. This is the chief remedy in the acute condition.

Silicea 200c   A suitable remedy for the less acute condition. The discharge is whitish and purulent. It will help to promote healing of ulcerated surfaces within the pouch. Dose: once daily for seven days.

Hydrastis 30c   This remedy is indicated if the discharge takes the form of a simple catarrh without purulent involvement. Dose: three times daily for two days.

Mercurius corrosivus 200c   The indications for this remedy are greenish coloured thin purulent discharge, possibly blood-

stained. This may accompany salivation and slimy diarrhoea.
Dose: three times daily for three days.

Kali bichromicum 30c   Pus bright yellow and stringy. Dose: once
daily for one week.

2. Tympanitis of the Guttural Pouch.

Foals between the ages of two months and one year have been known to suffer from this condition. It is caused by the accumulation of air in the pouch, which cannot then escape because of a blockage in the Eustachian tube. It is usually bilateral.

SYMPTOMS

The parotid region becomes the seat of a painless elastic swelling giving resonance on percussion. The swelling may extend downwards to include the throat region and when this happens interference with respiration and swallowing occurs.

TREATMENT

Calcarea carbonica 200c   This remedy is associated with an
accompanying ear discharge, which causes eruption around the
ear. Dose: once daily for one week.

Kali muriaticum 6c   Indicated when there is accompanying
swelling of associated glands. There may also be catarrhal
discharge from ear and nose. Dose: three times daily for three
days.

Mercurius dulcis 30c   This is a useful remedy for treating blockage
of the Eustachian tube, especially if associated with middle ear
discharge. Dose: three times daily for four days.

Pulsatilla 30c   Indicated when the ear becomes swollen, discharging a bland mucous catarrh. Dose: night and morning for four
days.

IV   Affections of the Nervous System

1. Encephalitis.   This term implies inflammation of the brain, or any inflammatory lesion occurring in brain tissue. It leads to loss of nervous function.

SYMPTOMS
Encephalitis is usually accompanied by fever and toxaemia; anorexia, depression and tachycardia occur also. Normal stimuli produce exaggerated responses, the animal being easily startled. There may be convulsions, accompanied by squinting of eyes and clamping of jaws. Paresis and ataxia may precede paralysis.

TREATMENT
Aconitum napellus 6c   If seen early enough, should be given in the febrile stage. Dose: hourly for four doses.
Belladonna 1M   This is a very useful remedy. There is an accompanying full bounding pulse, dilated pupils and a smooth hot skin. Dose: hourly for four doses.
Stramonium 30c   Indicated when signs of vertigo appear, such as a tendency to stagger and fall sideways. The eyes are usually wide open and staring. Dose: four times daily for two days.
Hyoscyamus 200c   Indications for this remedy include frequent head shaking and a tendency to muscular twitchings. There may be signs of abdominal discomfort. Dose: three times daily for three days.
Phosphorus 200c   This is a useful remedy in less acute cases, showing a tendency to recur. The animal becomes unsteady after rising. Dose: night and morning for one week.
Aethusa 30c   Indicated when there is accompanying photophobia and acute abdominal symptoms, e.g. the passing of flatus which

gives relief to the head symptoms. Dose: three times daily for three days.

Camphora 6c   Indicated when the body surface becomes cold and there is a tendency to collapse. A watery stool may accompany the condition. Dose: two hourly for four doses.

Cuprum aceticum 6c   The indications for this remedy are violent tenesmus and the passage of a slimy brown stool. Respirations are difficult and the animal moves the tongue in and out of the mouth frequently. Dose: three hourly for four doses.

Solanum nigrum 30c   Associated with coryza and eye symptoms such as alternate dilations and contractions of pupils. Dose: three times daily for three days.

Zincum metallicum 6c   Indicated when there is a tendency for the head to roll from side to side. Hyperaesthesia and hyperexcitability are present. Dose: three times daily for three days.

2. Meningitis.   Inflammation of the meninges is usually secondary to bacterial or viral disease.

SYMPTOMS

This condition is characterised by fever and muscle rigidity. Sensitivity of the skin is a common symptom. Trismus and opisthotonus may occur. There is retraction of the head and stiffness of neck muscles. Paresis of hindquarters is common.

TREATMENT

Aconitum napellus 6c   Should be given in the early febrile stage. The animal usually looks anxious and there is a rapid short pulse. Dose: hourly for four hours.

Apis 6c   This remedy is indicated if the condition in the nerve stage is accompanied by oedema of the meninges. Dose: every two hours for four doses.

Belladonna 1M   The indications for this remedy are an accompanying encephalitis, with dilated pupils and a throbbing pulse. The skin is smooth and hot; sweating is common. Dose: two hourly for three doses.

Helleborus niger 6c   Indicated when there are signs of considerable pain. The animal bores the head against any convenient object. Dose: two hourly for four doses.

Zincum metallicum 6c   Useful when the animal is easily startled. Rolling of the head is a common symptom. Paddling of the feet may occur. Dose: three times daily for three days.

Cicuta virosa 200c   Indicated where there is contraction of neck muscles and the head is twisted to one side. There is a tendency to stare fixedly and to squint. Dose: three times daily for three days.

Laburnum 6c   Useful when the spinal, as well as the cerebral, meninges are affected. There is difficulty in moving the fore feet and twitching of the facial muscles occurs. Unequal dilation of pupils is a common symptom. Dose: three times daily for three days.

Bryonia 6c   Indicated in cases showing vertigo. The animal resents movement and there is excessive dryness of mucous membranes e.g. seen in the mouth, where the lips show a parched appearance and there is great thirst. Dose: three times daily for three days.

Agaricus muscarius 200c   Useful in spinal meningitis showing a tendency to paralysis of the lower limbs. This is accompanied by twitching and vertigo which is accentuated in bright light. Dose: three times daily for four days.

Lathyrus sativa 6c   Indicated also in spinal meningitis with an accompanying myelitis. Movements are weak and tottering with muscle rigidity. Reflexes are increased and there is a tendency to emaciation of gluteal muscles. Dose: three times daily for three days.

Strychninum 200c   Indicated when there is violent jerking and twitching of muscles and opisthotonus. The limbs become stiff. Dose: three times daily for three days.

3.   Paralysis of the Facial Nerve.   This is of fairly common occurrence in the horse and may be unilateral, or bilateral. There are various causes, including traumatism and exposure to cold. A toxic form may arise as a sequel to some infectious disease, such as strangles or influenza.

SYMPTOMS
When the condition is unilateral, the lips are drawn towards the sound side. Bilateral involvement precludes grasping of food, while the lower lip hangs down. There is also difficulty in drinking. Occasionally the animal has difficulty in closing the eyelids.

TREATMENT

Gelsemium 200c   This is one of the main remedies in treating motor paralysis of various groups of muscles and nerves. It is especially useful if the paralysis is a sequel to infectious disease, particularly influenza. Dose: once daily for one week. It may be necessary to continue treatment with higher potencies.

Causticum 30c   This remedy is particularly useful if the condition has arisen as a result of exposure to cold. Dose: night and morning for five days.

Ammonium phosphoricum 6c   A lesser known remedy which should be remembered when there is an accompanying early morning coryza. Dose: night and morning for five days.

Zincum picricum 6c   Indicated in chorea-like twitchings of facial muscles together with general weakness and debility. Dose: night and morning for one week.

V Diseases of Respiratory Tract

1. Epistaxis – Nose Bleed. This condition may arise from injuries or over-exertion in which case the blood is usually bright red, but it can also be a symptom of various diseases, e.g. influenza or pneumonia and may be associated with ulceration of the nasal mucosa. In diseased conditions, the blood is usually discoloured. Slight bleeding may stop of its own accord, but when it is excessive, it demands immediate attention. When the bleeding is the result of constitutional illness, the underlying condition must be remembered when considering symptoms.

TREATMENT

Aconitum napellus 6c Bleeding results from over-exertion, and immediate treatment is advisable. Dose: every hour for four doses.

Arnica 30c Local injuries causing the nose-bleed. Dose: every four hours for three doses. Externally, the remedy should be given in tincture or liniment form by plugging the nostril with cotton wood soaked in tincture.

Ammonium carb. 6c Fat subjects, if the condition is dependent on constitutional upset. Dose: every three hours for four doses.

Belladonna 1M Feverish state, showing involvement of the central nervous system. Full pulse, dilated pupils and sweating. Symptoms relieved by keeping patient in a loose-box from which the light had been excluded. Dose: hourly for four doses.

Bryonia 6c Constitutional cases showing early morning bleeding. Animal better at rest. Dose: three times daily for three days.

China off. 30c After severe bleeding, great weakness. Dose: every four hours for four doses.

Hamamelis 6c Passive bleeding of dark non-coagulated blood. Throat veins engorged. Dose: three times daily for three days.

29

Ferrum phos. 6c   Animal nervous and sensitive, blood bright red. Dose: every three hours for three doses.

Ficus religiosa 1x   Accompanying bleeding from lungs, general respiratory distress. Dose: four times daily for two days.

Ipecacuanha 30c   Over-eating and digestive upsets. Blood bright red. Dose: every four hours for four doses.

Melilotus 6c   Muscular weakness. Nose may have polypi leading to haemorrhage which is usually profuse. Dose: three times daily for three days.

Millefolium 6c   Blood bright red, but there may also be blood from bowels or kidneys. Persistent high temperature. Dose: every two hours for four doses.

2. Coryza.   Inflammation of the nasal mucous membranes may arise from exposure to cold or damp and frequently attacks horses that are in poor condition or badly housed. Coryza has a tendency to extend to the laryngeal and lower respiratory area leading to a possible bronchitis or pneumonia.

SYMPTOMS

Early signs include sneezing and swelling of eyelids, followed by a thin mucous discharge from the nose. Discharge soon becomes thick and catarrhal. Most cases resolve quickly, but a chronic form may supervene in poorly nourished animals. Laryngitis and cough may accompany the condition, the former being associated with throat swelling.

TREATMENT

The patient should be put in a clean, well-ventilated loose-box and consideration given to the following remedies:-

Aconitum 6c   Early stages, when mucous membrane of the nose is dry and hot. Animal thirsty and feverish. Dose: hourly for four doses.

Arsenicum alb 1M   Discharge is acrid. Swollen eyelids, thirst for small quantities. Restless, worse after midnight. Dose every two hours for four doses.

Allium cepa 6c   Discharge bland, watery. Eyes red, showing lachrymation and photophobia. Dose: hourly for four doses.

Hepar sulphuris 200c   Sneezing, with ulceration of nostrils. Discharge thick and purulent, foul-smelling. Sensitive to pain resenting cold wind. Dose: three times daily for two days.

Natrum muriaticum 1M Discharge whitish, albuminous-looking. There may be violent sneezing. Dose: every two hours for four doses.

Hydrastis 30c Discharge catarrhal and bland. Dose: three times daily for two days.

Kali bichromicum 200c Discharge chronic, tends to become thick and tough. Dose: night and morning for five days.

Mercurius dulcis 6c Throat involved, nasal discharge greenish and thin. Dose: four times daily for one day.

Silicea 200c Discharge thin, greyish, associated with caries of nasal septum and neighbouring structures. Crusts form inside nose. Dose: once daily for six days.

3. Nasal Gleet. This term implies a chronic discharge caused by a catarrhal or purulent inflammation of long standing, which may extend to the facial sinuses.

SYMPTOMS
A copious purulent secretion appears in one or both nostrils. The character of the discharge varies from thin and mucoid to thick and purulent and may be accompanied by swelling and tenderness of the sub-maxilliary glands.

TREATMENT
Kali bichromicum 200c Secretion thick and lumpy, difficult to expel from the nostrils. Dose: night and morning for five days.

Hydrastis 30c Discharge catarrhal and non-purulent. Dose: three times daily for three days.

Mercurius corrosivus 200c Associated with disease of nasal bones. Discharge is purulent, greenish, sometimes streaked with blood. Dose: night and morning for four days.

Balsam of Peru 6c Discharge thick and foetid, frequently accompanied by catarrhal discharge elsewhere. Dose: three times daily for two days.

Pulsatilla 30c Greenish scales in nostrils, associated with catarrhal discharge, often worse in morning. Dose: three times daily for three days.

4. Ozaena. This is a form of nasal gleet producing symptoms like ordinary gleet, but with an extremely foul-smelling discharge.

TREATMENT

Cadmium sulph 30c   Nasal polypi, with ulceration and obstruction. Dose: three times daily for three days.

Aurum metallicum 30c   Extremely offensive odour with purulent bloody discharge. Nose swollen, discharge worse at night. Dose: three times daily for four days.

Lemna minor 30c   Nasal polypi and swollen turbinate bones. Worse in wet weather. Putrid smell from discharge. Dose: three times daily for three days.

Asafoetida 6c   Very offensive purulent discharge. There may be caries of nasal bones. Dose: three times daily for four days.

Mercurius corrosivus 200c   Perforation of nasal septum accompanied by a greenish thin discharge which may be blood-stained. Dose: night and morning for three days.

5.   Pus in the Facial Sinuses.   Catarrhal conditions of the upper respiratory tract may involve the sinuses, leading to a chronic sinusitis.

SYMPTOMS

There is a discharge of pus from the nostrils, with swelling over the nasal bones and maxillary region. Dullness on percussion is seen over the affected area.

TREATMENT

As an alternative to surgical intervention, the following remedies should be considered:–

Hepar sulphuris 200c   Sensitivity to draughts and cold. Extreme sensitivity to touch or pressure on the affected area. Dose: night and morning for one week.

Hydrastis 30c   Pus bland, flowing freely from nostrils. Dose: three times daily for six days.

Mercurius corrosivus 200c   Purulent material blood-stained, greenish. Dose: night and morning for five days.

Kali bichromicum 200c   Long standing cases showing tough stringy discharge. Dose: night and morning for five days.

Silicea 200c   Chronic cases showing thin, whitish pus associated with affections of maxillary and nasal bones. Dose: night and morning for five days.

Arsenicum alb 1M Discharge acrid, tending to excoriate the nostrils. Restless, worse after midnight. Dose: once daily for five days.

6. Laryngitis. The larynx may become inflamed, accompanied by secretion of mucus which may be profuse enough to interfere with the animal's breathing. It is frequently an accompaniment of catarrhal conditions or infections such as strangles or influenza.

SYMPTOMS
Breathing is quickened and attended by rough snoring sound and harsh cough which can be increased by pressure on the larynx. Breathing becomes more laboured when oedema of the glottis becomes profuse. The swelling and oedema appear on the anterior of the throat.

TREATMENT
Aconitum napellus 6c Early stages, febrile signs such as quickened pulse and respiration. Dose: hourly for four doses.
Apis 6c Oedema prominent symptom, throat becoming soft and swollen. Dose: three times daily for two days.
Spongia tosta 6c Severe attacks, with characteristic cough. Dose: three times daily for three days.
Belladonna 1M Inflammation extends to pharyngeal area. Difficulty in swallowing. Full bounding pulse, dilated pupils and smooth shiny skin. Dose: every two hours for four doses.
Mercurius cyanatus 30c Rough whitish membrane covers bottom of tongue and upper laryngeal area. Salivation is increased. Dose: three times daily for three days.
Sanguinaria 6c Threatened oedema of larynx. Cough with tenderness over wind pipe. Dose: three times daily for three days.

7. Bronchitis. Inflammation of the bronchial mucous membrane may arise independently of other illnesses, or may be a sequel to influenza or catarrhal states. The condition invariably involves lung tissue, being more a broncho-pneumonia than a pure bronchitis. It may arise simply by exposure to cold dry winds or to damp and cold.

SYMPTOMS
Breathing is accelerated, pulse becomes full and quick, accompanied by a frequent painful cough. Mucous secretion soon becomes purulent and may run from the nose as well as appear in the cough. Rattling respiratory sounds can be heard over the rib area.

TREATMENT
Aconitum napellus 6c Early stages, with hot, dry skin, feverish symptoms, and anxious expression. Dose: hourly for four doses.

Belladonna 1M Pulse full and bounding, with dilated pupils, sweating and excitement. Dose: every two hours for four doses.

Antimonium tartiaricum 30c Moist cough with threatened pulmonary oedema. Rattling sounds may be heard in the chest, respirations increased. Dose: three times daily for three days.

Bryonia 6c Cough hard and dry, pleura become affected. Relief from pressure over ribs. Dose: three times daily for three days.

Dulcamara 6c Condition has origin in damp surroundings and coughing worse after exertion. Dose: three times daily for three days.

Kali bichromicum 200c Phlegm in bronchial tubes difficult to expel. Nasal discharge. Dose: three times daily for three days.

Drosera 6c Coughing becomes spasmodic in character. Paroxysms follow one another rapidly. Dose: three times daily for three days.

Squilla 6c Coughing is accompanied by fluent coryza and much sneezing. Coughing produces slimy expectoration, brought on by drinking or exertion of any kind. Dose: three times daily for four days.

Arsenicum iodatum 6c Chronic cases with periods of quiescence alternating with bouts of coughing. Very useful remedy for bronchial conditions which fail to clear properly. Dose: night and morning for four days.

Spongia 6c Bouts of coughing eased by eating or drinking, worse by exposure to cold air. Dose: three times daily for four doses.

Sulphur 30c Give as a constitutional remedy when recovery takes place. Dose: once daily for five days.

8. Pulmonary Congestion. The term implies a sudden engorgement of the lungs and may occur after severe or long-continued exertion.

SYMPTOMS

Breathing is oppressed and laboured, nostrils become flayed in the effort to inhale. The pulse is strong and full and may reach ninety beats per minute. Occasionally blood may come from the nose. Legs and ears become cold and the eyes betray anxiety.

TREATMENT

Aconitum napellus 6c   A preliminary remedy, as soon as condition is suspected. Dose: hourly for four doses.

Ammonium caust. 6c   Increase in mucus and moist coughing, with exhaustion and muscular weakness. Dose: three times daily for three days.

Belladonna 200c   Hot dry skin, dilated pupils and excitability. Pulse full and bounding. Dose: every two hours for four doses.

Ferrum phos. 6c   Blood is coughed up and condition decreases in severity as night approaches. Dose: three times daily for three days.

Veratrum viride 6c   Congestion accompanied by scanty urine, rapid pulse of low tension. Dose: three times daily for two days.

Apis 30c   Pulmonary oedema severe, accompanied by extension of oedema to the laryngeal area. Dose: night and morning for four days.

9. Pleurisy. Injuries to the chest may lead to pleurisy and it may also arise from exposure to cold and damp.

SYMPTOMS

A quick, thready pulse precedes a bout of shivering. Signs of pain over the chest are indicated by abdominal breathing. There are general febrile symptoms such as discolouration of the conjunctiva and quickened pulse. The expression is anxious. Inspiration is difficult, but expiration is accomplished without much trouble. Cough is short, dry and hacking, with pain. Pressure over the ribs causes resentment. Sometimes the skin over the pleural area becomes thickened into folds. Occasionally oedema of the pleural cavities occurs leading to increased respiratory distress.

TREATMENT

Aconitum napellus 6c   The early febrile stage. Dose: hourly for four doses.

Bryonia 30c   Better at rest. Pressure over pleural area relieves. Cough usually hard and dry. Dose: every two hours for four doses.

Apis 30c   Oedema occurs in pleural cavities, urine scanty and high-coloured. Dose: three times daily for three days.

Cantharis 200c   Pleural effusion. Mucus expectorated with cough is usually blood-stained. Severe straining when trying to pass urine. Dose: three times daily for two days.

Guaiacum 6c   Articular surfaces of ribs more sensitive to pain than elsewhere. This may not be easy to diagnose, but coughing relieves the symptoms and expectoration eases the shortness of respiration. Dose: three times daily for two days.

Kali carbonicum 200c   Symptoms of pain worse on right side. Cough worse in early morning and there is usually a dry throat. Dose: three times daily for three days.

Senega 30c   In older animals, sneezing occurs after coughing. Useful also in exudative pleurisy. Dose: three times daily for three days.

Squilla 6c   Coughing provoked by drinking. Pain extends to abdominal muscles. Increased urination towards evening. Dose: three times daily for two days.

Arsenicum iodatum 30c   Chronic state, with persistent dry cough remaining after treatment. Useful generally for cases slow to respond or heal. Dose: once daily for one week.

Sulphur 30c   Use in the convalescent stage of pleurisy. Dose: once daily for six days.

Sanguinaria 6c   Cough raises rust-coloured sputum, with tenderness over right side. Cough always returns after each febrile attack. Dose: three times daily for three days.

10. Influenza.   This is due to various febrile agents. In its pure state, it consists of first a fever, and secondly a specific affection of the mucous membranes of the upper respiratory tract and eyes. It most commonly affects young horses and appears usually in spring and autumn.

SYMPTOMS
Febrile signs first appear and the animal is dull and listless. There is a fast, thready pulse. Urine may be scanty and high coloured. The congestive swelling of the nose extends down the respiratory tract, giving at first a mucoid, and later a purulent, discharge. The cough is harsh and dry and breathing is accelerated. The nervous system is also affected – state of general languor and muscular weakness. The conjunctivae are discoloured yellowish-brown.

TREATMENT
Aconitum napellus 6c   Early stage when febrile signs accompany anxious expression. Dose: every hour for four hours.
Belladonna 200c or 1M   Acute cases, with full pulse, dilated pupils. Skin hot and shiny. Excitement and head-shaking. Dose: every hour for four doses.
Gelsemium 1M   Languor, muscular weakness, incoordination of movement. Dose: every two hours for four doses.
Bryonia 6c   Harsh, dry cough. Pleuritic symptoms such as pain over chest and friction sounds are heard on auscultation. Relief on pressure. Short, grunting breathing. Dose: three times daily for three days.
Antimonium tartaricum 30c   Saliva appears accompanied by moist cough and the presence of mucous rales in auscultation. Dose: night and morning for four days.
Phosphorus 200c   Breathing short and rapid, pneumonia threatened. Dose: three times daily for two days.
Lycopodium 200c   Once pneumonia has set in and animal shows laboured movement of the alae nasi, independent of respiration. Dose: three times daily for two days.
Arsenicum alb. 1M   Symptoms generally worse towards or after midnight. Animal restless, drinks frequent small quantities. Skin dry and staring. Dose: every two hours for four doses.
Nux vomica 6c   Constipation and capricious appetite. Dose: every three house for four doses.
Ammonium caust. 6c   Pulmonary congestion supervenes, oedema threatens, with coldness of skin. Dose: three times daily for three days.

11. Pneumonia.   Inflammation of the lung tissue may appear as a result of overwork or chill. It is also a sequel to disease such as influenza or bronchitis.

SYMPTOMS

Frequent pulse rate, with discoloured conjunctivae, followed by laboured breathing and anxious or distressed look. As the condition progresses heaving on the flanks takes place and neck becomes extended as the animal seeks to take in more air. Legs and ears become cold and the mucous membranes of nose and mouth assume a dusky dark bluish tinge. Cough may be blood-stained or rust-coloured containing shreds of fibrin in the mucus.

TREATMENT

Aconitum napellus 6c   Should always be given first. Dose: every half-hour for six doses.

Bryonia 6c   Cough hard and dry and pleurisy is severe. Worse on movement and pressure over chest relieves. Dose: three times daily for two days.

Antimonium tartaricum 30c   Rattling of mucus, accumulation of frothy saliva. Dose: three times daily for three days.

Lycopodium 200c   Cases showing rapid wasting and involvement of the alae nasi. Dose: every two hours for four doses.

Phosphorus 200c   A main remedy, once hepatisation has set in. Pressure resented, particularly over left side. Sputum rust-coloured. Trembling of body. Dose: every two hours for four doses.

Iodum 30c   Hepatisation spreads rapidly, full pulse, absence of pain over chest. Temperature remains high, sputum blood-streaked. Dose: every hour for four doses.

Sanguinaria 30c   Heart symptoms such as valvular weakness appear and signs of accompanying pulmonary congestion set in. Urine may contain phosphates. Dose: night and morning for five days.

Tuberculinium aviare 200c   Chiefly for young foals with loss of strength and appetite. The apices of the lungs are more involved than other portions of lung tissue. Dose: night and morning for five days.

Sulphur 30c   Expectoration becomes greenish and purulent. Pulse rate decreases towards evening and rises again later in the evening. Dose: three times daily for three days.

Beryllium 30c Dyspnoea out of proportion to clinical findings. Also associated with skin symptoms. Dose: three times daily for three days.

12. Cough. While coughing is frequently associated with various pulmonary infections, it may arise as a seemingly independent syndrome, and takes various forms:–

1 Pleuritic cough. Short and dry and the animal shows pain when coughing.
2 Bronchitic cough. Starts dry and frequent, becomes moist and soft.
3 Pneumonic cough. Frequent, may contain rust-coloured fibrinous deposits in sputum.
4 Simple catarrhal cough. Usually moist and infrequent.
5 Stomach or intestinal cough. Various forms. Dependent on alimentary disorders.

TREATMENT

Bryonia 6c Pleuritic cough, dry, symptoms worse on movement. Better from pressure, or pressure over affected area. Dose: three times daily for three days.

Arsenicum iodatum 6c Cough lingers after chest infections such as influenza or bronchitis. Dose: three times daily for three days.

Belladonna 30c Cough accompanied by full pulse, hot smooth skin, dilated pupils, nervous symptoms. Dose: every two hours for four doses.

Drosera 6c Spasmodic cough of chronic nature. Sometimes associated with asthmatic symptoms, worse early morning. Dose: three times daily for three days.

Nux vomica 6c Origin in digestive upsets. Dose: three times daily for three days.

Causticum 30c Cough relieved by drinking. Expectorations scanty. Dose: night and morning for four days.

Arsenicum alb. 1M Cough worse after midnight, animal restless, thirsty with dry skin. Cough worse after drinking, even small quantities. Dose: night and morning for five days.

Spongia 30c Cough worse on inspiration and worse towards midnight. Relieved by drinking. Sometimes associated with heart disease. Dose: night and morning for three days.

Sticta 6c Cough originates more in the trachea, is worse in evening and during the night and on inspiration. Dose: three times daily for three days.

Stannum 30c Cough accompanies established influenza. Worse in latter part of the day. Expectoration forcibly expelled. Dose: three times daily for three days.

VI Diseases of the Circulatory System

1. Tachycardia. This is the name given to an increased heart rhythm and may be brought about by a fall in arterial blood-pressure, or by influences leading to pain and excitement. An independent form called paroxysmal tachycardia sometimes occurs in the horse. Disease of heart muscle may cause this form.

SYMPTOMS
The pulse is small and the heart sounds are increased. Exercise is poorly tolerated.

TREATMENT
Crataegus 6c This is very useful in the paroxysmal form to help restore strength to the heart muscle. Dose: four times daily for one week.

Lycopus 6c Indicated where there is palpitation from nervous excitement. Pulse is tremulous and weak. There may be passive haemorrhages. Dose: three times daily for four or five days.

Convallaria 6c Indicated in venous stasis and dyspnoea. Even slight exertion brings on palpitation. Pulse is very irregular and rapid. Dose: three times daily for five days.

Strophanthus 6c An irregular pulse, associated with myocarditis, will benefit from this remedy. The animal may show signs of pain on movement. Dose: three times daily for three days.

Aconitum napellus 6c Pain over left shoulder region, pulse full and tense, strained anxious expression. Dose: three times daily for four days.

Iberis 6c Palpitation accompanied by choking symptoms and an irregular, intermittent pulse. Palpitation easily induced. Dose: two hourly for four doses.

Lilium tigrinum 30c   Palpitation and very rapid pulse, associated with frequent urination, the urine being whitish and hot. There is also urging to defaecate and stool may be blood-stained and contain mucus. Dose: every two hours for four doses.

Naja 6c   Irregular pulse of low tension, associated with lethargy and threatened paralysis. Palpitation is common. Dose: every three hours for four days.

Phosphorus 30c   When this remedy is needed, there is violent palpitation. The pulse is weak and soft. Liver symptoms may be prominent giving tenderness over the hepatic region. Stools are clay-coloured and there may be purpura-like haemorrhages on mucous membranes and skin. Dose: three times daily for four days.

Thyroidinum 6c   Indicated when there is a weak, thready pulse and palpitation. The animal seldom lies down, due to numbness of lower front limbs. Pain is shown on movement and there may be a tendency to exophthalmos. Dose: three times daily for five days.

2. Bradycardia.   This term implies slowness of heart rhythm and is often due to some extraneous cause such as increase in blood-pressure. The heart muscle is invariably sound.

SYMPTOMS
The heart's action is heavy and slow.

TREATMENT

Abies nigra 30c   When there is dyspnoea with choking sounds in the throat. Coughing is frequent. Dose: three times daily for four days.

Veratrum viride 6c   Pulse of low tension may be felt prominently in any superficial vessel. Respiratory symptoms include dyspnoea and congestion of the lungs. Dose: three times daily for three days.

Opium 1M   Somnolent state, accompanied by severe constipation and stertorous breathing. Body surface usually very hot. Dose: three times daily for three days.

Gelsemium 200c   Slow pulse with spasmodic movements of the throat muscles leading to difficulty in swallowing. Respiratory symptoms prominent. Dose: night and morning for four days.

Aesculus 6c Abdominal discomfort such as liver dysfunction. Heart's action full and heavy. Urinary symptoms also prominent, e.g. dark and scanty. Dose: three times daily for three days.

Kalmia 6c Pulse weak and slow with muscular stiffness, especially over lumbar region. Shoulders may also show stiffness. Dose: three times daily for three days.

Apocynum 6c Valvular incompetence and dusky appearance of visible mucous membranes. Dose: three times daily for five to six days.

3. Pericarditis. Inflammation of the heart sac is rarely met with as a primary condition and is invariably a sequel to some bacterial or viral infection, such as influenza, and frequently follows pleurisy.

SYMPTOMS

The pulse becomes hard and wiry and is accompanied by febrile involvement. Pressure over the cardiac area causes resentment. Auscultation reveals a friction sound which ceases once effusion takes place into the pericardial sac. Fibrinous deposits may occur on the heart muscle leading to embarrassment of the heart's action. The friction sounds differ from those of pleurisy in that the latter are synchronous with respiratory movements while the former are independent of these and confined to the left chest-wall. The gait shows abduction with abdominal respiration.

TREATMENT

The animal should be isolated in a cool, well ventilated loose-box.

Aconitum napellus 6c Should be given as early as possible in the initial febrile stage. Dose: every hour for four doses.

Bryonia 30c Relief from pressure over the affected area. There may be a dry cough as a sequel to pleurisy. Dose: night and morning for three days.

Apis 30c This is one of the main remedies if effusion has occurred into the pericardial sac, indicated by absence of friction sounds. Dose: night and morning for one week.

Arsenicum alb. 1M Restlessness and prostration, with thirst for small quantities. Symptoms worse after midnight. Dose: night and morning for one week.

Spigelia 30c Trembling pulse, animal tends to lie on right side. Great distress from movement. Dose: night and morning for five days.

Colchicum 6c Low-tension pulse, thirst and flatulence, with increased salivation. Dose: three hourly for four doses.

Natrum muriaticum 200c Chronic state, showing wasting and increased thirst. Dose: night and morning for ten days.

Cantharis 200c Effusion. Urinary symptoms such as strangury; bloody urine may also be present. Dose: night and morning for five days.

Spongia 6c Hypertrophy of heart as a result of deposition of fibrinous deposits on the myocardium, leading to chronic pericarditis. Dose: three times daily for five days.

4. Myocarditis. Inflammation of the heart muscle is often secondary to bacterial or viral infections such as strangles or infectious anaemia, or navel-ill in foals. Degenerative lesions can arise from non-infectious causes and lead to functional or physical impairment.

SYMPTOMS

The animal usually shows a disinclination for exercise on account of this leading to embarrassment of heart's action. The heart's rate is increased and there may be an increase in the actual size of the heart, leading to respiratory distress. Bradycardia is the rule. Congestive heart states may supervene leading to a generalised oedema and severe dyspnoea.

TREATMENT

Crataegus 6c This remedy is indicated in most cases of heart muscle weakness. Exertion brings on severe breathlessness. Useful heart medicine during the course of infectious disease. Dose: three times daily for seven days.

Arsenicum iodatum 30c Condition a sequel to influenza or other respiratory infection. Dose: night and morning for five days.

Adonis vernalis 6c Marked venous engorgement. Cardiac dropsy. The condition may be associated with fatty degeneration of muscle. Pulse rapid and irregular. Dose: three times daily for six days.

Strophanthis 6x Weakness of heart muscle is accompanied by quick pulse and scanty albuminous urine. Dose: three times daily for five days.

Digitalis 6c Palpitation is brought on by the least movement. Slow, weak, intermittent pulse which quickens on movement of the animal. Dose: three times daily for seven days.

5. Endocarditis. This is inflammation of the membrane lining the heart cavities. It is of more frequent occurrence than pericarditis or myocarditis. It may arise as a sequel to rheumatic involvement. Most cases are bacterial in origin. It may also arise from parasitism due to strongyle infestation.

SYMPTOMS

Excitement of a febrile nature is accompanied by a small intermittent pulse. Body temperature may fall owing to a deficient peripheral circulation. Ulcerative lesions frequently appear on the heart valves leading to symptoms of congestive heart failure. In the horse aortic valves are usually affected, but the mitral valve may also suffer. The chief heart sound is a deep murmur varying according to which valve is affected. It frequently takes the form of a 'bellows' sound. Distension of the jugular vein may be seen.

TREATMENT

Calcarea fluorica 30c Fibrinous deposits occur on the heart valves and this remedy hastens their absorption. Dose: night and morning for five days.

Lycopus 30c Palpitation accompanies a weak intermittent pulse. Heart sounds are very intense. A wheezing cough may be present. Dose: night and morning for five days.

Naja 6c Lesions occur after bacterial or viral diseases. Suitable for both acute and chronic cases. Pulse irregular and body cold. Dose: three times daily for four days.

Convallaria 6c The pulse is extremely rapid and irregular. Venous stasis is prominent. Dose: three times daily for five days.

Adonis vernalis 6c If rheumatic involvement is suspected, with symptoms of vertigo. Venous engorgement also suspected. Dose: three times daily for five days.

Kalmia 6c Tumultuous heart action. Kidney involvement frequent. Signs of pain over left shoulder region. Dose: three times daily for one week.

Aconitum napellus 6c Tense full pulse, pulsation of carotid arteries. Animal appears anxious, with uneasiness and signs of pain. Dose: every two hours for five doses.

Cactus grandiflorus 6c Mitral valve incompetence. There may be cold sweating and signs of pain on movement. Blood pressure is low and heart sounds are increased. Dose: three times daily for one week.

Spigelia 6c Prominent dyspnoea. Animal tends to lie on right side, possibly due to pain over left shoulder area. The least movement aggravates. Dose: three times daily for four days.

6. Valvular Disease. Affections of the heart valves usually have their origin in endocarditis. Degenerative lesions of the aortic valves have been reported in horses. Valvular disease is diagnosed by murmurs heard on auscultation and may take the form of stenosis or incompetence.

Stenosis of Aortic Valves. This has little significance functionally unless accompanied by an abnormal pulse. The most audible sound is a harsh murmur associated with systole. It usually replaces the first heart sound and is heard posteriorly on the left side.

Incompetence of Aortic Valves. When this is sufficiently advanced, it is accompanied by a very full pulse, along with a high systolic and a low diastolic blood pressure. Sometimes the pulse may be seen in the small peripheral vessels.

Stenosis of the Mitral Valve. Passage of blood through a narrowed valve opening leads to a diastolic murmur, the duration of which being dependent on the severity of the stenosis. The murmur is most audible at the heart's apex on the left side and carries through the second heart to the beginning of the first. Incomplete filling of the left ventricle may lead to pulse changes.

Incompetence of the Mitral Valve. Leakage of blood during the heart's systole leads to a murmur heard at the apex of the heart on the left side. Normally there are no pulse changes.

Stenosis and Incompetence of Tricuspid Valve. This produces a symptom picture analogous to mitral valve affections, except that the heart murmur is found apically on the right side. A jugular pulse commonly accompanies tricuspid incompetence.

The diagnosis of these conditions depends on auscultation of the murmurs which replace normal heart sounds. These differ from pericardial friction sounds in being less audible and not differing in intensity with the heart's action.

TREATMENT

Lycopus 6c Tumultuous heart action, accompanies by a cough which contains blood. Dose: three times daily for four days.

Naja 6c Useful after infectious diseases, when body cold and pulse irregular. Dose: three times daily for five days.

Adonis vernalis 6c Marked venous engorgement with asthmatic symptoms and palpitation. Dose: three times daily for five or six days.

Crataegus 6c Weakness of heart muscle with slow, weak pulse. Dose: three times daily for six or seven days.

Spongia 6c Valvular incompetence with breathlessness and anxious expression. Peripheral veins are prominent and there is usually a dry, hard cough. Dose: three times daily for six days.

Spigelia 6c When rheumatic diathesis is suspected. Movement aggravates and animal lies on right side only. Pain and tenderness evident over left shoulder area. Dose: three times daily for five days.

Strophanthus 6c Heart muscle weak. Incompetence. Urinary symptoms. Dose: three times daily for five days.

Convallaria 6c Very rapid and irregular pulse. Dose: three times daily for seven days.

Laurocerasus 6c Mitral incompetence. Mucous membranes of mouth and nose become cyanosed and dusky. Dose: three times daily for five days.

VII Diseases of Blood and Blood-forming Organs

1. Dehydration. This arises when excessive fluid loss takes place and can be caused by super-purgation, polyuria and prolonged severe sweating. Depression of tissue fluid levels takes place and leads to a reduction in the fluid content of the blood.

SYMPTOMS
The main signs are dry shrunken appearance of the external skin and a harsh appearance of the coat. The eye becomes sunken. Muscular weakness and increased thirst are apparent. Urine becomes scanty and of a high specific gravity. The heart rate is increased and blood pressure falls.

TREATMENT
China off. 30c   This is the best remedy for this condition, helping to restore strength and promote a return to normal physiological condition. Dose: three times daily for three days.

2. Haemorrhage. This may take several forms, such as epistaxis, haemoptysis, metrorrhagia, haematemesis etc. and each case must be considered on its own symptomatology.

TREATMENT
Ipecacuanha 30c   Useful when the blood is bright red and profuse. Dose: every hour for four doses.
Phosphorus 200c   Indicated when there are extravasations of blood in the skin and mucous membranes. Purpura-like ecchymoses occur. Capillary bleeding is common. Dose: three times daily for three days.
Melilotus 6c   This remedy is associated with general congestive states. Throbbing of neck arteries is common. Dose: three days.

Ficus religiosa 6c Indicated when there is respiratory distress. Blood is usually bright red. Dose: every three hours for four doses.

Ferrum phosphoricum 6c Indicated in febrile states and urinary tract involvement. Blood is bright red. Dose: every two hours for four doses.

China off. 6c To control weakness associated with loss of blood. Helps to restore strength. Dose: every two hours for five doses.

Crotalus horridus 6c Indicated in dark haemorrhages of fluid blood which does not clot easily, especially from intestines and rectum. Dose: three times daily for three days.

Sabina 6c Indicated when the blood is bright red and, although fluid, clots immediately appear. Very useful in metrorrhagia. Dose: four times daily three hours apart.

Millefolium 6c Indicated in haemorrhages of bright red blood associated with combined febrile symptoms. This is a useful remedy in haemoptysis and also when blood is prominent in the urine. Dose: every two hours for four doses.

Hamamelis 6c Indicated in venous congestion with passive oozing haemorrhages. Dose: three times daily for two days.

Trillium pendulum 6c This is associated with general weakness and dizziness after loss of blood, particularly from the uterus. Dose: every two hours for four doses.

3. Shock. Shock can result from injury or surgical interference and can lead to peripheral circulatory failure.

SYMPTOMS

The skin becomes cold and temperature falls to below normal. There is a fall in blood-pressure and a weak pulse rate together with shallow respirations. Severe shock can lead to coma.

TREATMENT

Arnica 30c This remedy should be given in all cases. Dose: two doses usually suffice, two hours apart.

Bellis perennis 200c This is a useful remedy to combat shock after surgical intervention. Dose: every three hours for three doses.

Carbo vegetabilis 6c Indicated in cases of collapse and threatened coma. Body surface is cold. Dose: every two hours for four doses.

Veratrum album 200c   Useful in surgical shock and indicated when collapse is associated with cold perspiration. Dose: every hour for four doses.

4. Oedema.   This is the term given to any abnormal amount of fluid in tissue spaces. It can arise from various causes.

SYMPTOMS
Fluid swellings occur anywhere on the body surface and show pitting on pressure. The swellings may arise from some inflammatory condition or be dependent on poor peripheral circulation resulting from weak heart action. Oedema can also occur in body cavities such as the pleural and pericardial sacs.

TREATMENT
Apis 6c   This is the main remedy for oedematous states whether active from inflammation or passive as in chronic affections of pleura and weak heart action. Dose: three times daily for three days.
Antimonium tartaricum 30c   Indicated when oedema affects the lung tissue, associated with great increase of mucus. Dose: every two hours for four doses.
Prunus spinosa 6c   Useful in anascara and dependent parts such as feet and lower limbs. Dose: three times daily for three days.
Digitalis 6c   Indicated if weak heart action is present. Dose: three times daily for five days.
There are many other heart remedies to be considered, but they will be dealt with under diseases of the heart.

5. Anaemia.   This is the technical term for a deficiency of red blood cells or of haemoglobin.

SYMPTOMS
Anaemia is characterised by pallor of the mucous membranes and a weak, thready pulse. Jaundice and haemoglobinuria may occur. Weakness and lethargy are common.

TREATMENT
China off. 30c   A useful remedy when there is extreme weakness and when slow leakage of blood is suspected. Dose: every two hours for four doses.

Arsenicum alb. 200c   This is a good remedy in long standing cases or pernicious anaemia states. The animal is exhausted and restless. Thirst is prominent, for small quantities. Dose: three times daily for three days.

Trinitrotoluene 30c   This remedy is associated with jaundice and haemoglobinuria. Faintness and palpitation are common symptoms. The urine is highly coloured. Dose: three times daily for five days.

Natrum muriaticum 1M   Indicated in long standing cases depending on deficient salt metabolism. Dose: night and morning for five days.

Silicea 1M   When there is an increase in the number of white cells leading to interference in haemoglobin function, this is a very useful remedy. Dose: twice weekly for four weeks.

VIII   Diseases of Blood Vessels

1. Arteritis. This form of inflammation is common in horses infested with strongyle worms. It can lead to pathological changes in arteries such as the anterior mesenteric and the iliac, the former, when it occurs, giving rise to intermittent bouts of colic, and the latter to iliac thrombosis. Parasitic arteritis results in thickening of the artery walls due to inflammation. This can lead to the formation of a thrombus which in turn can lead to occlusion of the vessel. This is commonest in the anterior mesenteric artery. A specific form of arteritis also occurs and will be dealt with in the section on viral diseases.

TREATMENT

Calcarea fluorica 30c   Useful in removing fibrinoid deposits on the
    endothelium of the artery. Dose: three times daily for three days.
Kali hydriodicum 200c   Haemorrhagic infiltration of skin. Dose:
    three times daily for five days.
Note:– In all cases of arteritis affecting mesenteric and iliac
        arteries, attention should be paid to removal of strongyle
        worms.

2. Verminous aneurism. This is of common occurrence in the horse and can interfere with intestinal blood supply.

SYMPTOMS

Recurrent attacks of colic take place and if the aneurism becomes infected with pyogenic bacteria, temperature rise occurs. Signs of peritonitis such as hardening of the abdominal wall may arise.

TREATMENT

Accessory homoeopathic treatment after worming includes consideration of the following remedies:–

Veratrum viride 200c   Weak, intermittent pulse. There may by muscular twitchings and congestion of lungs. The animal is thirsty and the skin shows patches of sweating. Urine scanty. Dose: night and morning for four days.

Lycopodium 200c   Palpitation in thin subjects showing predisposition to liver disorders. Dose: three times daily for four doses.

Calcarea fluorica 30c   Glandular swellings with increased heart action. There may be an associated valvular incompetence. Dose: night and morning for four days.

3. Venous Thrombosis.   This may arise as a sequel to strangles and can affect large veins such as jugular or posterior vena cava.

SYMPTOMS
Pain on pressure over vein, engorgement and local oedema. The jugular vein, when affected, may stand out as a thickened cord-like structure.

TREATMENT
Vipera 30c   Associated jaundice and enlargement of liver. Dose: three times daily for five days.

Hamamelis 200c   Associated blood-shot involvement of eyes. Epistaxis is common and the veins of the throat become engorged. Dose: night and morning for four days.

IX Diseases of Lymphatic System

1. Lymphangitis. This term implies inflammation of the lymphatic vessels of the legs, more particularly the hind legs. It is commonly associated with rest on full rations after a period of exercise.

SYMPTOMS
Initial shivering is followed by signs of febrile involvement, viz. rapid pulse and breathing, with hot dry mouth. The affected leg is raised from the ground and the animal shows signs of pain or discomfort, looking round at the affected limb. Heat, swelling and tenderness are present in the leg. A painful cord-like swelling develops on the inside of the limb, developing along the course of the lymphatic vessels. The swelling starts first in the groin and extends down the leg towards the fetlock. The early swelling pits on pressure indicating oedema. Severe cases are accompanied by the expression of a honey-coloured fluid on the surface of the skin.

TREATMENT
Aconitum napellus 6x   Should always be given in the early febrile
  stage. Dose: every hour for four doses.
Kali bichromicum 200c   Indicated when a viscid, honey-coloured
  discharge appears. Dose: three times daily for four days.
Calcarea fluorica 30c   Useful in controlling involvement of
  associated lymph glands. Blood vessels are usually dilated.
  Dose: three times daily for four days.
Apis 6c   Indicated in the acute stage when oedematous swellings
  are prominent. Dose: three hourly for four doses.
Belladonna 200c   Useful when associated lymph glands are
  swollen and tender. Febrile signs are accompanied by dilation of
  pupils and a hot smooth skin. Dose: three hourly for four doses.

Lachesis 6c This remedy may be needed if septic lymphangitis occurs, the underlying tissues showing cellulitis and the skin becoming dark bluish. Associated blood vessels are dilated and blood may ooze from rectum, being dark and fluid. Dose: three times daily for two days.

Rhus toxicodendron 1M Associated with swelling and tenderness along the course of the lymphatic vessels, together with stiffness of the limb. The symptoms improve on exercise after rest. There may be an accompanying cellulitis. Dose: night and morning for four days.

2. Lymphadenitis. Inflammation of lymph glands may accompany bacterial infection or be associated with a neighbouring lymphangitis.

SYMPTOMS

Acute inflammation produces heat and swelling. Signs of pain are variable. Oedema accompanies lymphadenitis in the horse as a sequel to lymphangitis.

TREATMENT

Aconitum napellus 6c Should be given as soon as possible in the early inflammatory stage. Dose: every hour for four doses.

Belladonna 1M Indicated in acute cases when the glands are hot and tender. The animal shows excitement and dilated pupils. The pulse is full and bounding and the skin is hot and smooth. Dose: every two hours for four doses.

Phytolacca 30c A good general remedy for swelling of glands. If the submaxillary glands are affected, the swelling extends to the neighbouring parotid salivary glands. This remedy is of benefit in both acute and chronic cases. Dose: night and morning for three days.

Kali hydriodicum 30c A useful remedy when there is an associated local oedema. Coryza and lachrymation may be present. Dose: night and morning for five days.

Apis 6c Indicated in acute cases when oedema of the gland substance is suspected. Fluid swellings surround the affected parts. Dose: every two hours for four doses.

Mercurius iod rub 6c Especially suited for involvement of submaxillary glands which are enlarged and painful, especially on the left side. Dose: three times daily for three days.

Cistus 6c   A useful remedy in chronic lymphadenitis. The glands are indurated. The animal feels the cold and should be protected with a blanket. Throat glands may show a chronic suppuration. Dose: night and morning for one week.

Dulcamara 30c   Indicated when swelling and hardness of glands arise after exposure to cold and damp. Dose: night and morning for four days.

Hepar sulphuris 200c   This is a suitable remedy when suppuration of glands follows pyogenic infections. The animal is sensitive to cold and the glands are extremely tender and painful. Dose: night and morning for five days.

Silicea 1M   A good remedy for chronic involvement. Glands are hard and may contain inspissated pus. Dose: daily for one week.

3.   Angioneurotic Oedema.   This is the term used to denote oedema suddenly appearing, due to allergy and is usually of short duration. It is common in horses at pasture when flowers are in bloom. Affected animals commonly show recurrence after a previous attack.

SYMPTOMS

The head region is mostly affected, but lesions are frequently seen in the perineal region also. The eyes may become puffy and swollen along with similar involvement of the muzzle and cheeks. Lachrymation occurs along with salivation and occasionally rhinitis. Vulval swelling occurs in the mare when the perineal area is attacked.

TREATMENT

Apis 6c   This is a most useful remedy for oedematous swellings appearing especially round the eyes. Dose: every three hours for four doses.

Hypericum 1M   Indicated in cases associated with subcutaneous itching and a tendency to photosensitisation. Dose: every three hours for four doses.

Urtica urens 6c   Should be considered when the swellings are hot and itchy and there is general urticaria-like involvement over the body. Dose: every three hours for four doses.

Vespa 30c   Should be remembered as a possibly useful remedy when the condition is more confined to the face and eyes. Throat and mouth severely swollen. Dose: every three hours for four doses.

Phosphorus 200c Useful when the oedematous swellings are infiltrated with blood as a result of purpura-like haemorrhages. Dose: three times daily for two days.

Antipyrine 6c Associated with intense pruritis and urticaria. Dose: three times daily for three days.

4. Subcutaneous Haemorrhage. This is sometimes seen in horses which have been upset by eating mouldy sweet clover hay, leading to capillary damage. This is known as dicoumerol poisoning.

SYMPTOMS
The main sign is a soft swelling with no skin involvement. It is usually painless.

TREATMENT
Melilotus 6x Associated with general haemorrhage tendency: profuse epistaxis. Impaction of bowels occurs also. Dose: three times daily for four days.

Phosphorus 200c Indicated when capillary damage leads to purpura-like haemorrhages and multiple small swellings. Dose: three times daily for two days.

Millefolium 6c Haemorrhages of bright red blood occur from body orifices. Febrile symptoms are common with sustained high temperature. Dose: three times daily for three days.

Ficus religiosa 6c Indicated in a general haemorrhage diathesis when there are accompanying respiratory symptoms, with vomiting of blood when coughing. Dose: every two hours for four doses.

Ipecacuanha 6c A useful anti-haemorrhagic remedy when digestive upsets are present such as indigestion and slimy frequent stools. Dose: three times per day for three days.

Crotalus horridus 6c Associated with decomposition of blood and generalised haemorrhages of dark fluid non-coagulable blood. Septic involvement of lesions is common. Dose: every three hours for four doses.

Lachesis 30c Indicated when cellulitis is associated with purpura-like haemorrhages of dark blood. Sometimes there is throat swelling. Dose: three times daily for three days.

Arnica 30c If the condition has arisen as a result of injury or multiple bruising. The skin over the haemorrhage swelling is discoloured. Dose: twice daily for one day.

Hamamelis 6c Indicated in general venous congestion. Throat vessels are engorged. Passive haemorrhages of dark blood. The haemorrhages under the skin are associated mainly with venous circulation. Dose: three times daily for three days.

Secale 30c   Haemorrhages of dark, watery blood with a tendency to necrosis of tissue over the affected area. Epistaxis is common and the tongue is swollen making swallowing difficult. Dose: four times in one day.

X Diseases of Alimentary Canal

1. Stomatitis – Inflammation of Mouth. This may arise from various causes, internal and external.

SYMPTOMS

The mouth shows redness. Pain and swelling are usually present. Febrile signs accompany the mouth inflammation. Ulceration of the buccal mucous membrane may occur, leaving a raw, red surface which may discharge purulent material, as a result of secondary infection.

TREATMENT

Aconitum napellus 6c The early febrile stage. Dose: every hour for four doses.

Belladonna 200c No salivation, but mouth red and shiny, pupils dilated and skin hot. Dose: every two hours for four doses.

Rhus toxicodendron 1M Redness of tongue, with formation of small vesicles. Dose: every two hours for four doses.

Mercurius sol. 30c Profuse ropy salivation, with discharge of purulent material. Dose: three times per day for two days.

Nitric acid 200c Ulceration of the buccal mucous membrane occurs, leaving a raw surface. Dose: three times daily for two days.

Borax 6c Vesicular involvement. This remedy very useful when the animal is afraid to move forward or downwards. Dose: three times daily for two days.

Lachesis 200c Pronounced throat swelling, leading to difficulty in breathing and possible epistaxis. Dose: every hour for four doses.

Mercurius cyanatus 30c Inflammation extends to the throat, with formation of whitish membrane. Dose: three times daily for three days.

Kali chloricum 6c Signs of abdominal or hepatic disturbance. Dose: three times daily for three days.

2. Paralysis of Lips. This is usually seen as a result of injury or inflammation of nerves supplying the muscles of the lips.

SYMPTOMS

Lips appear flaccid and may hang loose, while saliva is not retained. Unable to pick food, or to drink water. If the condition is unilateral the lips are drawn away from the affected side.

TREATMENT

Gelsemium 200c Condition arises as a result of toxaemia. Dose: three times daily for two days, followed by one dose every second day for three doses.

Arnica 10M Paralysis results from an injury, one dose only, to be followed by other remedies according to indications.

Plumbum 30c Signs of weakness or paralysis elsewhere. Dose: three times daily for three days.

Causticum 200c Condition has origin in exposure to cold draughts. Dose: night and morning for three days.

Ammonium phos. 6c Accompanying signs of tremulous or tottering gait. Dose: three times daily for three days.

3. Ranula. A cyst-like swelling under the tongue caused by obstruction to a salivary duct.

SYMPTOMS

A globular swelling appears under the tongue and may be unilateral or bilateral.

TREATMENT

Thuja 200c Blisters on tongue, with inflammation of gums. Dose: three times daily for three days.

Apis 30c Fluid in the ranula will be reduced by this remedy. Dose: three times daily for one week, followed by one dose daily of the same remedy in potency 200c for four doses.

Belladonna 1M Inflammatory signs such as sensitivity to touch, with tenderness. Dose: every three hours for four doses.

Mercurius sol. 30c Profuse salivation. Dose: three times daily for two days.

4. Parotitis – Inflammation of Parotid Salivary Gland. This may arise from exposure to cold and may also be a sequel to infectious diseases like strangles.

SYMPTOMS

Normally the gland on one side only is affected and becomes swollen, hard and painful. This hardness usually persists, but rarely becomes suppurative.

TREATMENT

Aconitum napellus 6c Exposure to cold, producing an initial fever. This remedy should be used before giving any other. Dose: every hour for four doses.

Belladonna 1M Gland initially hot and swollen. Signs of delirium may show. Dilated pupils, throbbing dull pulse. Dose: every hour for four doses.

Pulsatilla 6c Right gland affected, with dry mouth and white coated tongue. Dose: three times daily for three days.

Calcarea fluorica 6c Gland is of stony hardness. Inflammatory symptoms are reduced and associated lymph glands become involved. Dose: three times daily for three days.

Bryonia 6c Origin is exposure to cold. Symptoms are relieved from pressure on the gland. Dose: three times daily for one day, followed by one dose night and morning of the potency 200c, for two days.

Baryta carb. 30c This remedy is particularly useful for very young, or very old animals. Swelling extends to tonsils and throat veins may become prominent. Dose: three times daily for three days.

Ferrum phosphoricum 6c A general hot feeling when the mouth is examined, with tonsillitis and ulceration of the throat. Dose: every two hours for four doses.

Kali bichromicum 30c Tough, stringy discharge from mouth and throat. Soft palate may have membranous deposits. Pulse soft and slow. Dose: three times daily for three days.

Mercurius corrosivus 6c Entire throat inflamed and swelling extends to lower neck. Inability to swallow. Salivation and slimy diarrhoea may accompany condition. Dose: three times daily for two days.

Phytolacca 30c Throat bluish-red with swollen tonsils which may be dropsical. Membranous deposits on throat. Lachrymation may accompany throat symptoms. Dose: three times daily for three days.

Rhus toxicodendron 1M Left gland usually affected. Small vesicles appear at corners of mouth. Tongue coated, red at edges. Throat red and inflamed. Redness and swelling of eyes, accompanied by orbital cellulitis. Dose: every two hours for four doses.

5.   Pharyngitis – Inflammation of Throat.   This condition may be dependent on change of weather or exposure to cold winds, or may be induced by change of food or work.

SYMPTOMS
Febrile symptoms first appear, accompanied by anorexia and difficulty in swallowing. The throat swells, becoming tender on pressure. Inflammation extends to the glands of the throat and under the ears. Respirations are increased and pulse is quickened.

TREATMENT
Aconitum napellus 6c In early febrile stage, always use this remedy first. Dose: every hour for four doses.

Belladonna 200c Full bounding pulse, dilated pupils. Tenderness and heat over throat glands. Hot, shiny skin. Animal usually excitable. Dose: every two hours for four doses.

Calcarea fluorica 6c Glands under jaw and behind throat become stony hard. Dose: three times daily for three days.

Mercurius cyanatus 6c Condition accompanied by membranous deposit on throat. Dose: three times daily for three days.

Rhus toxicodendron 1M Vesicular involvement of mouth and tongue, with left-sided inflammation of throat glands. Dose: every two hours for four doses.

Bryonia 6c Relief of symptoms on pressure over the throat, also when condition has arisen as result of exposure to cold dry winds. Dose: every two hours for four doses.

Alumen 6c Tonsils enlarged and hardened. There may be general enlargement of superficial lymph glands on the body. Dose: three times daily for three days.

Aesculus hip. 30c Veins of pharyngeal region swollen and distended. General abdomen discomfort. Liver dysfunction, signs of jaundice and pale stools. Dose: three times daily for two days, followed by one daily dose of potency 200c of 1M for four days.

Capsicum 6c Inflammation extends backwards to base of ears. Useful remedy in less acute involvement. Dose: night and morning for four days.

6. Acute Indigestion. Overeating or feeding on improper food accounts for this condition.

SYMPTOMS

These appear suddenly and include restlessness and signs of pain such as kicking at abdomen. Frequent rolling may accompany a tympanitic abdomen along with rising and lying down at short intervals. Sweating and increased pulse rate occur with discolouration of conjunctiva. The symptoms may abate and return just as badly after a short interval.

TREATMENT

Nux vomica 6c Especially if condition arises from ingestion of indigestible fodder. Constipation usually present. Dose: every two hours for four doses.

Colchicum 6c Tympanitic abdomen, animal passes flatus frequently. Dose: every two hours for three doses.

Colocynthis 6c Animal rolls in acute pain, with head turned towards flank. Dose: every two hours for four doses.

Arsenicum alb. 1M Animal restless, worse towards midnight, thirsty for small quantities of water. Skin dry and scurfy. Dose: every hour for three doses.

Abies canadensis 6c Condition due to overeating. Flatulence prominent. Dose: every two hours for four doses.

Lobelia inflata 6c Salivation and profuse sweating. Appetite often remains good. Flatulence often occurs. Dose: four times daily for one day.

Lycopodium 6c   Accompanying liver symptoms such as yellowish discolouration of conjunctiva and tenderness over liver region. Highly fermentable food aggravates. Dose: every two hours for four doses.

Carbo vegetabilis 6c   Abdomen tense due to flatulence, with comatose symptoms. Flatus every offensive. Symptoms worse lying down. Dose: every hour for four doses.

Nux moschata 6c   Excessive bloat. Difficulty passing a soft stool. Dose: every hour for four doses.

7. Stomach Staggers. In this condition, both stomach and nervous system are affected. If is more common in farm or heavy horses than in light breeds. It may arise if a horse gains access to corn after a period of fasting and then overeats.

SYMPTOMS

Constipation is present, dung being hard and shiny. Signs of colic appear and retention of urine is common. There may be passage of flatus and sweating is patchy in distribution. Mucous membranes of eye and mouth are tinged brick-coloured or yellowish. Symptoms of sleepiness and coma shortly appear and the animal may rest his head against any supporting object. The eyes are half-closed. Twitching of muscles may appear and the breathing is slow and laboured, while the pulse is full and hard. The eye-sight becomes affected and hind-leg paralysis may supervene. These symptoms may progress to a more violent involvement of the nervous system, when the animal bangs his head against a wall, stamps the ground, rears up and may fall backwards. Dilated pupils and staring eyes are prominent, with hard, frequent pulse.

TREATMENT

Nux vomica 6c   Early stages of constipation. Dose: every two hours for four doses.

Opium 10M   Signs of sleepiness and coma, with bowels completely inactive. Dose: one dose only.

Conium 30c   Hind-leg paralysis tending to move forward. Dose: three times daily for three days, after which it may be necessary to follow with ascending potencies at regular intervals.

Belladonna 10M   Severe encephalitis, dilated pupils and full bounding pulse. Dose: every two hours for three doses.

Agaricus muscaris 200c Head symptoms: falling over backwards, 'intoxication'. Dose: three times daily for three days.

8. Loss of Appetite – Anorexia. Although not a disease, this can be troublesome and can affect a horse's performance and usefulness. It may be a symptom of concurrent disease and should be investigated in order to eliminate this possibility.

TREATMENT

In the absence of specific trouble, anorexia may be treated as follows:–

Nux vomica 6c Condition dependent on weak digestion or full stomach. Dose: three times daily for three days.

Ornithogalum 1x Signs of abdominal pain in stomach region, due to pyloric spasm or stenosis. Dose: every hour for four doses.

Vitamin B12 3x This remedy frequently produces a return to appetite. Dose: three times daily for three days.

Anacardium 30c Indefinite cases where more selected remedies have not produced result. Dose: three times daily for three days.

Arsenicum alb. 1M Thirst for small sips of water. Dose: once daily for one week.

Hydrastis 6c Catarrhal conditions such as coryza and muco-purulent lachrymation. The anorexia due to catarrhal gastritis. Dose: three times daily for three days.

China off. 30c Bloated abdomen and general weakness. Bloating relieved by movement. Dose: every three hours for four doses.

9. Constipation. This condition accompanies many diseases, but may arise independently as a result of bad management, or allowing the animal access to rough forage. It may also be dependent on lack of sufficient fluid intake.

SYMPTOMS

Severe straining and passage of small hard lumps of dung, coated with slimy mucus. Spots of blood may be present on the lumps and in severe cases febrile signs may appear, such as reddened conjunctiva and quickened pulse.

TREATMENT

Nux vomica 6c Uncomplicated cases, when there is ingestion of indigestible food. Dose: every two hours for three doses, in mild cases. In animals subject to a more chronic condition, give potency 1M night and morning for two days.

Sulphur 6c   Abdomen sensitive to pressure and colicky symptoms after drinking. This remedy can most usefully be employed in conjunction with *Nux vom.*, giving the remedies in alternation.

Opium 1M   Somnolence and lack of abdominal straining. Animal usually recumbent. Dose: every two hours for two doses.

Hydrastis 30c   General catarrhal states. Signs of stiffness over lumbar region. Liver dysfunction and jaundice may be present. Dose: three times daily for three days.

Alumina 200c   Bleeding from rectum. Severe straining, difficulty in passing urine. Dose: three times daily for three days.

Magnesia muriatica 6c   Liver dysfunction, yellow tongue and other signs of jaundice may appear. Stools small and crumbly. Dose: three times daily for three days.

Collinsonia 6c   Young animals with tendency to rectal prolapse, with possible anal irritation and flatulence. Dose: three times daily for four days.

Bryonia 6c   Stools large, hard and may contain blood – especially in young animals. Dose: three times daily for three days.

Paraffinum 6c   Straining, particularly in foals and young horses. Dose: three times daily for four days.

10. Enteritis – Inflammation of Intestines.   This is a frequent occurrence and may be due to irritation from intestinal worms or to eating indigestible food. In acute cases, the inflammation may extend to the whole bowel.

SYMPTOMS
The condition usually arises slowly. Initial signs are restlessness, staring coat, dullness, rapid pulse and anorexia. Shivering may be present. Pain varies according to the severity of the condition. The abdomen is tucked up and is tender on pressure. There may be constipation, but when irritant materials have contributed to the cause, diarrhoea may be present. The conjunctiva becomes discoloured, while pulse is weak and thready. Prostration sets in as the condition advances, cold sweat appears and legs and ears become cold. Trembling and twitching also prominent symptoms in severe cases.

TREATMENT

Aconitum napellus 6c Early stages of febrile symptoms, animal anxious and restless. Dose: every hour for four doses.

Belladonna 1M Full bounding pulse, dilated pupils, hot shiny coat. Reddening of inside of nose and discolouration of conjunctiva. Dose: every two hours for four doses.

Mercurius corrosivus 30c Thirst and salivation. Slimy motions streaked with blood, with cold sweaty perspiration. Dose: four times in one day, three hours apart.

Arsenicum alb. 1M Restlessness, thirst for small quantities, weak thready pulse and symptoms worse after midnight. Coldness of legs and ears with watery motions, and cadaver-like odour. Dose: every two hours for four doses.

Colocynthis 6c Symptoms of great pain. Animal lies down, head bent toward abdomen. Stools dysenteric and slimy, brought on by eating or drinking. Dose: four times daily, three hours apart, for two days.

Croton tiglium 30c Severe diarrhoea results from inflammation of bowels. Stools watery and forcibly expelled. Dose: four times in one day only, three hour apart.

Sulphur 6c Chronic cases. Mucous membrane of lips and mouth usually intensely red. Dose: three times daily for two days.

11. Dysentery. Overwork or bad food can predispose to this condition. The acute form affects young animals particularly. Older animals may show a more chronic type.

SYMPTOMS

Anorexia, great thirst and small, rapid pulse. Respirations increased. Straining accompanied by signs of abdominal pain, such as kicking at abdomen. Motions are slimy and mucoid, containing whole blood. Fatty particles present.

TREATMENT

Aconitum napellus 6c Early stages of feverish signs – quickened pulse and anxious expression. Dose: every hour for three doses.

Mercurius corrosivus 6c Salivation accompanies condition. Worse at night. Dose: three times daily for two days.

Ipecacuanha 30c Fatty particles in stool. Accompanying cough. Less straining than with *Merc.* Dose: three times daily for three days.

Arsenicum alb. 1M Animal restless, motions watery and pale. Blood in the stool is diffused through the watery motion. Carrion-like odour from stool. Worse towards midnight, thirst for small quantities. Dose: every three hours for four doses.

Colocynth 6c Severe colicky pains accompany restlessness and distension of abdomen. Animal lies down, bending head towards abdomen. Dose: every two hours for four doses.

Phosphoric acid 30c Young animals show acute symptoms. Usually thin and may show skin irritation. Dose: every two hours for four doses.

Aloe 200c Lumpy, jelly-like stools with rectal bleeding. Pain when passing stool. Much flatus present, with tenderness over liver region. Dose: three times daily for two days.

Cantharis 6c Excessive tenesmus when passing stool. Shreds of mucus mixed with blood. Strangury, with small drops of bloody urine. Dose: every three hours for four doses.

Trombidium 30c Pain before and after stool. Dysenteric motions after eating, stools thin, with straining. Dose: every two hours for three doses.

12. Diarrhoea – Superpurgation. This may be an accompaniment of disease, or arise indefinitely as a result of improper feeding or change of diet.

SYMPTOMS

Frequently there is straining when passing evacuations and shreds of mucous membrane may be seen. Motions may be watery or mucoid, sometimes slimy, varying in colour according to the underlying cause. The stool may be passed with difficulty, shown by straining, or passively.

Superpurgation may arise from the overuse of purgatives or giving too large a dose. It may also be seen towards the end of febrile diseases, as a result of disordered metabolism, e.g. liver dysfunction.

There is passage of flatus accompanied by signs of abdominal uneasiness e.g. looking round at flanks. If too much fluid is lost, the legs may get cold and the body temperature may fall.

TREATMENT

Mercurius corrosivus 200c Motions slimy and may contain a little blood. The condition often worse during the night. Salivation. Dose: every two hours for four doses.

Arsenicum alb. 1M Motions pale, watery and excoriate skin round anus. Signs of abdominal pain, thirst for small quantities of water. Worse after midnight, with restlessness and weakness. Odour from stools carrion-like. Dose: every two hours for four doses.

Bryonia 6c Condition brought on by cold dry winds, or sudden change of temperature, or by drinking large quantities of cold water. Dose: three times daily for three days.

Nux vomica 6c Overeating or partaking of indigestible food. Diarrhoea may be preceded by attacks of colic.

Dulcamara 200c Attacks of diarrhoea follow exposure to damp. Stools green and slimy. More prevalent in summer, after sudden fall in temperature. Dose: every two hours for four doses.

Colocynth 6c Attack is accompanied by severe abdominal pain. Animal lies down and rises frequently, bending neck towards abdomen. Food and drink produces jelly-like slimy stools. Dose: every half-hour for four doses, followed by one dose every four hours for two doses.

Croton tiglium 6c Severe watery diarrhoea, with great expulsive movements, brought on even by small quantities of water. Dose: three times daily for two days.

China off. 30c Weakness due to loss of body fluid. This remedy is especially useful in chronic cases. Dose: three times daily for three days.

Podophyllum 6c Long-standing cases. Stools watery and foetid. Attacks worse in morning. There may be prolapse of rectum. Very useful in young animals. Dose: three times daily for three days.

13. Colic. This condition is referred to as spasmodic or flatulent, according to the symptoms arising. Spasmodic colic implies a cramping or spasm of the muscular coat of a portion of the large intestine. Animals of an excitable temperament are more disposed to the condition than those of a more lethargic nature. Flatulent colic, as the name implies, is accompanied by excessive formation of flatus. In each type the pulse becomes thready and the conjunctiva discoloured.

SYMPTOMS

Initially, there is restlessness, pawing the ground and kicking at the abdomen. The animal lies down and may roll violently, or it may lie flat, occasionally looking round at the flank. These spasms pass off but return after a short interval. The expression is anxious and respirations are increased. With flatulent colic there are additional symptoms, tympany and tense abdomen. There are rumbling noises from the bowel and frequent passage of flatus.

TREATMENT

Aconitum napellus 6c   Always in the early stages, one dose every hour for four doses.

Belladonna 1M   Full bounding pulse early in condition, sweating, dilated pupils and excitability. Skin hot and smooth. Dose: every two hours for four doses.

Colchicum 6c   Distension of abdomen and rumbling of flatus. Lower parts of the bowel become distended and can be felt on right side. Animal tends to remain standing. Dose: every hour for three doses.

Colocynth 1M   When spasmodic colic has severe pain and appears to result from having eaten green food. Motions watery, with wind. Dose: every four hours for four doses.

Nux vomica 6c   If attack brought on by eating indigestible food or overeating. Straining to pass dung and urinate. Animal lies on his side looking uneasy, bending head towards flank. Dose: every two hours for four doses.

Ammonium causticum 6c   Preponderance of wind, respiration becomes laboured and short, with discharge of mucus from nostrils. Dose: every two hours for four doses.

Note:–   In extremely acute cases, it may be necessary to administer medicines every ten or fifteen minutes. Generally five or six doses should be sufficient, followed by the extended times outlined above.

XI Diseases of Liver

1. Jaundice. This occurs as a symptom of inflammation of the liver. Sluggish function without inflammation may also produce jaundice. It is sometimes also associated with pneumonia. Obstruction of the bile ducts is also an obvious cause.

SYMPTOMS

The mucous membranes of the eye, mouth and nose become tinged with yellow and skin also shows this discolouration. Urine becomes dark green, because of the presence of bile. Constipation may be present, faeces light in colour. Oedema of limbs may supervene.

TREATMENT

Berberis vulgaris 30c Sluggish liver conditions with tenderness over lumbar region. Skin yellowish, urinary symptoms present. Dose: three times daily for three days.

Carduus marianus 6c Inflammation of liver accompanied by tenderness over hepatic region. Jaundice produces golden-coloured urine. Dose: three times daily for three days.

Chelidonium 6c Pain and tenderness over right shoulder area. Strong yellow discolouration of visible mucous membranes. Obstruction of bile ducts. Dose: three times daily for three days.

Chionanthus 6c Jaundice produces yellow putty-like stools. Liver enlarged. Dose: once daily for three days.

China off. 30c Weakness and debility. Abdominal pain. Stools yellow and fluid, increasing weakness. Dose: every three hours for four doses.

Hydrastis 30c Catarrhal state of bile ducts leading to a gleety condition of urine. Indigestion due to catarrhal gastritis. Pain and stiffness over back. Dose: three times daily for three days.

Lycopodium 200c   Flatulent state. Indifferent appetite. Abdominal tympany after eating. Mucous membranes greyish-yellow and urine loaded with red sediment. Dose: night and morning for five days.

Leptandra 6c   Jaundice cases showing bowel haemorrhage, giving black, foul-smelling stools. Tongue thickly coated and yellow. Portal circulation becomes disturbed. Dose: three times daily for three days.

Magnesia muriatica 30c   Enlargement of liver with difficulty in urination. Jaundice and abdominal pain pronounced. Dose: night and morning for four days.

2. Hepatitis. Inflammation of the liver parenchyma may be caused by a number of varying substances, some in horses being specific viral or other infectious agents. Acute and chronic forms are recognised.

SYMPTOMS

In the acute form, the animal is dull and disinclined to move. Muscular weakness and anorexia are common signs and there may be nervous excitability. Urine is scanty and high coloured. The faeces are clay-coloured and soft after initial constipation in the early anorexia stage. Yawning and lethargy are seen and there may be a tendency to fall forward or press the head against a wall or any convenient object. There is conjunctival discolouration and the mucous membranes of the mouth and nose are yellow and furred-looking. Pain over the right scapular areas produces slight lameness and is also evident on palpation of the liver area. Photosensitisation may occur in animals which are exposed to sunlight and fed on green food.

Chronic states may show oedema and jaundice more commonly than in the acute form. Ecchymotic haemorrhages are frequently seen and there is more tendency to head pressing.

TREATMENT

Phosphorus 200c   Acute form. Stools whitish, either soft or hard. Jaundice and purpura-like haemorrhages occur, urine shows haemoglobinuria and is muddy-looking. Pain in abdomen. Dose: three times daily for three days.

Aloe 200c Abdominal fullness, excessive flatus. Urine scanty, high-coloured. Stools contain much clotted mucus and are very loose. Dose: night and morning for three days.

Bryonia 6c Better at rest. Relief from pressure over liver. Dry coughing may accompany condition. Stools hard, dark, dry, urine scanty and hot. Dose: three times daily for three days.

Carduus marianus 6c Both acute and chronic cases. Urine deep yellow, due to jaundice. Stools deep yellow, alternate between constipation and diarrhoea. Ascites common in chronic state. Dose: three times daily for two days in acute stage; night and morning for two weeks in the more chronic.

Chelidonium 6c Acute stage, showing prominent jaundice, stiffness and pain over right scapular area. Dose: three times daily for three days.

Hydrastis 30c Catarrhal hepatitis indicted by gleety mucus in the urine and evidence of catarrhal inflammations elsewhere, such as rhinitis and catarrhal cough. Dose: night and morning for five days.

Hepar sulphuris 200c Suspected hepatic abscess, shown by presence of purulent material in urine, which has a greasy look. Suppurative involvement may be evident elsewhere, e.g. purulent rhinitis. Dose: night and morning for five days.

Lycopodium 200c More chronic form, in the early stages of cirrhosis. Ascites usually present. Urine contains reddish sediment, and is passed copiously during the night. Dose: night and morning for two weeks.

Mercurius dulcis 6c Chronic hepatitis, with loose, slimy stools, frequently blood-stained. Colitis may be present. Dropsical states common. Dose: three times daily for one week.

XII Diseases of Kidney and Bladder

1. Glomerulo-nephritis. Streptococcal infection may be a contributory cause of this condition in the horse.

SYMPTOMS

The main signs are oliguria and threatened anuria, while in the later stages uraemic signs appear, including increased respirations, sleepiness, intermittent diarrhoea and finally coma. The urine contains high protein together with albumen casts and erythrocytes. Chronic cases show a clear urine, with a low specific gravity and devoid of protein. The acute stage of glomerulo-nephritis is marked by swelling of the kidney substance together with tissue oedema. Pain and tenderness over the kidneys and loins is a fairly constant sign. Increased thirst may accompany the chronic form, owing to salt retention.

TREATMENT

Apis 6c Renal oedema in the acute form. Urine shows albuminous casts. Dose: every two hours for four doses.

Arsenicum alb. 6c Scanty urine showing high albumen content and drops of blood. The animal is restless and thirsty for small quantities. There is a harsh, dry coat. Symptoms worse after midnight. Dose: every two hours for four doses.

Belladonna 1M Acute cases showing excitement and dilated pupils. Full bounding pulse and hot smooth skin. Straining to pass urine which is scanty and loaded with phosphates. Haematuria is common. Dose: every two hours for four doses.

Berberis vulgaris 30c Marked tenderness over loins. Urine contains mucus and a reddish sandy sediment. Urination is frequent. Dose: every three hours for four doses.

Mercurius sol. 30c Urine scanty, with greenish mucus sediment which may contain pus and blood. Urine is dark-coloured. Dose: three times daily for four days.

Lycopodium 200c Urine profuse during the night. Tendency to retention with thick reddish sediment. Dose: night and morning for five days.

Thlaspi bursa 6c Frequent urination with haematuria and a tendency to sand and gravel. Urine heavy with phosphates. Dose: three times daily for two days.

Terebinthina 6c Urine bloody and difficult to expel. Pronounced sweetish odour. Condition often associated with infections. Dose: three times daily for three days.

Phosphorus 200c Acute cases showing blood in urine. Blood is diffused through urine, giving a brownish appearance. Dose: night and morning for three days.

Eucalyptus 6c Suppurative involvements following infections. Urine contains pus. Dose: three times daily for five days.

Kali chloricum 6c Associated jaundice and haemoglobinuria. Urine is albuminous, plentiful and high in phosphates. Dose: three times daily for three days.

Natrum muriaticum 200c Chronic cases showing a pale urine of low specific gravity. There is usually salt retention leading to thirst and anaemia. Dose: night and morning for one week.

2. Nephrosis. This term includes degenerative and inflammatory lesions of the renal tubules. It constitutes a chronic illness characterised by polyuria, emaciation and dehydration. It is frequently associated with toxaemia.

SYMPTOMS

In the acute stage diminution of urine occurs with increased protein in the urine. Chronic cases show polyuria, but degenerative changes in the glomerule sometimes produce a stage of oliguria. The chronic stage is also marked by urine of a low specific gravity.

TREATMENT

Aconitum napellus 6c Acute stage, urine scanty and reddish. Dose: hourly for four doses.

Arsenicum alb. 200c Urine hot and excoriating. There may be carrion-like diarrhoea. Urine contains casts. Symptoms worse after midnight. Dose: two hourly for four doses.

Acetic acid 6c   Chronic cases showing polyuria and pale urine. There may be an accompanying ascites. Dose: three times daily for four days.

Aesculus hip. 30c   Associated hepatic cases. Urine scanty and dark. Pain over left lumbar region. Dose: three times daily for four days.

Berberis vulgaris 30c   Sacral and lumbar pains. Polyuria alternates with oliguria. Dose: night and morning for five days.

Argentum nitricum 30c   Turbidity of urine with sweet smell. Frequent passage of urine and incoordination of movement. Dose: night and morning for four days.

Natrum muriaticum 200c   Emaciation, thirst and anaemia in chronic cases. Dose: night and morning for one week.

Cantharis 30c   Acute inflammatory stage showing severe straining and passage of bloody urine, which contains shreds of mucous membrane. Dose: two hourly for four doses.

Plumbum 30c   Frequent straining and signs of abdominal pain. Urine scanty and expelled drop by drop. Dose: night and morning for one week.

Conium 200c   Old animals showing weakness of hind limbs. Nervous weakness. Inability to expel urine properly. Dose: night and morning for five days.

Note:–   General signs of nephritis include a characteristic stance of the animal in the acute stage. The hind legs become stiff and straddled and there is disinclination to move. The loins are arched and hot and tender to the touch. Thirst is evident and the urine, which may contain blood, is passed with difficulty and in small amounts. The pulse is hard and quick.

3.   Diabetes Insipidus – Profuse Staling.   In this condition there is excessive passage of urine. It may be caused by damaged food, e.g. mouldy hay or oats.

SYMPTOMS
Appetite is diminished and the animal tires easily. Sweating is common. Thirst is prominent and the urine becomes profuse and clear.

TREATMENT
Phosphoric acid 6c   Polyuria worse during the night. Urine

contains phosphates and has a milky appearance. Dose: three times daily for five days.

Acetic acid 6c Excessive thirst and debility. Abdominal symptoms such as ascites are common. Dose: three times daily for five days.

Alfalfa 1x Increase in the amount of urea and phosphates in the urine. Frequency of urination accompanying the polyuria. Dose: four times daily for three days.

Uranium nitricum 6c Increase of sugar in the urine, plus increased flow. Accompanying emaciation with tendency to dropsy. Dose: three times daily for five days.

Argentum metallicum 30c Urine may be turbid, has sweetish odour. Dose: night and morning for three days.

Eupatorium purpureum 6c Strangury at beginning of urination. Urine appears milky and may contain blood. Dose: three times daily for two days.

Helonias 6c Urine is albuminous, profuse and clear. This remedy is especially indicated in mares and fillies. Dose: three times daily for four days.

Sinapis nigra 6c Frequent urging, flow copious. Dose: four times daily for one day.

4. Haematuria. Blood in urine may be associated with injuries or toxaemia from a systemic disease. It may be seen in mares after foaling.

SYMPTOMS

When due to injuries, the loins are hot and the condition tends to recur. When due to toxaemia, the usual febrile signs are present e.g. increased pulse and respiration.

TREATMENT

Aconitum napellus 6c Early febrile stage of toxaemic state. Animal tense and anxious. Dose: every hour for four doses.

Arnica 30c Condition due to injuries, urine shows dark brown sediment. Dose: night and morning for two days.

Terebinthina 200c Urine has sweetish odour. Strangury common, with tendency to suppression. Useful remedy in toxaemic states. Dose: night and morning for four days.

Belladonna 200c In haematuria, where there is no history of injuries or systemic affections. Passage of urine frequent, with signs of excitement. Dose: every three hours for four doses.

Coccus cacti 6c Great difficulty passing urine. Red sediment containing calculi and urates. Dose: four times in twenty-four hours.

Crotalus horridus 6c Urine dark and albuminous, containing casts. Associated with dark haemorrhages elsewhere. Dose: three times daily for three days.

Hamamelis 6c Increased urination, with venous congestion and passive haemorrhages. Dose: night and morning for five days.

Millefolium 6c When bright red blood in urine is associated with similar haemorrhages elsewhere. Dose: three times daily for three days.

Nitric acid 6c Urine contains albumin and smells strongly of ammonia. Cloudy phosphatic urine may alternate with clear urine in old animals. Dose: three times daily for three days.

Pareira brava 6c Thick urine containing much mucus, with great straining and signs of general pain. Dose: three times daily for three days.

Phosphorus 200c Acute febrile state, with signs of liver disturbance, e.g. jaundice and haemoglobinuria. Purpura-like haemorrhages may be seen on visible mucous membranes. Dose: night and morning for three days.

Uva ursi 6c Great accumulation of clotted blood and mucus in the urine, which may be bile stained and contain pus. Dose: three times daily for three days.

5. Cystitis. Inflammation of the bladder can arise from an extension of infection from some part of the urogenital tract. It may also arise as a sequel to calculus formation.

SYMPTOMS

There is general constitutional involvement; pulse and respiration are increased. There is trembling of the hind legs, accompanied by frequent straining to pass urine which may be so scanty as to pass drop by drop. Urine is blood-stained and contains mucus and sabulous material. Paralysis of the muscular coat of the bladder is common in chronic cases, shown by an inability to retain urine.

TREATMENT

Aconitum napellus 6c In the early febrile involvement when pulse and respiration are increased. Dose: every hour for four doses.

Cantharis 30c Much straining and scanty amounts of bloody urine. There is hyperexcitability and signs of sexual irritability. Dose: night and morning in chronic cases, for one week. In acute cases, give one dose every hour for four doses.

Thlaspi bursa 6c Chronic cystitis, when urine contains brick-coloured sediment of gravelly material. Dose: three times daily for one week.

Copaiva 6c Catarrhal cystitis, shown by increase of mucus in the urine. Pain over the bladder area and urine has a sweetish smell. Dose: three times daily for three days.

Nux vomica 30c When ineffectual urging is associated with digestive upsets. Dose: three times daily for two days.

Camphor 6c Strangury, associated with a general collapsed state. Pulse slow, body icy cold. Dose: every hour for four doses.

Cubebs 6c Frequent urination and catarrhal inflammation of the urogenital tract. A great amount of mucus in the urine. Dose: three times daily for three days.

Dulcamara 30c Catarrhal cystitis resulting from exposure to cold or damp. Urine contains a thick mucus or purulent sediment. Dose: three times daily for three days.

Eucalyptus 6c Catarrhal inflammation, while urine contains blood and pus. Urination profuse. Dose: four times daily, three hours apart, for one day.

Eupatorium purpureum 6c Animal shows uneasiness on passage of urine, which may be profuse and milky. Dose: three times daily for three days.

Oleum santali 1x Chronic state. Urine shows thick catarrhal deposit. Dose: three times daily for one week.

Uva ursi 6c Chronic state, where urine is slimy and accompanied by pain and tenesmus. Dose: three times daily for one week.

Sabina 6c Bright blood in urine. Pain over kidneys and bladder. This remedy may act better in mares or fillies, especially when there are uterine symptoms in the former. Dose: night and morning for one week.

6. Embolic Nephritis. This condition has been reported in foals as a sequel to infection by Shigella species.

SYMPTOMS

The urine contains blood and pus. Pain and tenderness over the kidney area accompanied by abdominal discomfort.

TREATMENT

Hepar sulphuris 200c   Animal shows extreme sensitivity to pressure or to cold draughts. Dose: night and morning for five days.

Silicea 30c   Excessive sweating, but symptoms less acute than those calling for *Hepar sulph.* Pus is thin and greyish. Dose: night and morning for six days.

7. Pyelonephritis.   This usually arises from ascending infection of the urinary tract.

SYMPTOMS

Presence of pus in the urine. This may arise from infection of the kidney pelvis, from a suppurative nephritis or from cystitis and urethritis.

TREATMENT

Hepar sulphuris 200c   There is frequently an accompanying suppurative lymphadenitis. Pain and swelling over the loins. Excessive reaction to cold winds or draughts or to touch on kidney area. Dose: night and morning for four days.

Silicea 30c   More chronic case. Pus in urine is creamy-white. Dose: night and morning for one week.

Streptococcus nosode 30c   A useful supplementary remedy to be given along with other indicated medicines. Dose: once daily for three days.

Mercurius corrosivus 200c   Urine is slimy and contains whole blood and greenish pus. Dose: night and morning for four days.

Benzoic acid 6c   When condition results from a primary catarrhal or suppurative cystitis. Urine strong-smelling with high uric acid content. Dose: three times daily for three days.

Kali bichromicum 200c   General catarrhal inflammation of mucous membranes, especially respiratory. Urine contains albumen and casts and is excessively mucous in character. Dose: night and morning for five days.

Uva ursi 6c   Slimy urine, with tendency to calculus formation. Often with urticaria and respiratory symptoms such as dyspnoea. Mucus and pus in urine has a sticky, colloidal character showing as large clots. Dose: three times daily for five days.

Epigea 1x When chronic cystitis leads to a secondary pyelonephritis. Urine contains fine gravel deposit, with pus and haemoglobinuria. Dose: three times daily for five days.

Populus tremuloides 1x Accompanying gastric symptoms, especially in the older animal, and particularly in pregnant mares. Dose: three times daily for five days.

8. Urolithiasis. This condition may arise from stasis of urine. Various factors contribute, but frequently the origin lies in sluggish liver function.

SYMPTOMS

Obvious difficulty in passing urine, which is scanty and blood-stained. Signs of pain include kicking at belly and looking round at the flanks. The penis is usually relaxed during attempts to urinate.

TREATMENT

Thlaspi bursa 30c Condition due to chronic cystitis. Blood in urine with brick-coloured sediment. Dose: night and morning for one week.

Lycopodium 200c Hepatic symptoms, with blood-stained urine containing red sediment – the early stages of calculus formation. Dose: night and morning for seven days.

Berberis vulgaris 30c Associated with liver dysfunction. Tenderness over loins and uric acid deposits in the urine, which also contains mucus. Dose: night and morning for five days.

Sarsaparilla 6c Pain at the beginning and at the end of urination, especially at the end. Urine contains gravelly deposit and is slimy. Dose: three times daily for three days.

Coccus cacti 6c Dark urine containing whole blood and urates. Small calculi may be present. Considerable urging and tenesmus. Dose: three times daily for five days.

Solidago 6c When urine is slimy and has thick sediment, but has a clear colour and offensive smell. Dose: three times daily for four days.

Ocimum ganum 30c Cases which show a uric acid diathesis. Long crystals of uric acid may appear in urine, which has a characteristic heavy smell. Urine thick and purulent. Dose: night and morning for five days.

9. Paralysis of the Bladder. In the early stages of paralysis, the bladder remains full and dribbling of urine takes place. The bladder wall loses its muscle tone and the result is a build up to a chronic cystitis.

TREATMENT

Gelsemium 200c   There is a profuse flow of pale urine which is expelled passively when the bladder becomes full. Dose: night and morning for five days.

Conium 30c   When passage of urine starts and stops frequently. There is difficulty in expulsion. Condition may be accompanied by weakness of back and hind limbs, shown by difficulty in rising. Dose: three times daily for four days.

XIII   Affections of the Skin

1. Pityriasis or Dandruff. The term implies an accumulation of bran-like scales on the skin. It has various causes, such as dietary, parasitic, fungoid, etc.

SYMPTOMS

There is an accumulation of scales on the skin, unaccompanied by itching. The scales are more prominent where there is long hair, e.g. under the mane. The coat is dry and harsh.

TREATMENT

Arsenicum alb. 1M This is especially adapted to fine-skinned animals. The temperament is usually restless and there is thirst for small quantities. Dose: once daily for two weeks.

Kali sulphuricum 6c Indicated where there are accompanying symptoms of gastric and respiratory upset. There may be an associated eczema showing papular eruption. Dose: three times daily for three days.

Lycopodium 200c Thickening of the skin which later becomes dry and shrunken. Dose: night and morning for one week.

Natrum muriaticum 200c When condition is associated with a greasy skin. There may be increased passage of urine with a low specific gravity. Dose: night and morning for one week.

Graphites 6c Skin rough and hard, showing a streaky discharge. Dose: three times daily for one week.

Sulphur 6c Skin generally unhealthy-looking and dirty. There may be a musty smell. Folds of skin tend to become excoriated. Dose: three times daily for one week.

2. Parakeratosis. This is a condition where keratinisation of epithelial cells is incomplete.

SYMPTOMS

The condition shows as a lesion often confined to the flexor aspects of the joints. It is shown first as reddening, followed by thickening of the skin. A greyish discolouration becomes super-imposed. Fissuring takes place and a raw red surface remains.

TREATMENT

Kali arsenicum 30c   Lesions worse under warm conditions. There may be an associated itching. Dose: night and morning for one week.

Cantharis 200c   Acute state, showing itching and reddening of skin. Straining at urination probable, urine being passed drop by drop. Dose: night and morning for four days.

Graphites 6c   Persistent dryness of skin with, or without, exudation. Dose: three times daily for four days.

Sulphur iodatum 6c   Accompanying papular eruption, usually with reddening and itching. Dose: night and morning for one week.

3.   Impetigo.   This condition is characterised by the appearance of small vesicles surrounded by an erythematous zone. It is usually staphylococcal in origin, and found frequently on the hairless parts of the body.

SYMPTOMS

The vesicles at first contain a clear fluid, but later become pustular and then go on to scale formation. They remain separate as a rule. Secondary infection after rupture of the pustule can lead to pyogenic involvement.

TREATMENT

Antimonium tartaricum 6c   Vesicles and pustules are surrounded by a bluish red mark. There may be an accompanying respiratory distress. Debility and sweating are prominent symptoms. Dose: three times daily for three days followed by one dose daily for four days.

Mezereum 30c   Condition associated with stiffness and involvement of bones. Intense itching of vesicles which have a reddish surround. Dose: night and morning for five days.

Cantharis 200c   Vesicles intensely itching and burning, together with accompanying strangury, the urine being blood-stained and

passed drop by drop. Dose: three times daily for two days
followed by one dose daily for three days.

Rhus venenata 30c Underlying skin dark red. Itching and
erysipeloid inflammation. Dose: night and morning for four
days.

Hepar sulphuris 200c Secondary infection leads to the formation
of purulent small ulcers. Dose: night and morning for five days.

4. Urticaria. This is an allergic condition characterised by
wheals or raised oedematous plaques on the skin. They appear
quickly and are usually multiple.

SYMPTOMS
The plaques are tender to the touch. If dependent on insect bites or
stings, itching may be present, but otherwise this is absent.
Diarrhoea is usually present.

TREATMENT
Antimonium crudun 6c Much itching and plaques are small and
numerous. Dose: three hourly for four doses.

Apis 6c Plaques hot and tender and contain fluid and are usually
large. Dose: two hourly for four doses. Abdomen mainly
affected, with tendency for the condition to become chronic.
Dose: three times daily for four days.

Antipyrene 6c Condition accompanied by angio-neurotic oedema,
which appears very suddenly. Dose: two hourly for four doses.

Fragaria 6c Accompanying erysipelatous inflammation, with an
associated body swelling. Dose: three hourly for four doses.

Astacus fluv. 30c Liver complaints, e.g. jaundice accompany the
condition. Cervical lymph glands swollen. Dose: three times
daily for three days.

Natrum muriaticum 200c Accompanying alopecia and passage of
large quantities of pale urine. Dose: once daily for ten days.

Urtica urens 6c Plaques hot and itchy, with a tendency to oedema.
Urine usually contains uric acid deposits. Dose: three times daily
for three days.

5. Eczema. This term covers skin complaints which produce an
inflammation of epidermal cells. It can arise from internal or
external factors. It may be environmental in origin, or be dependent
on excessive sweating or repeated wetting.

SYMPTOMS

The initial lesion is erythematous, followed by weeping of the skin. Itching is usually intense and alopecia may occur.

TREATMENT

Sulphur 30c Lesion red and looks wet. Itching intense, worse from warmth. Dose: night and morning for five days.

Arsenicum alb. 1M Dry eczema. Animal is thirsty and seeks warmth. Symptoms worse after midnight, animal becoming more restless. Dose: once daily for two weeks.

Rhus toxicodendron 1M Condition is vesicular and itchy. Stiffness is relieved by movement. Dose: once daily for five days.

Bovista 6c Pimply eruption with crust formation and abnormal pain. Dose: three times daily for four days.

Antimonium crudum 6c Eczema accompanied by stomach upsets. Worse at night. Dose: night and morning for three days.

Anacardium 200c Nervousness. Skin reddish and very itchy, with vesicular eruption. Dose: night and morning for five days.

Petroleum 200c Blistery eruptions with tendency to suppuration of cracked skin, which bleeds easily. Skin usually dry. Dose: night and morning for one week.

Psorinum 30c Dry, lustreless skin with severe pruritis. The associated lymph glands are swollen. Sometimes an oily skin has ulceration which heals slowly. An unpleasant smell accompanies the eczema. Dose: night and morning for one week.

Graphites 6c Discharge of sticky, honey-coloured fluid. Dose: three times daily for three days.

Cantharis 200c Severe vesicular eczema. Strangury and blood-stained urine. Dose: night and morning for five days.

Kali arsenicum 30c Severe pruritis in chronic states. Worse from a change of weather. Lesion dry and scaly. Dose: night and morning for ten days.

6. Dermatitis. This term implies an inflammation of the true skin – the dermis – and the epidermis. It may be bacterial, mycotic or viral in origin and an allergic form is common in the horse.

SYMPTOMS

Erythema is the first sign. Vesicular lesions may then occur followed by oedema of the subcutaneous tissues in severe cases, leading to cellulitis if the condition persists. Shock may be present in the early stages and toxaemia may occur.

TREATMENT

Arsenicum alb. 1M Dry dermatitis. Thirsty, restless and worse after midnight. Dose: one dose per day for ten days.

Rhus toxicodendron 1M Vesicles may form in the early erythematous stage. Stiffness of joints. Dose: one dose three times daily for two days.

Antimonium tartaricum 30c Early stages of vesicular formation. Respiratory symptoms sometimes accompany this condition. Dose: one dose night and morning for three days.

Arnica 30c Shock symptoms in the early stages. Dose: one dose six hourly for two doses.

Aconitum napellus 6c Febrile symptoms and toxaemia. Dose: one dose two hourly for four doses.

Thuja 200c Chronic state, showing thickening of the skin. Dose: one dose per day for two weeks.

7. Photosensitisation. This condition in which the unpigmented parts of the skin show sensitivity to sunlight is sometimes seen in piebald or skewbald animals. It is a sensitisation of the superficial layers of the skin to light and may lead to dermatitis.

SYMPTOMS

Lesions are restricted to unpigmented areas and may accompany liver disturbance such as jaundice. The lesions are always confined to the upper part of the body. The early signs may be erythema and oedema.

TREATMENT

Hypericum 1M Accompanying pruritis. Dose: three hourly for four doses.

Chelidonium 1M Signs of jaundice, pain and stiffness over the right shoulder area. Dose: once daily for one week.

Rhus venenata 30c Dermatitis and blister formation. Dose: night and morning for four days,

Antimonium crudum 6c Skin dry and itchy, with tendency to scab formation. Dose: night and morning for five days.

8. Alopecia. Loss of hair may be due to metabolic or dietetic errors. The skin may appear shiny and thinner than usual.

TREATMENT

Lycopodium 200c Frequent skin ulceration together with gastric and hepatic disorders. Dose: night and morning for one week.

Pix liquida 6c Skin irritation accompanied by respiratory disorder. Dose: night and morning for five days.

Calcarea fluorica 6c Helpful in skin condition which heal slowly, e.g. ulcers and fissures. Dose: three times daily for three days.

Thyroidinum 200c In generalised alopecia when it is suspected that the thyroid gland is at fault. Dose: once daily for two weeks.

Note:– It may be necessary to continue treatment on a higher potency and for a longer period, if there is only partial improvement with any of the above remedies.

9. Seborrhoea. This is excessive secretion of sebum on the skin. In horses one of the main types is greasy heel starting as a dermatitis or eczema and leading to secondary infection. Greasy heel is commonest in the hind feet of horses accustomed to standing for long periods in damp, unhygienic stables.

SYMPTOMS

The skin becomes thick and greasy and small vesicles appear. In cases of greasy heel, lameness appears first, followed by pain due to abrasions on the skin which may extend down to the coronary band.

TREATMENT

Arsenicum alb. 1M Use in the early stages before secretion of sebum becomes profuse. Dose: once daily for one week.

Graphites 6c Secretion is sticky and honey-coloured, skin generally rough and dry. Eczematous lesions appear in the fissures of the skin and bends of the joints. Dose: three times daily for five days.

Antimonium crudum 30c Vesicles appear, accompanying thickening of the skin. Dose: night and morning for one week.

Thuja 200c A most valuable remedy in greasy heel. Dose: once daily for ten days.

Note:– Externally an application of *Arsenicum* lotion is useful. Other applications such as *Sulphuric acid* and *Thuja* lotions may be used.

10. Hyperkeratosis. In this condition keratinised cells accumulate on the skin surface.

SYMPTOMS
Skin becomes corrugated and hairless. Excessive thickening occurs accompanied by dryness and scale formation. Fissuring occurs and may lead to secondary infection.

TREATMENT
Arsenicum alb. 1M Useful when continued over several weeks with intervals between treatments. Dose: once daily for one week, followed by several weeks of no treatment. If, during the interval, improvement has been noted, but ceases, it is then advisable to continue with this remedy in a higher potency. e.g. 10M.
Kali arsenicum 6c Pruritis aggravated by warm conditions. Fissuring in the bends of the joints. Dose: night and morning for one week.
Sulphur iodatum 6c When there is danger of a secondary infection occurring. Dose: night and morning for ten days.
Thuja 200c Long-standing cases. There may be enlargement of associated glands. Dose: once daily for two weeks.
Hydrocotyle 6c This remedy often gives success when the better known remedies fail to act. Dose: night and morning for ten days.

11. Acne Infection of hair follicles by a special bacillus or by any pyogenic bacterium e.g. staphylococcus. A non-specific form is common in the horse and lesions can occur in pressure areas, e.g. under the saddle.

SYMPTOMS
Lesions commence as nodules quickly becoming pustular and spreading to other neighbouring follicles.

TREATMENT
Hepar sulphuris 200c It is probable that this remedy, given where the symptoms are uncomplicated, may have to be repeated in

increasingly higher potencies. First dosage: night and morning for one week.

Sulphur iodatum 6c Associated eczema with reddening of the skin. Dose: night and morning for one week.

Arsenicum alb. 1M When skin is dry and itchy. Animal restless and thirsty. Dose: once daily for ten days.

Silicea 200c Sweats easily, with lesions which coalesce quickly and penetrate the subcutaneous tissues. Dose: once daily for two weeks.

Kali bromatum 6c When lesions affect shoulder and head. Skin is insensitive to pain. Dose: night and morning for one week.

Ledum 6c Acne associated with facial eczema. Itching made worse by warmth. Dose: night and morning for one week.

Hydrocotyle 6c Pustules worse on the chest, associated with skin desquamation and severe itching. Dose: night and morning for one week.

Antimonium crudum 6c Warty excrescences and dry skin. Hard scabs appear over the pustules. Dose: night and morning for five days.

12. Sporotrichosis – Mycotic Dermatitis. This is a contagious disease of horses caused by a specific fungus. It leads to the development of nodules on the skin and ulceration of the lower limbs. The disease may be spread either by direct contact, or through contaminated bedding or harness.

SYMPTOMS

Groups of small nodules develop on the skin of the legs particularly about the fetlock. The nodules develop scabs which discharge pus, but they are usually painless. The condition has a tendency to spread and form new nodules and three may, or may not, be an associated lymphangitis.

TREATMENT

Sepia 30c Useful in fungal conditions. Dose: once daily for two weeks.

Bacillinum 200c In mycotic conditions, this is a very good remedy. Dose: once weekly for three doses.

Arsenicum alb. 1M An excellent skin remedy and can often be combined with other treatment. Dose: once daily for ten days.

Calcarea iodata 200c When the condition is combined with swellings of the associated glands. Dose: once daily for five days.

Silicea 200c When the nodules discharge pus and the ulcers are slow to heal. Dose: once daily for one week.

13. Ringworm. Ringworm lesions in the horse may be superficial or deep, the former being the more common, producing desquamation and alopecia with development of thick crusts.

SYMPTOMS

Irritation and itching may first occur, the lesions developing initially on the rump and trunk and spreading to other parts. When deeper structures are involved, small suppurative foci develop in the hair follicles, producing a small scab over the follicles.

TREATMENT

Hydrocotyle 6c When there are scaly lesions on the trunk. There is exfoliation of scales of the skin. Dose: night and morning for one week.

Bacillinum 200c Rough, dry skin. Give as a constitutional remedy. Dose: once per week for three doses.

Sepia 1M Associated with unpleasant musty odour. Dose: once a week for four doses.

Pix liquida 6c Tendency to alopecia. Eruptions scaly and itchy. Dose: night and morning for one week.

14. Sebaceous Cysts. Occasionally these occur in the horse, being sited mainly on the sheath and the false nostril and the lips. The cysts contain fatty material along with dead cells and are due to the retention of sebaceous material in the glands. They are usually soft and fluctuating in the early stages, but may become firm and doughy later. Inflammatory symptoms appear if the cyst is subject constant irritation.

TREATMENT

Baryta carb. 30c Cysts prominent on the head and face. Dose: twice daily for five days.

Benzoic acid 6c Cysts on face, accompanied by cystitis with dark offensive urine. Dose: three times daily for five days.

Conium 200c   Long standing cases when cysts are usually firm and hard. Dose: once daily for seven days.

Apis 30c   Early stages when there is an abundance of fluid present and inflammatory symptoms appear. Dose: every three hours for four doses.

XIV   Affections of the Female Reproductive System

1. Infertility. Hormone dysfunction can occur frequently in the form of cystic ovaries, and ovaritis without cyst formation. Leucorrhoea, endometritis and vaginitis also occur.

Ovaritis.   Inflammation of the ovary may lead to irregularities in ovarian function and can result in extension of inflammation to oviducts and the formation of adhesions in the ovarian bursa.

SYMPTOMS
The mare exhibits signs of pain in the pelvic area, kicking at one or other of the flanks. Temperament may change, e.g. a normally docile animal may become difficult. Rectal examination reveals an increase in the size of the ovary concerned.

TREATMENT
Aconitum napellus 6c   Early acute stage. Febrile signs – rapid, firm pulse and increased respiration. Dose: hourly for four doses.
Apis 6c   Inflammation with swelling due to hyperaemia leading to oedema. Dose: three times daily for two days.
Bryonia 6c   Right ovary affected, shown by animal kicking at right pelvic flank. Animal prefers to be still and quiet. Dose: three times daily for two days.
Lilium tigrinum 200c   Accompanying signs of uterine inflammation such as discharges. Hind legs weak, frequent straining movements. Dose: three times daily for three days.
Cimicifuga 30c   Left ovary affected. Pains extend across lumbar region and downwards towards the udder. Heart action weak and irregular. Dose: night and morning for four days.

Hamamelis 6c General venous congestion with this complaint. Blood vessels of throat usually enlarged. Pain extends over whole abdomen and there may be a metrorrhagia. Dose: three times daily for three days.

Iodum 6c Thin animals showing excessive appetite and dryness of skin. Mammary glands appear shrunken. Dose: three times daily for one week.

Cantharis 30c Furious excitement and severe strangury. Urine contains blood and its passed drop by drop. Vesication of skin may occur. Dose: two hourly for four doses.

Palladium 30c Right ovary affected, with leucorrhoea and flatulence. Dose: night and morning for one week.

2. Cystic Ovaries. This condition is associated with an over-development of the Graffian follicle and its persistence in the ovaries. It may be associated with an absence of heat or, at the other extreme, a state of nymphomania may occur. Between these extremes are signs of irregular heat. The condition sometimes resolves itself, but when extreme, the enlarged follicle becomes filled with fluid and is referred to as cystic.

SYMPTOMS

In mares which do not show heat periods, there are usually one or two large cysts present. These are detected by rectal palpation. Mares showing cystic ovaries are usually uncertain in temperament. When the condition occurs in animals which show continuous or irregular lengthy heat periods, multiple small cysts develop and a state of nymphomania supervenes.

TREATMENT

Apis 6c As one of the main remedies for dropsical conditions, this should be tried as an initial treatment. Dose: three times daily for four days.

Aurum mur. nat. 6c When a chronic metritis is suspected, and whitish discharge shows. Ovaries may be indurated. Dose: three times daily for four days.

Colocynth 6c Nymphomania, with multiple small cysts. Symptoms of great abdominal pain. Dose: night and morning for one week.

Oophorinum 6c   Accompanying skin disorder, e.g. a non-pruritic eczema. Dose: three times daily for one week.

Platina metallicum 30c   Nymphomania, with constipation and abdominal pain extending to pelvis. Dose: night and morning for one week.

Aurum iodatum 6c   Accompanying degenerative lesions in other areas, e.g. chronic inflammatory conditions of serous membranes. Dose: three times daily for one week.

3. Leucorrhoea. This condition implies a whitish mucoid, catarrhal or purulent discharge from the vulva. It may be associated with increased activity of the uterine glands and usually has its origin in ovarian dysfunction when there is failure to ovulate despite good follicular activity.

SYMPTOMS

There is passive non-inflammatory bland discharge from the vulva, usually whitish and mucoid. Secondary infection of the uterine mucous membrane leads to a purulent discharge. If the discharge becomes acrid, the skin around the vulva becomes excoriated.

TREATMENT

Pulsatilla 30c   Discharge acrid, thick and creamy. Urinary symptoms such as pain during and after micturition. Dose: night and morning for five days.

Alumen 30c   Chronic state. Discharge has yellow colour and there may be necrosis of areas of the vagina. Dose: night and morning for one week.

Hydrastis 30c   Discharge bland and catarrhal. Mucous membranes elsewhere may also show this type of discharge. Dose: three times daily for five days.

Kali muriaticum 6c   Discharge bland and milky-white. There may be accompanying glandular swellings and a thick white-coated tongue. Dose: night and morning for one week.

Kreosotum 30c   Discharge greenish-yellow and acrid, has a pungent odour. There may be swellings and ecchymotic haemorrhages on the skin. Dose: night and morning for one week.

Nitric acid 6c   Vaginal mucous membrane ulcerated and there is brown, watery discharge. Small ulcers may also appear in the mouth. Dose: once daily for one week.

Psorinum 1M Harsh dirty coat showing rough eczematous patches. Skin has heavy, musty odour. Discharge contains lumps of mucous material and there are signs of weakness, especially along the back muscles. Dose: once daily for five days.

Thuja 200c Wart formation on various parts of the body, especially round the vulva. Discharge thick and greenish. Dose: once a week for one month.

4. Endometritis. This is commonly associated with a difficult parturition or with retained foetal membranes especially after abortion. These conditions cause a delay in involution of the uterus which leads to the metritis.

SYMPTOMS
There is a vulval discharge which at first is mucoid, but soon becomes purulent, due to secondary bacterial invasion. The inflammation extends to the anterior area of the vagina and produces a thickened corrugated condition of the uterine cervix and vagina. Febrile symptoms in acute cases following protracted labour or retention of foetal membranes following abortion. These signs include rapid, wiry pulse, shallow respiration and sweating. Signs of pain include kicking at the flank and looking round to the pelvic area. Straining is a common symptom.

TREATMENT
Aconitum napellus 6c   Give early in the acute febrile stage. Animal anxious and restless. Dose: hourly for four doses.

Belladonna 1M Acute cases, when there is full pulse, dilation of pupils and a hot, smooth skin. Dose: every two hours for four doses.

Echinacea 6x Puerperal fever, or septicaemia sets in after abortion or retention of unhealthy foetal membranes. Dose: two hourly for four doses.

Sabina 6c Discharge of bright blood, partly clotted. Especially useful is condition results from abortion. Urine blood-stained. Dose: three times daily for four days.

Secale 30c Puerperal metritis after abortion, where discharge of blood is dark and fluid. Dose: three times daily for four days.

Arsenicum alb. 200c Chronic endometritis in restless animals, showing thirst for small quantities. Worse after midnight. Dose: one dose daily for ten days.

Mel cum sale 6c   Chronic endometritis when cervix is particularly affected and at commencement of inflammatory process. Dose: three times daily for three days.

Sulphur 200c   This can usefully be given in chronic cases, in combination with other indicated remedies. Dose: one dose weekly for three days.

Note:– As this condition is frequently associated with streptococcal infection, it will be found profitable to combine treatment with the use of Streptococcus nosode, giving one dose per day for three consecutive days at the beginning of treatment.

5. Vaginitis.   Inflammation of the vagina can arise as a sequel to or complication of coitus and parturition. It is also seen in mares when a heat period coincides with a feverish illness such as influenza.

SYMPTOMS

The vaginal mucous membrane becomes red and thickened and a mucous discharge appears which becomes purulent, due to secondary infection. Straining is a common sequel.

TREATMENT

Aconitum napellus 6c   Febrile signs accompanying the acute phase. Dose: every two hours for three doses.

Hydrastis 30c   Discharge is catarrhal and bland. There may be catarrh of other mucous membranes. Dose: three times daily for two days.

Cantharis 200c   Severe urinary symptoms: urine is passed drop by drop and contains blood. Mare strains violently and kicks at lower abdomen. Dose: every two hours for four days.

Mercurius sol. 30c   Secondary purulent discharge, greenish and streaked with blood. Slimy blood-stained stools and salivation. Dose: three times daily for three days.

Pulsatilla 30c   Discharge bland and creamy. Signs of colic. Dose: three times daily for three days.

Nitric acid 200c   Ulceration on posterior vagina. Discharge thin, watery and brown. Possibly mouth ulcers and diarrhoea. Dose: night and morning for four days.

Arsenicum alb. 200c   Discharge acrid and burning, excoriating skin round vulva. Mare restless, thirsty, worse after midnight. Dose: three times daily for three days.

6.   Abortion.   This can arise from various causes, some of which are specific and are dealt with under specific diseases. Non-specific causes include injuries and over-exertion and may also follow an attack of severe colic.

SYMPTOMS
The signs are those of approaching parturition, viz. loosening of the sacral and pelvic ligaments, discharge of blood-stained fluid, kicking at abdomen and general restlessness. The pulse is quickened and becomes firm and wiry.

TREATMENT
Aconitum napellus 6c   Give immediately on first signs of impending abortion. Dose: every hour for four doses.
Arnica 30c   Abortion results from injury. Dose: every three hours for three doses.
Opium 200c   Abortion resulting from severe fright. Dose: twice in one day only.
Secale 200c   Will help control post-abortion haemorrhage when accompanied by much straining. Blood dark and clotted. Dose: every three hours for four doses.
China off. 30c   Much loss of blood, with great weakness. Dose: every two hours for four doses.
Sabina 6c   Haemorrhage, with bright red blood, partly clotted. Dose: every three hours for four doses.
Pyrogenium 1M   Septic abortion associated with retention of foetal membranes, producing a low grade fever characterised by discrepancy of pulse and temperature, e.g. a weak thready pulse with high temperature, or a full pulse with low temperature. Dose: every three hours for four doses.
Note:-   Treatment should always be directed towards the associated effects such as retained placenta, endometritis, uterine discharge, etc.

7.   Retained Placenta.   This is not a common occurrence in the mare, but may occur occasionally after a normal parturition. It is more commonly seen after abortion and can be accompanied by severe symptoms such as laminitis and septicaemia. Normally the foetal membranes are expelled shortly after parturition but if not expelled after two hours one or other of the following remedies should be given.:-

Sabina 6c Dose: every hour for four doses.
Pulsatilla 30c Dose: every three hours for three doses.
Secale 30c Dose: every two hours for three doses.
Pyrogenium 1M Dose: every three hours for three doses.

8. Inflammation of Udder. This may arise in a nursing dam, due to exposure to cold and sometimes as a result of an inability on the part of the foal to suck enough milk.

SYMPTOMS

There may be an initial febrile involvement, such as rapid pulse and increased respiration. The mouth may be hot and constipation is usually present. Local symptoms include heat and tenderness of the gland which is swollen and firm in acute cases. Softening of the swelling is accompanied by the formation of cheese-like curds which may contain blood.

TREATMENT

Expression of the contents of the udder should be accompanied by the use of one of the following:-

Aconitum napellus 6c Early in febrile symptoms. Dose: every hour for four doses.
Phytolacca 6c Associated lymph glands are involved. Udder swollen and tender. Dose: three times daily for two days.
Belladonna 1M Acute case, excitability, dilated pupils, full bounding pulse. Udder hot and swollen. Dose: every two hours for four doses.
Bryonia 6c Gland hard, but less hot than when *Belladonna* is indicated. Dose: three times daily for three days.
Hepar sulphuris 200c Suppuration, udder extremely tender, mare resents touch. This remedy in low potency, e.g. 6x will hasten expression of purulent material, but in higher potency, will hasten resolution. In either case, one dose three times daily for two days, of the appropriate potency, should suffice.

Mercurius sol. 30c Secretion greenish, blood-stained. Udder tissue firm after evacuation of contents. There may be an accompanying blood-stained diarrhoea. Dose: three times daily for three days.

Silicea 200c When superficial ulcers appear and are slow to heal, showing thin, creamy pus. Dose: once daily for five days.

S.S.C. 30c This is a combination of *Sulphur*, *Silicea* and *Carbo veg.* and may be used to ease expression of clotted milk. Dose: three times daily for three days, followed by one dose daily for three days.

XV Affections of the Musculo Skeletal System

1. Myopathy. This term implies degeneration of muscle tissue, non-inflammatory in origin. A common form in saddle horses is the condition known as polymyositis.

SYMPTOMS

The affection shows clinically as muscle weakness. It can develop suddenly during exercise and can lead to necrosis of muscle tissue of the hind quarters. The skeletal muscles become rubbery and swollen and the animal moves with a short, painful gait, or may be disinclined to move at all.

Myopathy has been reported in the thoroughbred foal up to about four months of age, appearing in spring or early summer. A per-acute form exists in which dejection, stiffness and disinclination to move are the chief symptoms. Less acute cases may move more readily but are stiff and lethargic. The subcutaneous tissues over the gluteal muscles become swollen and firm and this occurs also at the base of the mane. Excessive salivation has been noted, also superficial ulceration of the tongue.

TREATMENT

Sarcolactic acid 30c Muscles of the neck and back affected. Muscular prostration and possibly dyspnoea. Dose: night and morning for four days.

Picric acid 6c Muscular weakness and involvement appear to deteriorate in an ascending manner. Symptoms worse after motion. Dose: night and morning for one week.

Thuja 200c Sweating accompanied by twitching of muscles. Dose once daily for one week.

Cuprum metallicum 1M   Cramping accompanies a general hardening of muscles. Dose: once daily for one week.

2. Muscular Spasm.   Spasm of muscle may take one of two forms: (a) tonic or continuous spasm, and (b) clonic or intermittent. The former can occur in such diseases as tetanus, but can also arise after prolonged exertion and may appear up to twelve hours after discontinuing exercise. Clonic spasms are more usually associated with poisoning or certain nervous diseases.

TREATMENT

Arnica 30c   After prolonged or violent exercise. Dose: every three hours for two doses.

Cuprum metallicum 1M   Clonic spasms accompanied by cramping of muscles. Dose: hourly for four doses.

Agaricus muscarius 6c   Twitching, with cramp-like condition of lower limbs. Dose: every two hours for four doses.

Strychninum 200c   Pronounced clonic spasm of any muscle group. Dose: every two hours for four doses.

Cicuta virosa 6c   Extensive tonic spasms. Muscles of nape of neck and head chiefly involved. Dose: every three hours for four doses.

Strophanthus 6c   Clonic spasms, especially muscles of the upper part of the body. Dose: every two hours for four doses.

Cimicifuga 30c   Heaviness of lower limbs accompanied by twitching. The animal is usually restless and shows signs of pain. Dose: every three hours for four doses.

3. Rupture of Muscles.   Muscle rupture may result from excessive contraction and relaxation and may involve associated tendons. Violent injury or strain may also lead to rupture.

SYMPTOMS

Inflammation and swelling are early signs, the latter often due to extravasated blood. Lameness will be evident if limb muscles are involved.

TREATMENT

Arnica 30c   All cases. Dose: every two hours for two doses.

Ruta graveolens 30c   If there is an associated rupture of tendon at its insertion. Dose: three times daily for three days.

4. Myositis. Inflammation of muscle tissue may have its origin in an open wound or in infection, or it may be the result of severe straining.

SYMPTOMS
Local heat in the muscle is an early sign, followed by stiffness or lameness if leg muscles are involved. Febrile signs will accompany infectious conditions.

TREATMENT
Arnica 30c Should always be given in the early inflammatory stage. Dose: every two hours for two doses.
Apis 6c Oedema accompanies inflammation. Dose: every three hours for four doses.
Hepar sulphuris 30c Infection from an open scratch or wound. Dose: three times daily for three days.

5. Muscular Atrophy. Wasting of muscle tissue may follow myositis or be dependent on an impaired nerve supply.

SYMPTOMS
These are obvious, comprising reduction in muscle size and loss of muscular function.

TREATMENT
Arnica 30c All cases, in as much as injury of one kind or another has been the original cause. Dose: every two hours for two doses.
Gelsemium 200c Local paralysis of nerve supply, provided there has been no permanent damage. This remedy helps loss of nerve function. Dose: three times daily for three days.
Curare 30c Muscular paralysis associated with trembling of limbs and various groups of muscles. Dose: three times daily for four days.
Lathyrus sativa 200c Atrophy of gluteal muscles and those of stifle and hock. Dose: three times daily for five days.
Plumbum 1M Generalised paralytic involvement leads to affection of various groups of muscles. Feet often become swollen. Extensor muscles are more involved when this remedy is indicated. Dose: once daily for seven days.

Thallium 30c Paralysis of lower limbs leading to atrophy. Evidence of recurring pains. Dose: twice daily for five days.

Abrotanum 6c Marked wasting of the lower limbs, accompanied by stiffness of joints. Dose: three times daily for four days.

Acetic acid 6c Wasting of muscles accompanied by oedema of feet and legs. Dose: twice daily for seven days.

6. Osteodystrophy. This term implies failure of normal bone development, or abnormal growth of already developed bone.

SYMPTOMS

The main symptom is distortion and enlargement of bones and susceptibility to fracture. Gait is interfered with. Rickets of young animals and osteomalacia of adults are manifestations, caused by deficiencies of calcium, phosphorus and vitamin D. A spondylitis occurs in the horse and can affect racing performance. It is thought by some authorities to start as a disc degeneration. Weakening of bones leads to fractures and deformities depending on the age of the animal. Bony enlargements occur especially at the ends of large bones.

TREATMENT

Calcarea phosphorica 200c Signs of pain accompanying enlargements at ends of long bones. This remedy has given excellent results in young animals. Dose: once daily for two weeks.

Phosphoric acid 6c Debility in young, growing animals. Periostium frequently affected. Dose: night and morning for one week.

Iodum 30c Painful enlargements of joints, with dry, withered-looking skin. Dose: once daily for one week.

7. Osteoarthritis. Degenerative lesions of joint cavities, non-inflammatory in origin are grouped under this heading. These lesions can accompany bone diseases such as osteodystrophy.

SYMPTOMS

In affections of limbs, lameness occurs and in severe cases there is distension of joint capsule together with crepitus. The articular surfaces of the cervical vertebrae are sometimes affected in the horse. This may cause pain and difficulty of movement. More frequently compression of spinal nerves is the cause rather than the affection of the bone itself. Involvement of the stifle joint may lead to fracture of the head of the tibia causing complete recumbency. When the hip joint is affected reduction in the head of the femur takes place.

TREATMENT

Osteoarthritis nosode 30c   This remedy may help alleviate some of the painful symptoms. Dose: once a week for four doses.

Rhus toxicodendron 1M   Amelioration of symptoms of pain when the animal moves. Dose: once daily for one week.

8.   Arthritis.   This condition differs from osteoarthritis in being inflammatory in origin, commonly bacterial. In new-born foals a common cause is Salmonella abortus-equi.

SYMPTOMS

Pain, stiffness, heat and swelling occur, due to inflammation of the synovial membrane. The hock, stifle and carpus are the joints chiefly affected, while in foals involvement of several joints is common, leading to severe lameness and recumbency.

TREATMENT

Apis 6c   In the early stage, when the joint is swollen and there is an increase in synovial fluid. Dose: every two hours for four doses.

Rhus toxicodendron 30c   Lameness improved by exercise. There may be an associated stiffness of muscles and tendons. Dose: night and morning for four days.

Belladonna 200c   Joints are very hot and swollen without excess of joint fluid. Various joints may be simultaneously affected. The animal is usually excitable. Dose: every two hours for four doses.

Bryonia 30c   Pressure over joints relieves. The animal is worse on movement. Dose: night and morning for four days.

Note:–   Brucellosis is a disease which has now become recognised as a cause of bacterial arthritis in the horse, e.g. in the atlanto-occipital bursa, the navicular bursa and the vertebral joints of the withers. Before commencing any of the above remedies, it would be helpful to administer one dose of the *Brucella abortus nosode* 30.

XVI   Affections of Bursae

1.   Acute Bursitis.   Bursa is the term generally employed to include all synovial sacs and refers to the true bursa situated between tendon and bone, or between two tendons and also includes joint capsule and synovial sheath. Bursitis may be dry, serous or purulent and arises as a result of open wound infection or contusion.

SYMPTOMS
The dry form quickly leads to the serous or purulent forms. There is a swelling at a particular site which contains either clear, serous fluid or purulent material.

TREATMENT
Bryonia 30c   In the initial inflammatory stage, there is relief from pressure and symptoms are worse on movement. Dose: every three hours for four doses.
Apis 6c   Excess of fluid formed by inflammation. Dose: every two hours for four doses.
Hepar sulphuris 200c   Purulent bursitis. Extreme tenderness and sensitivity to touch. Dose: every three hours for four doses.

2.   Chronic Bursitis.   This may take the form of a cystic swelling or of a fibrous enlargement. It may follow the acute form or arise independently. The cystic form contains a clear fluid while the fibrous form is firm and contains only a small amount of fluid.

SYMPTOMS
Distension and enlargement are the only prominent signs and there is evidence of lameness or pain.

TREATMENT

Calcarea fluorica 30c Swelling. This remedy, given over a long
period is beneficial. Dose: twice daily for seven days, followed
by one dose weekly for three weeks.

Apis 6c Cystic form, with excess fluid. Dose: twice daily for
seven days.

XVII   Bacterial Diseases

A.   Streptococcal

1.   Strangles.   This disease is usually acute and is characterised by upper respiratory tract inflammation together with abscess formation in the sub-maxillary glands. Young animals are principally affected. There is a high incidence when groups of horses are exposed to inclement conditions.

SYMPTOMS

The disease commences with fever and nasal discharge, at first mucoid, but soon becoming purulent. Cessation of feeding occurs. Throat involvement is usual, in the form of an acute lymphadenitis. A persistent moist cough is present in most cases. The temperature, high in the initial stage, usually falls in two to three days, but may recur once abscesses develop in the throat glands. These become hot, swollen and tender to touch. Accompanying this abscess formation is an increase in purulent nasal discharge. The abscesses may rupture, discharging a thick, creamy pus. Extension to neighbouring lymph glands is the rule in severe cases, while accumulation of pus in the guttural pouches can result from neglected cases. Metastatic spread of infection results in complications such as pneumonia and arthritis.

TREATMENT

Aconitum napellus 6c   Always the first choice remedy in early febrile stage. If given early enough, this remedy alone may bring about resolution of the disease. Dose: hourly for four doses.

Belladonna 1M   Full bounding pulse, dilated pupils, nervous excitability. Dose: every two hours for four doses.

Phytolacca 30c   Neighbouring lymph glands or salivary glands in the throat become firm, tender and swollen. Dose: three times daily for four days.

Pulsatilla 6c Yellow mucous discharge from nose. Pharyngeal area tender. Dose: night and morning for three days.

Mercurius sol. 200c Salivation and possibly slimy diarrhoea. Nasal discharge oily and greenish, possibly blood-stained. Dose: night and morning for three days.

Hepar sulphuris 200c Low potencies will help abscesses to mature. In higher potency, condition will be aborted without rupture of the abscesses. Dose: low potency, e.g. 6x, three times daily for one day. Higher potency: night and morning for two days.

2. Neo-natal Streptococcal Infection. S. pyogenes is frequently involved in infection of the umbilicus, resulting in bacterial spread to other organs, especially the joints. The source of the infection is contamination by uterine discharges from an infected mare, the infection presumably taking place through the umbilicus. Septicaemia sets in from the patent umbilicus producing suppurative lesions throughout the body. Although arthritis is the most usual complication, ophthalmia can also develop in foals which are affected when they become two to three weeks old.

SYMPTOMS
Initially there is swelling and pain of the umbilicus and there is usually an oedematous plaque surrounding the naval. Patent urachus is common and there may be a purulent discharge from the umbilicus. Febrile symptoms are slight. The joints commonly affected are the hock and stifle and occasionally the carpus. Lameness may be severe and recumbency is common.

TREATMENT
Streptococcus nosode 30c This nosode should always be employed. Sometimes it will be curative by itself. Dose: once daily for three days, followed by one dose every second day for three doses.

Apis 6c Synovitis severe. Joints puffy, tender to touch. Dose: every two hours for four doses.

Rhus toxicodendron 1M Arthritis, when animal improves on movement. Dose: three times daily for three days.

Benzoic acid 6c   Indicated when the carpus is involved. Accompanying tenderness and swelling of the Achilles tendon. Urine dark brown, offensive. Dose: three times daily for two days.

Bryonia 6c   Joints swollen, hot and tender. Pain better from pressure, symptoms worse on movement. Dose: three times daily for three days.

Lycopodium 200c   Shoulder and elbow joints affected. Accompanying sweating of the limb and possibly hepatic symptoms. Dose: night and morning for three days.

Natrum phosphoricum 30c   When the carpus is especially involved. Affected joints show crepitation. Dose: night and morning for one week.

Note:–   Prevention of this condition is possible, by administering the nosode to the in-foal mare, giving one dose per month for the last four months of pregnancy, followed by two doses in the last week. This will help to mitigate symptoms in the young animal and possibly prevent infection entirely, as it is thought by some authorities that intra-uterine infection can occur. An additional preventive measure is to give the foal one dose of nosode immediately at birth and repeat every day for four days.

3.   Genital Tract Infection of Mares.   Streptococcal infections of the genital tract can occur in mares and show usually as metritis, which can led to abortion and sterility. Coitus is thought to be the cause of its spread.

SYMPTOMS

Metritis in the acute stage is evidenced by fever and signs of toxaemia. The pulse rate is increased, respiration is more rapid and sweating is common. Systemic involvement may lead to laminitis. The inflammation in the uterus may extend to the vagina producing a corrugated thickening and a vulval discharge at first mucoid, later purulent. If abortion occurs retention of foetal membranes follows. Chronic metritis may lead to sterility and is associated with changes in the endometrium accompanied by chronic discharges.

TREATMENT

Streptococcus nosode 30c   Always commence treatment with this remedy. Dose: three times daily for two days.

Aconitum napellus 6c   Early stages of acute infection. Dose: every hour for four doses.

Echinacea 6x   Puerperal involvement follows the metritis. Dose: every two hours for four doses.

Pyrogenium 1M   Metritis resulting from abortion. Retention of foetal membranes. Rapid, thready pulse in contrast to a low temperature, or weak faint pulse and high temperature. Dose: every three hours for four doses.

Sabina 6c   Haemorrhages of bright blood from the uterus. Retained foetal membranes. Dose: every hour for five doses.

Belladonna 1M   Mare excitable, with dilated pupils, full bounding pulse, sweating and hot skin. Dose: every two hours for four doses.

Sepia 200c   Chronic metritis. Intermittent uterine discharge. Dose: once weekly for four doses.

Hepar sulphuris 6c   Purulent involvement in chronic cases. Dose: three times daily for five days.

4. Ulcerative Lymphangitis of Foals.   This is a streptococcal disease affecting foals only and is distinct from the commoner lymphangitis associated with corynebacteria occurring in older animals.

SYMPTOMS
Swelling of lymphatic vessels occurs and neighbouring lymph glands show firmness, if the condition is very acute. Normally, however, there is only slight involvement of these glands. The lymphatics become corded due to the development of abscesses. When these mature and burst, ulceration of the lymphatic vessels occur discharging pus of a creamy, thick nature. The surrounding tissue becomes swollen due to cellulitis.

TREATMENT
Streptococcus nosode 30c   Give once daily for three days.

Silicea 200c   Ulceration having occurred, this remedy will rapidly heal the abscess and resolve necrotic tissue. Dose: night and morning for three days.

Hepar sulphuris 6x–200c   In low potency, abscess material will be expelled, while the higher will abort the process. Dose: three times daily for two days of potency 6x, or one dose night and morning for three days of potency 200c.

B. Corynebacterial Infections

1. Contagious Acne – Contagious Pustular Dermatitis.

This disease is characterised by the development of pustules in pressure areas, caused by C. pseudotuberculosis. Spread from animal to animal is by infected grooming utensils or harness.

SYMPTOMS

The hair follicle is first affected, leading to local suppuration and eventually pustular formation. There is an initial papular lesion which is sometimes painful, but not itchy, and this develops into a pustule which eventually ruptures, liberating a greenish pus.

TREATMENT

Arsenicum alb. 1M   Thirst, restlessness, worse after midnight. Lesions sometimes attended by local oedema. Dose: once daily for one week.

Antimonium crudum 6c   Accompanying gastric symptoms. Itching made worse by warmth. Dose: three times daily for three days.

Hepar sulphuris 200c   Tendency to suppuration. Dose: night and morning for five days.

Sulphur 6c   This is a good general remedy to be used as a constitutional aid to elimination of toxins from the blood and may profitably be combined with other remedies. Dose: night and morning for three days.

Sulphur iodatum 6c   Inter-current throat affections. Skin surrounding lesions is red and itchy. Dose: night and morning for ten days.

2. Corynebacterial Pneumonia of Foals.

This disease of young foals produces pneumonia and respiratory lesions generally and is caused by C. equi. It is a frequent cause of death in breeding stables and most commonly affects animals one to two months old, but may cause illness in foals up to six months old.

SYMPTOMS

There is an initial fever which is caused by a bacteraemia leading to development of suppurative lesions in various organs but particularly the lungs. The younger the animal, the more severe the clinical symptoms. Pneumonia develops quickly in these cases, accompanied by lesions in the joints, causing an acute arthritis. In older animals, a moist cough leads to a slowly developing pneumonia and emaciation. The animal may continue to suck, but gradually loses condition. Profuse diarrhoea often accompanies the respiratory disease. Upper respiratory involvement is uncommon.

TREATMENT

Aconitum napellus 6c   In the initial febrile stage. Dose: every hour for four doses.

Arsenicum alb. 6c   The older foal showing emaciation, restlessness, frequent thirst, dry skin and diarrhoea. Dose: three times daily for one week.

Antimonium tartaricum 30c   Moist cough, with rattling mucus and dyspnoea. Dose: three times daily for four days.

Lycopodium 200c   Laboured breathing involving the alae nasi and accompanied possibly by liver symptoms. Dose: night and morning for one week.

Phosphorus 200c   Rapid onset, blood-stained cough which contains fibrinous shreds. Dose: three times daily for two days.

Arsenicum iodatum 30c   When the more severe conditions have been resolved, this remedy will aid recovery. Dose: once daily for one week.

Tuberculinum aviare 200c   Young animals showing acute broncho-pneumonia with weakness and debility. Dose: once daily for four days.

3. Ulcerative Lymphangitis. This is a contagious disease caused by C. pseudo-tuberculosis, infection due to scratches on the lower limbs. It can spread quickly when horses are grouped together in large numbers.

SYMPTOMS

Beginning with skin infection, spread takes place to the lymphatic vessels, producing abscesses along their course. Swelling of the pastern usually follows initial infection, frequently producing lameness. Subcutaneous nodules appear over the fetlock area and eventually discharge a creamy pus, sometimes green tinged. The ulcer which develops becomes indolent and necrotic. The lymphatic glands associated with the area become infected and fresh abscesses and ulcers develop, producing hardening and thickening. The disease can persist for many months in untreated cases.

TREATMENT

Calcarea fluorica 30c   Lymph glands and vessels are hard, before suppuration begins. Dose: three times daily for three days.

Phytolacca 200c   Lymph glands swollen and hot. Dose: night and morning for five days.

Silicea 200c   Chronic cases, when ulcers tend to spread and become fistulous. Indolent ulcers and necrotic patches will heal quickly under this remedy. Dose: once daily for five days.

Hepar sulphuris 6x–200c   Lower potencies of this remedy hasten maturation of abscesses. Higher potencies resorb the condition. Dose: three times daily for one day of potency 6x, and one dose night and morning for two days of potency 200c.

C.   Clostridial Disease

1.   Tetanus.   This disease is caused by the bacillus Cl. tetani, which produces a toxin which has a predilection for nervous tissue. The toxin is formed in deep punctured wounds which have become infected by the tetanus bacillus. The organism can produce the toxin only in the absence of free oxygen, hence the liability of the disease to show after the occurrence of a deep wound in the susceptible animal. An idiopathic form of the disease also occurs in which there is no observable wound, infection probably taking place from an internal wound.

SYMPTOMS

After an incubation period of one to three weeks, there appears a general stiffness of all muscles accompanied by muscle tremors. Clamping of jaws supervene and prolapse of the third eyelid occurs. The tail is held straight out behind the body. The expression is invariably tense and alert with retraction of the lips and erect positioning of the ears. There is exaggerated response to stimuli. Constipation and retention of urine are present and there is inability to feed or open the mouth. In prolonged cases there is arching of the back and tetanic convulsions eventually appear along with opisthotonus and extreme extension of the limbs. Sweating may be profuse along with marked pyrexia. Death occurs by paralysis of respiration.

TREATMENT

Animal should be kept in darkened loose-box, in absolute quiet.

Aconitum napellus 6c If seen early enough after the initial injury and also during the febrile stage, should there be one. Dose: every hour for four doses.

Belladonna 1M Great excitement, dilated pupils, full bounding pulse, skin hot and smooth. Dose: every two hours for four doses.

Nux vomica 1M Stiffness of limbs and constipation severe. Dose: every four hours for four doses.

Ledum 6c When origin of disease is a deep, punctured wound and is *not* idiopathic. Give immediately wound is sustained. Dose: every two hours for three doses.

Hypericum 1M Damage to nerve endings. The remedy will prevent infection ascending the nerve paths. It should be combined with *Ledum* in alternate doses. Dose: every two hours for three doses.

Strychninum 200c When tetanus spasms and muscle rigidity first appear. This remedy alone has been known to effect a cure if the disease process has not advanced too far. Dose: three times daily for one week.

Arnica 30c Since the source of the disease is not only injury, but is accompanied by shock, give early in the course of the disease – two doses four hours apart.

Tetanus nosode 30c Give early in course of disease. It will aid action of other remedies. One dose daily for five days.

2. Botulism. This condition is essentially a motor paralysis caused by the absorption from the stomach or intestine of the toxin of Cl. botulinum. It is usually sub-acute in the horse and produces a picture of progressive muscular paralysis.

SYMPTOMS

The muscles affected are usually those of the limbs, jaw and throat. Weakness and paralysis commence in the hind quarters and ascends to the forelegs and head region. Stumbling and knuckling occur and there is inability to raise the head. The animal later becomes recumbent with its chest on the ground and head turned towards the flank. Paralysis of the tongue causes it to protrude from the mouth. Involvement of the chest muscles produces a laboured abdominal breathing.

TREATMENT

This should always begin with the administration of the Cl. botulinum nosode and should be given three times daily for three days.

Conium 30c   Conditions showing ascending paralysis. It may be necessary to give ascending potencies at short intervals. Dose: three times daily for three days.

Gelsemium 200c   Weakness and paralysis of the head region. Dose: three times daily for two days.

Plumbum metallicum 200c   Paralysis may be accompanied by a cold feeling of lower limbs and associated with bouts of colic. Dose: night and morning for five days.

D.   Salmonellosis

1.   Paratyphoid Disease.   Disease caused by Salmonella usually takes the form of an acute septicaemia or an acute or chronic enteritis. The chief organism concerned is S. typhimurium and foals are principally affected. Adult horses which are overfed prior to transport are also susceptible.

SYMPTOMS

Septicaemic symptoms are seen in young foals, producing fever and depression. This form may produce early fatalities. An enteric form is associated with dysentery or diarrhoea according to the severity of the infection. Shreds of intestinal mucous membrane may be evident in the faeces. Thirst is prominent and acute abdominal pain is nearly always present. Polyarthritis is a common sequel to the disease in foals.

TREATMENT

Salmonella typhimurium nosode 30c   This should be given three times daily for two days at the beginning of treatment.

Mercurius sol. 200c   Stools slimy and dysenteric, often worse during the night. Dose: three times daily for two days.

Baptisia 30c   Thin, dark stools often blood-stained with tenderness over the abdomen. Dose: three times daily for three days.

Camphor 30c   Threatened collapse. The body surface is cold. Dark watery stools. Dose: every two hours for four doses.

Veratrum album 6c   Watery diarrhoea accompanied by pain. Stools forcibly evacuated, followed by prostration. Dose: three times daily for three days.

Arnica 30c   Congestive venous states accompany blood-stained putrid stools. Dose: three times daily for two days.

Arsenicum alb. 1M   Restlessness, worse at night, thirst for small quantities. Dose: three times daily for three days.

2.   Salmonella Abortion in Mares.   This infection, caused by S. abortus equi is confined to horses and donkeys. Natural infection can occur from ingestion of contaminated feed, usually from uterine discharges from other mares, while transmission by coitus is thought probable also. Infection can persist in uterus and cause subsequent abortion.

SYMPTOMS

Infection by ingestion leads first to a bacteraemia, the bacteria subsequently becoming lodged in the placenta, resulting in abortion. Less virulent infection can result in viable first term foals but these may be infected, disease being spread via the umbilicus. Abortion usually occurs at about seven or eight months and is accompanied by difficult expulsion of the foetus. Retention of foetal membranes and metritis are common sequelae.

TREATMENT

Caulophyllum 200c   The entire process of pregnancy can be usefully controlled by this remedy. Dose: once a month until the final month, when the dose should be one dose at two-weekly intervals.

Sabina 6c   If abortion has occurred, this remedy will help to reduce discharges and also to expel the placenta. Dose: every hour for four doses.

Secale 30c   Post-abortion discharges, contaminated by dark-coloured blood will be helped by this remedy. Dose: every four hours, for one day.

3. Testicular Lesions. S. abortus equi has been implicated in testicular lesions in the stallion, leading to oedema of the prepuce, followed occasionally by orchitis and atrophy of testicular tissue. Arthritis may also occur.

TREATMENT

Salmonella abortus equi nosode 30c This should be used as a preliminary to the use of other remedies. Dose: daily for five days.

Belladonna 1M Acute orchitis, with excitability and dilated pupils, full bounding pulse, testicles swollen and hot. Dose: once daily for five days.

Rhododendron 6c Testicular lesions indurated, left testicle being more involved. Dose: three times daily for three days.

Spongia 6c Testicular swelling extends to the epididymis. Pain and tenderness in testicles. Dose: three times daily for three days.

Aurum metallicum 30c Testicular swelling is long-lasting leading eventually to induration. Dose: night and morning for one week.

Pulsatilla 30c Testicular swelling extends along the abdomen, with urethral discharge. Dose: night and morning for five days.

Apis 30c Oedema of the prepuce prominent. This remedy will also reduce testicular swelling when due to oedema. Dose: three times daily for two days.

XVIII   Miscellaneous Bacterial Infections

Among the conditions which are important to consider are Brucellosis, E. coli infection, Shigella disease of foals and Leptospirosis.

1. Brucellosis.   In the horse the organism Brucella abortus has been associated with bursitis of various joints, poll evil, and fistulous withers being considered prominent examples. The sacro-iliac joint is one that is frequently affected and lameness in this joint should be considered as possibly due to brucellosis. Some authorities have recently attributed the inflammation of the navicular bursa to this organism. Arthritis of the lower joints is also thought to be due to brucellosis, leading to intermittent lameness and transient fever. This disease can also cause hygromatus swellings on the skin which may yield a honey-coloured viscid fluid arising from numerous small vesicles.

TREATMENT
Brucellosis abortus and Brucellosis melitensis nosode 30c   The combined use of these nosodes is always indicated at the beginning of the course of treatment. Dose: night and morning for three days.
Hepar sulphuris 30c   As brucellosis is a pyogenic infection, the use of this remedy invariably produces good results, especially when the condition is accompanied by extreme sensitivity to cold and wind. Pain and tenderness exist over affected areas such as fistulous withers. Dose: every three hours for four doses. It may be necessary to continue treatment at regular intervals with ascending potencies.

Silicea 200c The more chronic and neglected case, when abscess formation has taken place, the underlying tissue having become necrotic leading to fistulae. Dose: once daily for seven days.

Apis 6c Acute synovitis, joint showing tenderness, swelling and heat. Dose: every two hours for four doses.

Rhus toxicodendron 1M Joint ligaments involved, with improvement on exercise. Dose: night and morning for one week.

Bryonia 6c Acute swelling and firmness of joints. Worse on movement. Dose: three times daily for three days.

2. E. Coli Infection. Colibacillosis.
The septicaemic form of this infection is the more usual, although arthritis can be a common sequel in foals which recover.

SYMPTOMS

There is usually a cold skin and sub-normal temperature, slowness of heart and signs of impending coma in the very acute type. Less acute cases show depression, weakness and increased heart rate. The initial high temperature falls and diarrhoea sets in. This takes various forms and ranges from watery to pasty consistency and may be tinged with blood. The stool has a characteristic rancid odour and soils the buttocks. Abdominal signs include colic and kicking at belly and there may be tympany and tenesmus.

TREATMENT

E. coli nosode 30c The use of this nosode has given good results, a peculiarity being that it does not have to be prepared from the particular strain of organism concerned in the illness. Experience has shown that nosode made from many different strains is effective. Dose: three times daily for two days.

Arsenicum alb. 6c Diarrhoea is watery and tinged with blood. Animal restless, thirsty, worse after midnight. Dose: three times daily for three days.

Ipecacuanha 30c Less acute cases, when faeces less watery, slimy, green. Dose: three times daily for two days.

Colchicum 6c Signs of tympany appear, with signs of colic. Dose: every two hours for four doses.

Colocynth 6c Should be considered when severe abdominal pain is evident. Animal rolls and looks round at flanks. Dose: every hour for four doses.

China off. 6c   Profuse watery stools. Great weakness. Dose: every
   two hours for four doses.

Mercurius corrosivus 200c   Disease takes the form of severe
   enteritis, with passage of slimy blood-stained stools, accompanied by salivation. Stools more frequent during night. Dose:
   three times daily for two days.

3.   Shigella Disease of Foals.   This is an acute septicaemic
disease of foals, particularly the new-born. It is limited to horses.
Foals may contract infection through the umbilicus, or become
infected *in utero*.

SYMPTOMS
Suppurative lesions develop internally in animals which survive an
acute attack. An early symptom is a febrile reaction and increased
respiration. Diarrhoea and dysentery may occur. Foals frequently
show comatose or sleepy symptoms. Arthritis develops in animals
which survive acute attacks.

TREATMENT
Aconitum napellus 6c   Give in early febrile stage. Dose: every
   hour for four doses.

Arsenicum alb. 1M   Enteric symptoms. Diarrhoea usually acrid
   and has carrion-like odour. Straining, with restlessness and
   thirst. Dose: three times daily for two days.

Rhus toxicodendron 1M   Arthritis cases which show improvement
   on movement. Joints hot and stiff. Dose: night and morning for
   three days.

Note:– A nosode could be prepared from the causative organism
   Shigella equirulis which could be cultured from the stool of
   infected foals. This nosode would be a useful complement
   to other indicated remedies.

4.   Leptospirosis.   This infection, due to leptospira species is
usually mild in the horse, although occasionally blindness has
resulted, possibly as a result of an associated ophthalmia.

SYMPTOMS
There is an initial fever and a degree of haemoglobinuria. Jaundice
is a fairly common sequel and abortion may follow.

TREATMENT

Aconitum napellus 6c   Give in the early febrile stage, one dose hourly for three doses.

Chelidonium 30c   Jaundice, with tenderness or lameness over right shoulder region. Dose: night and morning for three days.

Berberis vulgaris 30c   Haemoglobinuria present. Tenderness over lumbar region. Dose: three times daily for four days.

XIX   Virus Diseases

D.N.A. Viruses Affecting the Horse

The main groups are as follows:

A. **Papoviruses** causing warts and papillomata.
B. **Adenoviruses** causing adenovirus infections.
C. **Herpes Viruses** associated with rhinopneumonitis, abortions and coital exanthema.
D. **Pox Viruses** associated with horse pox and grease.

Homoeopathic remedies which may favourably influence treatment of these conditions include the following:

A.   Papoviruses

1.   Thuja which has a beneficial action on the Papillomatous warts viz. those which are jagged and bleed easily. They are usually found in the scrotal region but may also appear elsewhere. Treatment should commence with the 30c potency giving one dose three times per week for four weeks. This should be followed by 200c potency one twice weekly for four weeks, followed by 1m potency one per week for four weeks.

2.   Sabina This is a remedy which may favourably influence treatment in mares especially in the genital area. Potency 200c should be considered giving a dose twice weekly for six weeks.

3.   Dulcamara This remedy is associated with loose bowels especially when cool evenings follow warm days, and also in autumn. Animals which have warts and show clinical symptoms as above described may benefit from this remedy. A potency of 200c twice weekly for four weeks should be given.

4. Calcarea carbonica   This is a useful remedy for warts which are sessile especially in the young animal. A potency of 200c once per week for four weeks should be followed by a potency of 1m weekly for four weeks.

5. Causticum   is a remedy which should be considered in the treatment of small sessile warts which assume a cauliflower-like appearance. A potency of 30c three times per week for eight weeks may be necessary.

B. Adenoviruses.   These viruses cause acute and sometimes fatal infections of young horses characterised by fever and pneumonia. The chief clinical signs are a deep soft cough yielding a muco-purulent phlegm and purulent rhinitis. Discharges develop from the eyes and ulcers may appear around the nostrils and mouth. These symptoms are also associated with immune deficiency disease affecting Arab horses, becoming subject to infection once passive material antibody levels decline. This may not show until about four weeks. Remedies which may help deal with respiratory infection include *Phosphorus* 200c giving one dose per day for seven days, *Bryonia* 30c in the same way and *Antimonium tartaricum 30c* once daily for ten days. Depending on response these remedies may have to be continued in higher potencies once or twice per week for four weeks. The remedy *Acidum nitricum* should be considered for treatment of ulcers around mouth and nose, using a potency of 30c daily for ten days.

C. Herpes Virus Infection

Equine Herpes 1. Infection is associated with respiratory disease, abortions, and in a chronic form neurological disease. The respiratory form is seen as outbreaks of purulent rhinitis with or without pneumonia. The chronic or neurological form becomes shown as hind-limb weakness with or without oedema of the leg. Crossing of the legs is a common feature. Peripheral nerve paralysis may also occur e.g. facial or pharyngeal.

Equine Herpes 4. Infection is also associated with respiratory disease, while Equine Herpes 3. Infection is associated with coital exanthema in mares.

Nosodes (oral vaccines) are available for both treatment and prevention of these viral infections and can be combined with selected remedies such as *Aconitum* or *Belladonna* in the acute stages, while *Phosphorus*, *Bryonia*, and *Antimonium tartaricum* should be considered as follow-on remedies for respiratory disease. In-foal mares should be given the remedies *Viburnum opulis 30c* and *Caulophyllum 30c* as these are proven remedies which help prevent miscarriage. *Viburnum* should be given during the first two months of pregnancy (one twice weekly for eight weeks) while *Caulophyllum* should be reserved for the last month giving one dose twice weekly. This remedy should also help to ensure a good parturition.

E.H.V. 3. Infection causing coital exanthemata should be treated by remedies such as *Acidum nitricum 200c* one twice per week for eight weeks and *Variolinum 30c* daily for ten days. This should be given first, followed by the previous one.

Useful remedies for the neurological form of the disease include *Conium* and *Lathyrus* together with the nosode. The remedy *Conium* may need to be given in ascending potencies starting with 30c daily for ten days going on to 200c potency three times per week for four weeks. Refractory cases may need still higher potencies e.g. 1M to cM. *Conium* is the main remedy but the remedy *Lathyrus* should not be overlooked as it may well be that some cases will need this rather than the *Conium*. A potency of 1M should be considered, three times per week for four weeks. These remedies can be combined with the nosode in 30c potency giving one dose per day for ten days.

D. Pox Viruses. Horse pox is relatively uncommon but remedies such as *Antimonium crudum* and *Variolinum* will prove useful in treatment using 30c daily for ten days in each case. The main remedies for grease are the nosode *Malandrinum 30c* giving it daily for ten days, followed by *Graphites 1M* three times per week for four weeks.

RNA Viruses affecting the Horse

The main ones are:

    A. Myxoviruses causing Influenza A equi 1 and 2 and Influenza C which is less important.

    B. Paramyxoviruses causing Parainfluenza 3 associated with upper respiratory infection and rabies: also vesicular stomatitis.

    C. Arboviruses causing eastern and western encephalitis.

    D. Oncoviruses causing equine infectious anaemia.

Influenza.   In its pure form it presents as a fever and secondly as involvement of the mucous membranes of the upper respiratory tract and eyes. It most commonly affects young horses and appears in spring and autumn.

SYMPTOMS

Febrile signs accompany a dull and listless appearance. The pulse is fast and thready and urine may be scanty and high coloured. The congestive swelling of the nose extends down the respiratory tract producing at first a mucoid and later a purulent discharge. The cough is harsh and dry and respirations are increased. The nervous system is also affected manifested by a state of general languor and muscular weakness. The conjunctiva are discoloured.

TREATMENT

Aconitum should always be given as early as possible in the febrile stage. Suggested potency 10M one dose every two hours for four doses.

Belladonna   This should follow *Aconitum* when indicated by a fast pulse and dilated pupils. The skin may be hot and the animal may show excitement. Suggested potency 1M one dose every two hours for three doses.

Gelsemium   Languor, muscular weakness and incoordination of movement are present when this remedy is indicated. Suggested potency 200c one dose every two hours for four doses.

Bryonia may be needed when a harsh dry cough is present. Pleuritic symptoms such as friction sounds on auscultation are frequently present, giving relief on pressure. Suggested potency 30c three times daily for four days.

Antimonium tartaricum   Saliva is abundant accompanied by moist cough and presence of rales on auscultation. Suggested potency 30c three times daily for five days.

Phosphorus   When this remedy is indicated the breathing is short and rapid, threatening a pneumonia. Suggested potency 200c three times daily for three days.

Lycopodium If pneumonia supervenes leading to laboured respiration and an aggravation of symptoms in early evening this remedy should prove useful. Faeces may be dry and shining. Suggested potency 1M daily for ten days.

Hippozaeninum This nosode is a useful accompaniment to other remedies when there is purulent rhinitis. Suggested potency 30c one dose daily for 10 days.

Equine influenza nosode can be given along with other remedies preferably early in the course of the disease. Suggested potency 30c one dose three times daily for two days.

Vesicular Stomatitis. This viral disease presents as vesicular lesions appearing on the mouth and feet.

SYMPTOMS

A primary viraemia develops localisation occurring in the mucous membranes of the mouth and the skin around the coronet. Lesions in the horse are more usually found in the mouth, dorsam of tongue or on the lips. The external genital organs may also show involvement. Rupture of vesicle produces a ropy saliva.

TREATMENT

Aconitum When primary viraemia sets in this remedy will be useful in controlling the febrile reaction. Suggested potency 10M one dose every two hours for four doses.

Antimonium crudum Indicated when lesions principally affect the area around the mouth and on the skin of the genital area. The tongue may be heavily coated. Suggested potency 6c three times daily for five days.

Borax A very useful remedy when lesions appear on the tongue and around the coroney band. Ropy saliva is profuse. The animal is reluctant to move especially in a downward manner. Suggested potency 6c three times daily for seven days.

Acidum nitricum Indicated when ulcers extend to the soft palate. The area around the lips is severely affected also. This is a very useful remedy for eczematous conditions affecting areas where skin and mucous membranes meet and could be indicated also therefore in the genital area. Suggested potency 200c daily for seven days.

Kali muriaticum When aphthous whitish ulcers are present accompanying a shiny coating of the tongue. Suggested potency 30c three times daily for four days.

Viral Encephalomyelitis. A viral infection characterised by derangement of consciousness leading to paralysis after an initial motor irritation. Infection in horses is accidental from birds and spread by vector, possibly mosquitoes and ticks. Eastern and western encephalitis do not occur in Britain. They are mentioned here principally because the symptoms displayed do not differ in any material way to those exhibited by horses suffering from non-specific disease.

SYMPTOMS
Early viraemia evidenced by fever and depression may be transitory or persistent according to the strain of virus. This follows an incubation period of 1–3 weeks. Hypersensitivity is the earliest nervous sign and disturbances of vision soon follow. Involuntary muscle twitching occurs. Somnolent states are common as the disease progresses. Paralysis of various muscles is the rule and when the mouth is affected the tongue protrudes. Incoordination of gait is common and the disease may progress to total paralysis.

TREATMENT
The early viraemic state should be countered by the remedy *Aconitum* given in 10M potency every two hours for four doses. The following remedies may all be indicated depending on symptoms portrayed.

Hyoscamus which should help control hypersensitivity and early nervous signs. Suggested potency 30c three times daily for three days.

Agaricus muscaris General ataxia with vertigo accompany the need for this remedy. Suggested potency 30c three times daily for seven days.

Strychninum Chorea and muscular twitchings are indications for this remedy. Suggested potency 200c one daily for seven days.

Opium Somnolent states associated with bowel stasis indicate this remedy. Suggested potency 200c one every hour for three doses.

Plumbum met. Indicated in general paralytic states especially involving the larger motor nerves. Suggested potency 1M daily for seven days.

Conium When this remedy is indicated there is an ascending paralysis starting on the lower hind limbs. This remedy may need different potencies starting with 30c three times daily for seven days followed by 200c, 1M and possibly 10M given weekly for four weeks.

Cicuta virosa and *Stramonium* are other remedies which could also be indicated (see section on Materia Medica).

Equine Infectious Anaemia, African Horse Sickness, Equine Viral Enteritis and Borna Disease are mentioned in the text for readers outside the UK who may have an interest in those diseases.

1. Infectious Equine Anaemia. This is a contagious disease of horses which produces a chronic illness, caused by a specific virus which attacks all age groups. The disease is usually confined to summer and autumn and shows an incubation period of two to four weeks.

SYMPTOMS

Early signs are depression, incoordination and rapid wasting. Febrile symptoms are intermittent and follow an undulating pattern. Petechial haemorrhages appear on the conjunctiva while jaundice and oedema become evident. The heart's action is increased and the sound is intermittent. Epistaxis may occur and an increase in the size of the spleen may be felt on palpation. Relapses are common, leading to further emaciation and weakness. There may be a watery diarrhoea, but it is an inconstant sign. Abortion may occur.

TREATMENT

There is no specific treatment, but the following remedies will produce alleviation of symptoms:-

Aconitum napellus 6c In the early febrile involvement. Dose: every hour for four doses.

Phosphorus 200c Petechial haemorrhages occur on mucous membranes. Dose: three times daily for three days.

Chelidonium 20c Jaundice. Possible stiffness over right shoulder area. Dose: night and morning for four days.

Apis 6c In oedematous states, this remedy will help control the amount of fluid in the tissues. It will have to be combined with other indicated remedies. Dose: three times daily for two days.

China off. 6c   Great loss of strength in anaemic states. Dose: three
 times daily for three days.

Note:– If possible, a nosode should be made from infected blood
 drawn from the patient about the fifteenth day after
 infection, when the febrile reaction is usually at its height.
 Such a nosode could be used both prophylactically and
 therapeutically.

2.   African Horse Sickness.   This disease has recently spread to
Europe. It is caused by various species of virus and follows an
acute, mild or chronic course. The incubation period is from five to
seven days.

SYMPTOMS

The acute type takes a pulmonary form producing an initial fever,
dyspnoea and coughing. Nasal discharge of yellow frothy material
occurs, followed by sweating and incoordination of gait. The mild
or sub-acute type has a longer incubation period of up to three
weeks and symptoms develop more slowly. Oedema of the head
region is the main outward sign, showing particularly on the eyelids
and lips and may spread to the pectoral region. Petechial
haemorrhages are seen under the tongue, and the mouth shows a
bluish colour. Hydropericardium is common in the more chronic
type and endocarditis may occur. Pulmonary oedema, if it occurs,
is dependent on the weak heart action. Sometimes the cardiac and
pulmonary forms co-exist, one type developing into the other.

TREATMENT

Aconitum napellus 6c   In the early febrile stage. Dose: every hour
 for four doses.

Antimonium tartaricum 30c   Pulmonary signs, showing dyspnoea
 and coughing. Dose: three times daily for three days.

Apis 6c   Oedematous state. This remedy will control the amounts
 of fluid present in the pulmonary and cardiac forms. Dose: three
 times daily for two days.

Kali bichromicum 200c   Yellowish discharge from nose. Dose:
 three times daily for three days.

Phosphorus 200c   Petechial haemorrhages on mucous membranes.
 Dose: three times daily for two days.

Conium 200c Incoordination of gait and weakness of hindquarters. Dose: three times daily for three days.

Note:– A nosode can be made from infected blood, the virus being present in the blood-stream from the first day of clinical illness. It could be used both prophylactically and therapeutically.

3. Vesicular Stomatitis. This is an infectious disease caused by a virus producing crops of vesicles on the mouth and feet.

SYMPTOMS

A primary viraemia develops and localisation takes place in the mucous membranes of the mouth and the skin around the coronet. The lesions in the horse are more usually found in the mouth, on the dorsum of the tongue, or on the lips. The external genital organs can also show involvement. When the vesicles rupture, a ropy saliva is produced.

TREATMENT

Aconitum napellus 6c When the primary viraemia sets in, this remedy will be useful in controlling the febrile reaction. Dose: every hour for three doses.

Antimonium crudum 6c Tongue heavily coated and eczema appears round the mouth. Dose: three times daily for three days.

Borax 6c When vesicles appear both in the mouth and above the coronet. The animal is disinclined to move. Dose: three times daily for four days.

Natrum muriaticum 200c Dry mouth and vesicles extend to the lips. Dose: night and morning for three days.

Argentum nitricum 30c Papillae of tongue unduly prominent. There may be bleeding from the gums. Dose: night and morning for four days.

Nitric acid 200c Associated ulcers on soft palate. Tenderness of feet. Vesicles appear mainly on the side of the tongue. Dose: night and morning for four days.

Kali muriaticum 30c Aphthous whitish ulcers develop. Slimy coating on tongue. Dose: three times daily for three days.

4. Equine Viral Rhinopneumonitis. This disease of the upper respiratory tract may also cause abortion and is usually mild in character, although abortion may be of frequent occurrence if the disease appears among brood mares. Transmission is by droplet infection or ingestion of contaminated material. Carrier animals are common and are a frequent cause of continued spread of the disease. The incubation period is two to ten days.

SYMPTOMS

The pregnant uterus becomes infected after an initial viraemia. Infection of the respiratory tract causes rhinitis and interstitial pneumonia, followed by pyraemia, conjunctivitis and coughing. Submaxillary lymphadenitis may occur. Some months after respiratory involvement, abortions may occur, shedding of the placenta taking place with the expulsion of the foetus. There is pronounced leucopenia.

TREATMENT

Aconitum napellus 6c   If seen early enough in the initial viraemic state, give one dose hourly for four doses.

Kali hydriodicum 200c   Conjunctivitis, cough and pulmonary oedema. Dose: three times daily for three days.

Antimonium tartaricum 30c   Interstitial pneumonia with moist cough and rattling of mucus. Dose: night and morning for three days.

Arsenicum alb. 200c   Animal restless, thirsty and has foul-smelling diarrhoea. This remedy will help associated rhinitis and pneumonia. Dose: every two hours for four doses.

Phytolacca 200c   Cases showing lymphadenitis. Dose: three times daily for four days.

Caulophyllum 30c   The use of the remedy will be found helpful in regulating pregnancy and allaying the tendency to abortion. Dose: once a month of pregnancy, with two doses during the last month.

Viburnum opulus 6c   Another useful remedy in controlling abortion. Dose: once a week for the first three months.

Note:– A nosode could be made from any infective material and employed as an oral vaccine and also therapeutically.

5.   Infectious Equine Pneumonia.   This virus disease produces a severe lobar pneumonia accompanied by septicaemic complications. It may arise when large numbers of horses are brought together from different regions.

SYMPTOMS

Primary virus involvement is fairly mild, but secondary bacterial invasion produces the severe symptoms. Lobar pneumonia follows a primary viraemia. The incubation period may be as long as thirty days, associated with fever and increased heart rate. Respiratory signs come later accompanied by sanguineous nasal discharge. Consolidation of lung tissue soon follows along, with exudation. Moist rales are heard on auscultation and harsh friction sounds are heard over the pleura.

TREATMENT

Aconitum napellus 6c Early febrile stage. Dose: every hour for four doses.

Phosphorus 200c Hepatisation. Severe dyspnoea with rust-coloured nasal discharge. Dose: three times daily for three days.

Antimonium tartaricum 30c Moist cough and mucous rales. Dose: night and morning for four days.

Bryonia 6c Pleuritic involvement. Pressure on chest relieves, worse on movement. Dose: three times daily for two days.

Lycopodium 200c Symptoms worse late afternoon. There may be signs of liver involvement, jaundice. Dose: night and morning for five days.

Ferrum phosphoricum 6c Blood coughed up. Symptoms appear better at night. Dose: three times daily for three days.

Iodum 6c This remedy may be useful when condition is accompanied by a dry withered look of the skin. Animal worse in warmth and seeks cool air. Dose: three times daily for three days.

Sanguinaria 6c Nervous animals showing dilation of blood vessels, easy sweating and blood-stained rust-coloured mucus when coughing. Dose: three times daily for three days.

6. Equine Viral Arteritis. This disease is characterised by an acute upper respiratory tract infection and abortion. The small arteries show specific lesions. The chief economic significance is loss of foals due to abortion and mares of all age groups are susceptible. Infection is presumed to be air-borne or by ingestion of contaminated material.

SYMPTOMS

After an incubation period of up to six days fever develops and a muco-purulent nasal discharge takes place. Conjunctivitis and lachrymation are common sequelae. Cough and pulmonary congestion occur leading to severe dyspnoea. Vascular damage occurs to small arteries and a haemorrhagic arteritis develops causing diarrhoea or dysentery. Pulmonary and limb oedema occur and occasionally jaundice. Abortions in this disease occur much earlier than in equine viral rhinopneumonia and differ also in that there are no lesions in the foetus. The vascular lesions produce a haemorrhagic picture in many of the internal organs, petechiae being present on most of the serous surfaces.

TREATMENT

Aconitum napellus 6c Give early in the febrile stage, one dose hourly for four hours.

Arsenicum alb. 1M Rhinitis and diarrhoea. Animal is restless, thirsty. Dose: every two hours for four doses.

Kali hydriodicum 200c Conjunctivitis and lachrymation. Pulmonary oedema. This is one of the remedies most likely to alleviate symptoms. Dose: three times daily for four days.

Antimonium tartaricum 30c Moist cough accompanies pulmonary congestion. Mucous rales prominent. Dose: three times daily for three days.

Phosphorus 200c Petechial haemorrhage, liver involvement and jaundice. Dose: three times daily for three days.

Millefolium 6c General haemorrhagic diathesis with tendency to continued febrile involvement. Dose: three times daily for three days.

Apis 6c This remedy will help to control oedema. Dose: three times daily for two days.

Crotalus horridus 30c This remedy also will help control a haemorrhagic tendency especially purpura-like ecchymosis and will have value in controlling uterine involvement. Dose: three times daily for three days.

7. Viral Encephalomyelitis. This is an infectious disease characterised by derangement of consciousness leading to paralysis after an initial motor irritation. Infection in horses is accidental from birds and spread is by vector, possibly mosquitoes and ticks.

SYMPTOMS
Viraemia is common to begin with and may be transitory or persistent according to the strain of virus. The incubation period is one to three weeks and initial symptoms are fever and depression. Hypersensitivity is the earliest nervous sign and disturbances of vision soon follow. Involuntary muscle twitching occurs. Somnolent states are common as the disease progresses. Paralysis is the rule and when the mouth is affected, the tongue protrudes. Incoordination of gait is common and the disease may progress to total paralysis.

TREATMENT
Aconitum napellus 6c   Give early in viraemic stage, one dose every hour for four doses.
Hyoscyamus 30c   Will help control hypersensitivity and early nervous signs. Dose: three times daily for three days.
Agaricus muscarius 6c   Vertigo and depression. Dose: three times daily for three days.
Strychninum 200c   Muscular twitchings and chorea prominent. Dose: three times daily for three days.
Opium 200c   Somnolent state associated with paralysis of bowel movement. Dose: twice in twenty-four hours.
Plumbum metallicum 30c   General paralytic state, worse at night. Extreme hyperaesthesia, associated with bouts of pain. Dose: night and morning for four days.
Gelsemium 200c   Paralytic involvement of head and tongue are the most prominent symptoms. Dose: three times daily for two days, followed by one dose weekly of potency 1M for three weeks.
Conium 30c   Ascending paralysis, starting in the hind legs. Dose: three times daily for three days. It has sometimes been found necessary to use ascending potencies after an interval.

8. Borna Disease. This is an infectious encephalomyelitis caused by a virus which is fairly resistant to environmental factors. The incubation period is up to one month.

SYMPTOMS
Febrile signs are slight and hyperaesthesia and muscle tremors occur. Swallowing becomes difficult owing to paralysis of the throat region. Lassitude and general paralysis takes place.

TREATMENT
Hyoscyamus 30c Hyperaesthesia, with head shaking. Naturally excitable animals will benefit from this remedy. Dose: three times daily for three days.

Strychninum 200c Muscular twitching and chorea, with tendency to muscular rigidity. Dose: three times daily for three days.

Gelsemium 200c Motor paralysis prominent in throat region, making swallowing difficult. Dose: night and morning for three days.

Conium 200c Paralysis affecting hindquarters and limbs, showing a tendency to ascend. Dose: night and morning for four or five days.

Agaricus muscarius 6c Lassitude, hyperaesthesia and vertigo. Dose: three times daily for three days.

9. Horse Pox. This condition is usually benign and is characterised by typical pox lesions on the limbs and on the lips. Badly affected animals may lose condition severely.

SYMPTOMS
The lesion commences as a small papule and progresses to vesicle, pustule and scab formation. When the leg is affected, the lesions are usually seen on the back of the pastern. Those on the mouth form on the buccal mucosa. Lameness may supervene and stomatitis may develop.

TREATMENT
Thuja 200c This will help resolve the lesions and promote rapid healing of scabs without scarring the skin. Dose: once daily for one week.

Antimonium crudum 6c Scab formation is accompanied by a honey-coloured secretion. Itching may occur towards night. Dose: night and morning for one week.

Borax 6c Lesions develop into ulcers on the palate, producing stomatitis. Dose: night and morning for five days.

Nitric acid 200c Ulceration of the soft palate, with diarrhoea and ulceration of the external genitals. Dose: night and morning for five days.

10. Papillomatosis. Warts of this nature are caused by a virus. In the horse they are usually confined to the muzzle, nose and lips and are invariably sessile.

TREATMENT

Thuja 200c This is the main remedy for papillomatous warts, especially those which bleed easily. Dose: once daily for ten days.

Causticum 30c This remedy may be indicated for hard warts associated with weakness and tremors of the foreleg muscles. The warts are usually worse on the nose. Dose: night and morning for one week.

Calcarea carbonica 200c Warts small, hard and do not bleed easily. Dose: once daily for one week.

Conditions Affecting the Foal

The young foal can be subject to a variety of infective and non-infective conditions, chief among which are intestinal and respiratory infections, hepatitis (usually associated with inherited herpes virus) also kidney and central nervous system complications, and joint-ill.

Bowel involvement usually takes the form of scour and depending on the nature of the loose faeces the following remedies will be found useful.

E. coli This nosode which is marketed simply as E. coli should always be given to begin with, one dose of 30c three times daily for three days, followed by one every second day for three doses. In the great majority of cases this remedy should suffice.

Aloe The stools are lumpy and jelly-like with signs of pain when passing stool. There is tenderness over the liver region. Suggested potency 200c daily for five days.

Arsen alb. The foal is restless the motions being offensive and possibly blood-stained. There is thirst for small quantities and conditions are worse towards midnight. Suggested potency 1M three times daily for four days.

Mercurius corr.   The motions are slimy and may contain blood, and symptoms are worse from sunset to sunrise. Suggested potency 200c three times daily for two days.

China off.   This remedy could be combined with others as it is the prime one for restoring strength after loss of body fluids. Suggested potency 30c three times daily for five days.

Dulcamara Attacks of diarrhoea follow exposure to damp, producing stools which are green and slimy. This type of diarrhoea is more prevalent in late summer when cool nights may follow a warm day. Suggested potency 200c three times daily for three days.

Podophyllum   This remedy is more useful in refractory cases and stools are worse in the morning. Suggested potency 1M daily for seven days.

Veratrum alb.   With this remedy there is a general appearance of collapse with signs of abdominal pain preceding the onset of diarrhoea. Stools are watery and forcibly evacuated, while body sweating is present as a rule. The foal is cold and visible mucous membranes may assume a bluish tinge. Suggested potency 30c three times daily for four days.

Pulsatilla   When this remedy is indicated it will be found that the character of the stool changes frequently, e.g. at one stage it may contain a significant amount of mucus while at others it may be watery. Changeability of symptoms is a keynote of this remedy. Suggested potency 30c three times daily for five days.

Streptococcus 30c   As various species of streptococcus are some-times associated with this trouble it could be beneficial to give a daily dose for five days of 30c potency. It combines well with selected remedies.

Hepatitis.   This condition in the young foal is invariably associated with Herpes infection and leading to jaundice and other complications such as anaemia and involvement of the central nervous system. Remedies which may help include:

Chelidonium   For acute cases showing jaundice of mucous membranes with stiffness over the right-shoulder area. Suggested potency 10M one twice daily for three days.

Phosphorus also indicated in acute forms giving whitish stools which may be either soft or hard. Purpura-like haemorrhages sometimes appear while the urine shows haemoglobinuria. Suggested potency 200c three times daily for three days.

Chionanthus A good general liver remedy when stools are clay coloured accompanying a high coloured urine. There is often rapid loss of condition. Suggested potency 30c daily for ten days.

Cuprum met. A useful remedy when central nervous system symptoms are prominent leading to convulsions. Suggested potency 30c twice daily for seven days.

Herpes nosode (1) should also be given along with other selected remedies in a potency of 30c daily for seven days.

Kidney involvement. Sometimes in the young foal referred to as a Shigella dysenteria, presented as sleepiness, lethargy and convulsions probably due to retention of toxins following kidney failure. Treatment could be unrewarding and should comprise remedies such as *Apis mel*, *Eel serum* and *Plumbum*. *Apis* may help if the foal is thirstless and may help promote urination. A potency of 6c every four hours for four doses is indicated. *Eel serum* in 30c potency will help the circulation and also promote urination, giving a dose three times daily for three days. If convulsions are present *Plumbum* 1M one three times daily for four days may be needed. This is also a good general kidney remedy.

Convulsions. These take the form of meningeal complications which can vary in severity. Remedies to consider are potencies of various heavy metals such as *Cuprum*, *Plumbum* and *Zinc*: and also remedies such as *Cicuta*, *Stramonium* and *Belladonna*. The metals should be used in 30c potency for *Cuprum*, twice daily for seven days, *Plumbum* 1M daily for ten days, and *Zinc* in 200c potency three times per week for three weeks. When *Cicuta* is indicated the head may be thrown back or the neck twisted in an S bend; a potency of 30c should be used three times daily for ten days. A similar potency used in the same way is indicated for *Stramonium* when the head deviates to the left side. *Belladonna* gives a picture of excitement, dilated pupils and throbbing pulse.

Joint-Ill. This condition is associated with various species of streptococci with occasionally infection by Salmonella typhymurium. Lameness is a prominent symptom with enlargement of joints such as stifle and carpus. Both nosodes *Streptococcus* and *Salmonella* in 30c potency may give encouraging results in treatment using a 30c potency three times daily for three days and following with one dose every second day for three doses. Residual swelling of joints once acute symptoms have been resolved may need remedies such as *Calc fluor* 30c daily for fourteen days of *Silicea* 200c one dose three times per week for four weeks.

Before leaving this short account of infective conditions affecting the young foal we must mention one or two remedies which will prove extremely useful in the rearing of these young animals. To begin with foals which show immaturity at birth or are born prematurely should be given the Bach Flower Rescue Remedy. This (although not a potentised homoeopathic remedy) will help revive any such foal, a few drops given on the tongue at regular intervals over a few hours will quickly revive them.

Over a longer period, the main remedy to promote proper growth of bones and muscle is *Calc phosph* 30c. Given over a period of three months a twice weekly dose will lay the foundations for the development of a better animal than otherwise would be the case. From three to six months the dose can be reduced to one per week.

XX   Protozoal Diseases

1. Babesiasis. This disease is characterised by fever and intravascular haemorrhage or haemolysis producing an anaemic state, along with haemoglobinuria. The causative organism is transmitted by ticks.

SYMPTOMS
An initial pyrexia is followed by anorexia and weakness. The conjunctivae are at first bright red, but soon become pale due to anaemia. Jaundice may supervene in the later stages. Mares if pregnant may abort. Haemoglobinuria is rare in the horse, but oedema of various parts is common, e.g. in the supraorbital fossa. Colic and petechial haemorrhages on the conjunctiva have been observed.

TREATMENT
China off. 6c   This is a good supportive remedy in anaemic states, helping to maintain strength and control pyrexia. Dose: every two hours for four doses.
Ferrum arsenicum 6c   Enlarged spleen, accompanied by dry skin. Dose: night and morning for one week.
Phosphorus 200c   Petechial haemorrhages. Dose: night and morning for four days.
Silicea 1M   This remedy has some reputation in restoring red cells and stimulating haemopoiesis. Dose: once weekly for four weeks.

2. Dourine.   This contagious disease is caused by *Trypanosoma equiperdium*, a flagellate protozoon. It is transmitted by coitus and affects principally the external genital organs. It produces lesions also on the skin and in some cases paralysis.

SYMPTOMS

Local oedematous swellings occur after initial infection and systemic involvement follows. The incubation period may be up to one month and sometimes longer. Swelling of the penis and scrotum are the first signs in the stallion and the oedema may extend forward as far as the pectoral region. Urethral discharge occurs and there is involvement of the regional lymph nodes.

Vulval oedema occurs in the mare accompanied by vaginal ulceration and discharge. As in the stallion the oedema spreads downwards and forward. Nervous symptoms appear in both sexes leading to incoordination of movement, and in the later stages, paralysis, preceded by atrophy of the hindquarters. In severe cases there may be sexual excitement and more severe oedema. Skin lesions in the form of plaques appear over the neck and various parts of the body.

TREATMENT

Apis 6c   Oedema of genitalia. Oedematous plaques on skin. Dose: three times daily for five days.

Urtica urens 6c   Itch accompanies formation of oedematous areas. Dose: three times daily for five days.

Rhus toxicodendron 1M   Scrotal skin becomes erythematous and itchy with initial swelling. Dose: three hourly for four doses.

Conium 200c   Paralysis. This remedy helps to prevent hindquarter atrophy. Dose: night and morning for one week.

3.   Coccidiosis.   This contagious disease takes the form of an enteritis caused by a protozoon parasite, *Eimeria leukarti*. Characteristic of the condition is dysentery, followed by emaciation and anaemia. The disease may affect a group of young animals, if they are kept in close confinement, e.g. foals running together in a paddock. Animals become infected by ingestion of contaminated feed or water.

SYMPTOMS

After a variable incubation period of fourteen to twenty-one days, a mild febrile reaction occurs. Diarrhoea, usually severe, is the first noticeable sign, the faeces containing mucus and whole blood, sometimes dark, but more often bright red. This is accompanied by severe straining which can persist long after faeces are passed. If much blood is lost in the stool, signs of anaemia occur, e.g. paleness of mucous membranes and conjunctivae, together with weak, rapid pulse and general weakness. Appetite is lost and dehydration sets in. Mild cases may show only diarrhoea and stunted growth, without loss of blood.

TREATMENT

Aconitum napellus 6c Signs of fever in early stages of the disease. Dose: every hour for three doses.

Arsenicum alb. 1M First stages of diarrhoea, especially if faeces are evil-smelling and worse after midnight. Dose: every two hours for four doses.

Ipecacuanha 30c Protozoal infection of the intestine. Faeces contain abundant mucus, shreds of mucous lining and whole blood, usually bright red. Dose: three times daily for three days.

Millefolium 6c Accompanying haemorrhages from urinary tract and from the nose. Dose: three times daily for three days.

China off. 30c Great loss of strength after loss of blood. Dose: three times daily for two days.

Mercurius corrosivus 200c Stools bloody, excessively slimy, passed more often during the night. Dose: three times daily for three days. This remedy is particularly useful for straining unaccompanied by stool.

XXI Miscellaneous Diseases

1. Haemolytic Anaemia of New Born Foals. The predisposing factors of this disease occur during pregnancy, but the foetus is not affected. Symptoms show only after birth when the young animal has ingested colostrum. The foal inherits red cell antigens from the sire and these pass the placental barrier into the dam's circulation. If these antigens are not normally present in the dam, antibodies are produced in the dam's circulation against the foal's red cells. These antibodies are produced late in pregnancy, but do not pass the placental barrier, so the foetus remains unaffected. The antibodies against the foal's red cells are present also in the dam's colostrum and are soon absorbed into the foal's circulation after it has sucked for the first time. These produce intravascular haemolysis because of the interaction of antibody and red cells resulting in anaemia and jaundice.

Vaccination against rhinopneumonitis has been suggested as a possible cause, especially if this is done twice during pregnancy in the last three months, using a vaccine which has been prepared from foetal tissue.

SYMPTOMS

Clinical signs appear only if the colostrum has been ingested and are evident after two to four days in the average case. There may be per-acute, acute or sub-acute involvement. Early signs include lassitude and disinclination to suck, the foal usually lying on its chest. The heart rate is increased and the cardiac sounds are intensified, having a metallic tone. A jugular pulse is evident. Once anaemia develops, respiration becomes laboured and yawning is frequent. Haemoglobinuria is present in per-acute cases, jaundice being absent. Sub-acute cases show a reversal of these two findings.

TREATMENT

Replacement of affected blood in the foal by transfusion is normal practice and is usually effective. The following remedies will aid recovery:–

China off. 30c This remedy will quickly help the foal to regain strength and regulate heart and respiration. Dose: every two hours for four doses.

Phosphorus 200c This remedy will help to promote a healthy peripheral circulation and restore liver function. Dose: three times daily for two days.

Note:– If there is cause to believe that this disease may arise because of a history of pneumonia vaccination, the above remedies should be given to the foal immediately at birth, prior to having the affected blood replaced by transfusion. Replacement of orthodox or allopathic vaccination by a nosode or homoeopathic oral vaccine will reduce the likelihood of the disease occurring.

3. Purpura haemorrhagica. This is a non-contagious disease characterised by oedematous and haemorrhagic swellings in the subcutaneous tissues. Mucosal and visceral haemorrhage also occur. It frequently follows an attack of an infectious disease such as strangles, infectious arteritis or pneumonitis. The incidence is highest where there are large numbers of horses at risk in an outbreak of strangles.

SYMPTOMS

Subcutaneous swellings characterise the initial stages of the disease; these are oedematous and are seen particularly around the muzzle and lips. They are painless and may appear suddenly or over the course of a few days. Oedema of the limbs is confined to areas above the knee or hock. Oozing of serum may take place from the swellings. Petechial haemorrhages occur on the conjunctiva and submucous haemorrhages in the mouth and nasal passages. Colic may occur due to visceral oedema and haemorrhage. The heart rate is increased but the temperature usually remains normal.

TREATMENT

Apis 6c This remedy should be employed as soon as oedematous swellings first appear. Dose: every two hours for four doses.

Phosphorus 200c This is indicated for petechial haemorrhages. It will also help visceral haemorrhages especially if hepatic in origin. Dose: three times daily for three days.

Kali bichromicum 30c This will prevent further development of oedematous swellings. It is also useful in controlling the oozing of serum from swellings. Dose: three times daily for three days.

Crotalus horridus 200c This is a valuable remedy for general haemorrhagic diathesis, with oozing of dark blood from petechial haemorrhages. It is particularly useful if jaundice is present. Dose: four times daily for two days.

Lachesis 30c This remedy may be indicated when generalised petechial haemorrhages are accompanied by throat swelling and epistaxis. Dose: three times daily for three days.

Hamamelis 6c This is an important remedy. There is a generalised venous congestion with enlarged throat veins. Purpura and petechiae are accompanied by pain. Dose: three times daily for three days.

Sulphuric acid 30c This remedy is especially useful if the condition has arisen as a result of strangles. Petechiae are associated with a skin irritation. Dose: three times daily for three days.

If there is a history of previous infectious disease, the appropriate nosode should be administered at the commencement of treatment. If may be combined with indicated remedies. Dose: once daily for three days.

3. Allergic Dermatitis. This extremely itchy condition is due to a hypersensitivity to insect bites. The majority of cases occur during the summer months, especially if the weather is humid. The condition is confined to horses and all ages are affected. Stabled animals clear themselves of the condition. Affected areas are the base of the tail, the rump, along the back to the withers and forward to the ears.

SYMPTOMS

Pruritis is intense and is worse at night. Constant scratching causes shedding of the hair and secondary infection may occur in the hair follicles. In mild cases, the skin may appear scaly with loss of hair.

TREATMENT

Arsenicum alb. 30c This is one of the main remedies. It may have to be given in progressively high potencies. Dose: once daily for ten days.

Sulphur iodatum 6c This is useful in long standing cases, showing a tendency to secondary infection. Dose: three times daily for one week.

Hepar sulphuris 200c This is indicated when the hair follicles have become infected and localised suppuration has occurred. It is especially useful if the lesions are tender to the touch. Dose: night and morning for one week.

Mezereum 30c This remedy will be found useful in neglected cases where scab formation has developed around the lesion. Dose: three times daily for two days, followed by one dose daily for five days.

4. Fistulous Withers. This is the term applied to a sinus or fistula which develops along any part of the withers. As in poll evil abscess formation and necrosis affect the ligamentum nuchae in this region, but involvement of spinous processes and cartilages is also of common occurrence. When bone is involved the lesion is carious.

SYMPTOMS

An extremely tender inflammatory swelling of the withers occurs. Various openings discharge purulent material and the disease tends to move downwards and forwards, affecting deeper tissues. Secondary septicaemic involvement is common, with febrile symptoms.

TREATMENT

Aconitum napellus 6c If seen early enough, this should be given to prevent febrile complications. Dose: every hour for three doses.

Apis 6c This remedy is indicated to control synovitis which may occur in the small joints involved. Dose: every two hours for four doses.

Hepar sulphuris 200c This is a most useful remedy, the guiding principle being extreme sensitivity to pain, which almost always is present in the acute stage. This remedy will also help once suppuration has occurred, promoting resolution and relieving pain. Dose: three hourly for four doses.

Silicea 200c   This remedy is indicated in more neglected cases, once fistulae have appeared. Its use will prevent necrosis and promote healthy granulation of ulcers. Dose: once daily for seven days.

Brucella abortus nosode 30c   As brucellosis is frequently implicated in this disease, the nosode should be given for three consecutive days at the commencement of treatment. Dose: once daily.

Externally, a lotion of *Calendula* and *Hypericum* will promote quick healing and aid the action of indicated remedies.

5. Poll Evil.   This condition is a bursitis, affecting the atlanto-occipital joint, leading to necrosis of the ligamentum nuchae and resulting in a sinus or purulent fistula of the poll region.

SYMPTOMS
Heat, tenderness and swelling of the area first occur, the joint becoming extremely sensitive to touch. Secondary infection leads to suppuration which tends to invade the surrounding tissues and may infect adjacent bone. Fistulous involvement occurs, caused by necrosis of tissue in the ligamentum nuchae.

TREATMENT
Brucella abortus nosode 30c   This nosode should be given at the commencement of treatment. Dose: once daily for three days.

Aconitum napellus 6c   This remedy should be given in the early febrile stage. Dose: every hour for four doses.

Apis 6c   If synovitis of the joint is suspected, in the acute stage, this remedy will relieve pain and reduce the joint fluid. Dose: every two hours for four doses.

Hepar sulphuris 30c   This remedy will be of considerable benefit if given either in the early inflammatory stage, showing extreme sensitivity to pain, or when suppuration has set in. Dose: every two hours for four doses.

Silicea 200c   This is a valuable remedy in the more chronic case, once fistulous involvement has occurred with the development of purulent channels. Dose: once daily for seven days.

Externally, a compress of *Hypericum* and *Calendula* lotion will hasten healing.

6. Leuco-encephalomalacia. This condition is sometimes seen as a result of horses feeding on mouldy corn, which arises as a result of wet grain being stored allowing moulds to develop.

SYMPTOMS

Early signs of disturbance include weakness accompanied by tremors of various groups of muscles. This animal may walk in circles and staggering and incoordination may appear. The reflexes become sluggish, while abdominal disturbance is manifested by jaundice in a proportion of cases. Febrile signs are absent.

TREATMENT

Agaricus muscarius 6c   This remedy will help those cases showing depression of consciousness and incoordination of movement. Dose: every two hours for four doses.

Curare 30c   This remedy is indicated in the early stages showing muscle weakness and tremors. Dose: hourly for four doses.

Plumbum metallicum 30c   When the main symptom is walking in circles, with a tendency to paralysis, this remedy should help. Dose: three times daily for one week.

Phosphorus 200c   The administration of this remedy will help liver function and control petechial haemorrhages which may occur in some parts of the central nervous system. Dose: every three hours for four doses.

Chelidonium 1M   This is a useful remedy when there is jaundice, accompanied by muscle stiffness over the right shoulder area. Dose: three times daily for three days.

7. Snake Bite. The adder-type of bite causes a local swelling and severe pain. Dyspnoea can arise from bites near the throat. Other types of bite may produce vesicular involvement leading to haemorrhages and secondary infections.

SYMPTOMS

The area surrounding the bite becomes swollen and discoloured, sometimes assuming a bluish or purplish appearance.

TREATMENT

Apis 6c   This remedy is indicated for adder bites when accompanied by local oedema. Dose: three times daily for two days.

Naja 6c This remedy will be of use when underlying tissue oedema is accompanied by purplish discolouration of the skin above. There is usually much salivation. Dose: every two hours for four doses.

Crotalus horridus 200c Indications for this remedy include haemorrhage and localised secondary infection. The blood is dark and fluid. Dose: every two hours for four doses.

Echinacea 6x Indicated when there is secondary infection from venous wounds. This takes the form of blood poisoning with involvement of lymphatics. Dose: every hour for five doses.

Tarentula cubensis 6c This remedy will be useful when there is a puffy swelling round the bite, with early suppuration. The underlying skin is purplish. Dose: every two hours for four doses.

Lachesis 1M When the skin surrounding the wound appears bluish, with systemic symptoms involving the region of the throat, this remedy will be found to be useful. Dose: hourly for four doses.

Anthracinum 200c This nosode is indicated when the subcutaneous tissues become indurated and necrotic. The blood is dark, with the associated lymph glands becoming swollen and tender. Dose: every two hours for four doses, followed by one dose daily for three days.

8. Calcium Deficiency. This may occur among horses during training, if kept indoors for much of their time, and is usually associated with vitamin D deficiency.

SYMPTOMS
Signs are commoner in the young animal and show usually in retardation of growth and poor or abnormal development of teeth. In older animals anorexia, stiffness and a tendency to recumbency occur, together with a predisposition to fracture of the long bones.

TREATMENT
Calcarea phosphorica 30c The most useful remedy for restoring a healthy, calcium metabolism. Dose: night and morning for two weeks.

9. Osteodystrophia Fibrosa. In this condition fibrous tissue is deposited in place of calcium, which becomes deficient due to excessive phosphate feeding. It can be induced by Ca:P ratio of one to three or more. Diets which contribute to this condition include cereal hay, together with heavy grain or bran feeding. The imbalance of calcium and phosphorus produces a demineralisation of bone, leading to a susceptibility to fractures and separation of the attachment of muscles and tendons.

SYMPTOMS

Lameness appearing in different legs is the first obvious sign and there may be an arching of the back. Joint lesions sometimes occur, producing a crackling sound when the animal moves. Different parts of the skeleton produce their own picture of involvement, e.g. the facial bones may become swollen and the ribs flattened. Joint swellings and bending of long bones are seen in advanced cases.

TREATMENT

Calcarea phosphorica 30c This is the remedy which should be tried first, helping as it does to restore the calcium and phosphorus ratio. Dose: night and morning for two weeks.

Calcarea fluorica 30c Where joint exostoses and any dental involvement occur, this is the remedy of choice. Dose: night and morning for seven days. This is a form of treatment which may have to be repeated at monthly intervals.

Phosphoric acid 6c The young, rapidly growing animal responds well to this remedy. Dose: once daily for ten days.

10. Copper Deficiency. Primary copper deficiency is rare in adult horses, but foals may show abnormalities of the limbs, if reared in copper deficient areas. Such animals, if untreated, usually remain unthrifty and slow growing.

SYMPTOMS

Enlargement of joints and stiffness are early signs. The flexor tendons are subject to contraction, shown by the animal putting the toe to the ground when walking. Severe cases may show knuckling.

TREATMENT

Cuprum metallicum 200c This remedy should be administered once a day for one week, followed by a dose twice weekly for four weeks.

11. Iodine Deficiency. Deficiency of this element may be primary, produced by an insufficient intake, or it may be secondary when it is then associated with too much calcium in the feed.

SYMPTOMS
Iodine deficiency assumes its greatest importance as a main contributory cause of still births, or weakly viable foals. This weakness may be severe enough to prevent the foal standing unaided. The fetlock and pastern areas of the fore limbs sometimes show excessive flexion, coupled with a corresponding extension of the same areas in the hind leg. Thoroughbreds and hunters in affected areas may show thyroid enlargement in the adult animal.

TREATMENT
Iodum 6c   This should be given twice daily for one week, but it may be necessary to continue treatment for longer periods, depending on response.
Kali hydriodicum 12x   The iodide of potassium is a more suitable preparation for weakly foals, influencing, as it does, the extremities. Dose: twice daily for seven days.

12.   Horsetail Poisoning.   This may occur from time to time, as a result of young or immature plants being incorporated into a hay crop. Animals rarely show symptoms when grazing.

SYMPTOMS
Incoordination of movement, along with swaying from side to side are early signs. The hind legs may be splayed out and crossing of the fore legs is not uncommon. Muscle tremors arise, followed by arching of the back, leading to recumbency. Coma may eventually set in, preceded by opisthotonus and possibly brain symptoms such as convulsions.

TREATMENT
Agaricus muscarius 6c   In the early stages, associated with muscle twitchings and tremors, this remedy will prove useful. Dose: every two hours for four doses.
Strychninum 200c   This remedy is indicated to control a tendency to opisthotonous and will also help severe muscle twitching. Dose: four times daily for two days.

Gelsemium 200c Muscular incoordination will be helped by the use of this remedy. It should also prevent paralytic symptoms appearing. Dose: three times daily for three days.

Opium 200c Indicated when somnolent states arise, or signs of coma appear. Dose: every two hours for three doses.

13. Lead Poisoning. Chronic poisoning is occasionally met with, especially among animals grazing near factories, which use lead for processing, or those in the vicinity of lead mines.

SYMPTOMS

The recurrent laryngeal nerve shows paralysis leading to difficulty in inspiration. This may extent to the pharyngeal area, when difficulty in swallowing will be noticed, while paralysis of the lips is a common sequel. These signs accompany a dry skin, together with muscular weakness and stiffness.

TREATMENT

Gelsemium 200c This remedy will probably be of most benefit in treating laryngeal and other paralyses of the head and throat. Dose: three times daily for four days. It may be necessary to prolong treatment with a lower potency, reducing the frequency of administration.

Cuprum metallicum 1M Those cases showing muscular weakness and stiffness may be helped by *Cuprum*, more especially when there is muscular rigidity. Dose: once daily for seven days.

Curare 30c Indicated in general muscular weakness, associated with excessive trembling of limbs. Dose: three times daily for three days.

Conium 200c This remedy will be of especial benefit if the hind limbs show paralysis, symptoms gradually moving upwards and forwards. Dose: once daily for one week. It may be necessary to continue treatment with ascending potencies.

14. Chronic Selenium Poisoning – Alkali Disease. This may occur when there is a gradual intake of selenium, by horses grazing on soils or pasture containing large amounts of selenium-rich plants.

SYMPTOMS

Emaciation, stiffness and lameness occur, together with loss of hair on the tail. Abnormality of the hooves occur, including coronitis leading to severe lameness.

TREATMENT

Cuprum metallicum 1M   This remedy will be of assistance when there is generalised muscle stiffness. Dose: once daily for seven days.

Arsenicum alb. 6c   This remedy will help control loss of hair along the base of the tail and will also promote appetite. Dose: night and morning for two weeks.

Calcarea fluorica 30c   When hoof abnormalities are prominent, this remedy will be of value. Dose: once daily for three weeks.

XXII   Diseases of Unknown Etiology

1. Post-Vaccinal Hepatitis.   This condition has been recorded as a sequel to infectious encephalomyelitis and may occur up to three months after contraction of the disease. It is usually related to the use of serum and vaccine used in controlling the disease, but some cases can arise independently. It has been reported in mares vaccinated against virus abortion and also in horses vaccinated against other diseases.

SYMPTOMS
The chief symptom is severe jaundice. Oliguria is present and nervous symptoms appear also. The head is pressed against any convenient object and the gait becomes incoordinated.

TREATMENT
Phosphorus 30c   Faeces pale. Petechial haemorrhage may occur on visible mucous membranes. Dose: three times daily for three days.
Chelidonium 30c   Yellow discolouration of the conjunctiva and visible mucous membranes. Possible tenderness over right shoulder region. Dose: three times daily for three days.
Carduus marianus 30c   Tenderness over liver region, with yellow stools. Dose: three times daily for four days.
Chionanthus 6x   Head symptoms. Conjunctiva yellow, stools yellow. Urine dark. Dose: three times daily for seven days.
Lycopodium 200c   Oliguria prominent. Urine contains sediment, reddish, and there may be abdominal distension. Dose: night and morning for one week.
Mercurius dulcis 6c   Bloated abdomen. Stools slimy, possibly blood-stained. Dose: night and morning for five days.

2. Grass Sickness. This is a non-infectious disease character-ised by paralytic involvement of the nerve endings of the alimentary tract. It produces emaciation and extreme bowel stasis. The age group commonly affected is three to six years and foals do not contract the disease. While an occasional case has been recorded in stabled animals, the great majority occur at pasture in the early summer months.

SYMPTOMS
Acute, sub-acute and chronic types occur. In the acute form, initial signs are anorexia and inability to swallow water. Bowel move-ments cease and slight tympany is present, together with frequent urination. Patchy sweating occurs and fine muscle tremors are seen especially over the shoulder region. Stomach contents run from the nose and frequently there is difficulty in rising, the animal assuming a 'sitting-dog' posture. Rapid, wiry pulse and brick-red discolou-ration of conjunctiva are indicative of severe systemic disturbance. Sub-acute cases show a gaunt 'herring-gut' appearance and wasting of gluteal and femoral muscles. Extreme restlessness causes the animal to pace round the field in an aimless manner, and he may dip his head frequently into a water trough in an attempt to drink. Bowel stasis is not quite so severe in the sub-acute form, small quantities of soft faeces being passed infrequently. This form may show a temporary improvement, but soon lapses into a chronic form characterised by intermittent bouts of abdominal pain, sweating and excessive muscular weakness. Such cases invariably degenerate and if they are allowed to survive show acute symptoms the following year.

TREATMENT
No effective treatment has yet been devised, probably because there are no prodromal signs indicating disease. Once symptoms appear, they worsen very rapidly and are invariably terminal. Opportunities for studying and treating this disease are much fewer than formerly when there were more susceptible animals of the draught type to be found. The following remedies are worthy of consideration and trial:–

Gelsemium 1M In this high potency, it may be possible to influence favourably the paralytic involvement of the throat and mouth.

Plumbum metallicum Generalised paralysis, especially of the gut, can be helped by this remedy.

Conium When hind-leg paralysis occurs as in the 'sitting-dog' posture, this remedy may have great value.

Zincum metallicum Useful in controlling muscle tremors and patchy sweating.

Cocculus Associated lower limb paralysis and abdominal tympany.

Nux vomica This remedy may have some influence in helping bowel stasis especially in restlessness.

Lathyrus sativa The provings of this remedy suggest that it may be of value in restoring nerve function, if not completely lost.

Thallium Paralysis associated with this remedy extends to the lower abdomen and as such it may be of use in helping bowel stasis.

3. Colitis – Rudiosa Disease. This little known disease has assumed importance in the last decade or so. It takes the form of acute enteritis of the large bowel and affects mainly the adult animal.

SYMPTOMS

The inflammation is of very sudden onset and early signs are depression and discolouration of the conjunctivae. The pulse is very fast and thready and there is patchy sweating. Restlessness occurs with evidence of bowel pain, such as kicking at belly and looking round at the flanks. Foul smelling diarrhoea may occur but is not a constant symptom as the disease may be per-acute and leave no time for such a development. Dehydration occurs in less acute cases. The lesion in the caecum and colon is one of necrotic enteritis with haemorrhagic infiltration. The contents of the large bowel are fluid and foul smelling.

TREATMENT

In the less acute cases, which give room for medication, the following remedies should be tried:–

Arsenicum alb. 1M Give every hour for four or five doses.

Arnica 30c Passage of bright red blood accompanied by colic.
  Dose: every hour for four doses.

Baptisia 200c   Tympanitic signs, especially on right side. There may be considerable flatus. Stools dark and watery. Dose: three times daily for three days.

Mercurius corrosivus 200c   Slimy mucus in stool, along with blood-stained lining of gut. Symptoms worse during the night. Severe colicky signs also present. Dose: every two hours for four doses.

4.   Thoroughbred Foal Disease.   This condition, occurring only in thoroughbred studs, is sometimes associated with too early cutting of the umbilical cord with consequent interference with blood supply to the foal from the dam's placenta.

SYMPTOMS

Early signs are convulsions and paddling movements of the limbs. Recovery from this stage may lead into other stages showing different nervous symptoms. The disease commences during the first twenty-four hours. Weakness and aimless movements are accompanied by blindness. Nystagmus and sweating are prominent signs during convulsions and the foal may injure itself by striking the head on the floor. A comatose stage may supervene after which the animal passes into a stage in which reflexes are lost and blindness persists. In this stage the foal can walk, but blindness causes aimless wandering movements.

TREATMENT

Agaricus muscarius 6c   Give at the first suspicion of the disease developing. Dose: one hourly for five doses.

Belladonna 1M   Convulsions occur and the foal may strike the head on the ground. Dose: one hourly for five doses.

Stramonium 1M   Useful if nystagmus is a prominent symptom, also when aimless wandering occurs. Dose: one dose every two hours for four doses.

Opium 200c   For the comatose stage. Animal usually lies perfectly still. Dose: two doses four hours apart.

Hyoscyamus 200c   When blindness supervenes and early nervous signs appear, such as head shaking and early aimless movements. Dose: two doses three hours apart.

5. Enzootic Ataxia. This disease affects young horses, principally thoroughbreds and saddle horses. The onset of the disease may have its origin in a fall or in some violent activity.

SYMPTOMS

Incoordination of movement is the first sign and in mild cases may not be noticeable unless the animal is ridden or exercised. Pressure over the cervical vertebrae causes pain. Knuckling occurs if the animal is pulled up sharply. Swaying of the hind-quarters is common. Intermittent dragging of feet and a disinclination to move or rise are seen in many cases. It is thought that symptoms are produced by compression of the spinal cord and this view is reinforced by the post-mortem finding of projections of vertebrae into the spinal canal. Inflammation of the articular processes of the thoracic and cervical vertebrae may be present.

TREATMENT

Conium 30c Weakness and incoordination of hind-limbs. Difficulty in rising. Dose: three times daily for three days.

Gelsemium 200c Knuckling and tendency to recumbency. Dose: three times daily for three days.

Lathyrus sativa 30c Spastic movements accompany rigidity of muscles. Difficulty in straightening up. Dose: three times daily for four days.

Agaricus muscarius 6c Pain over back, with tottering gait. Dose: three times daily for three days.

6. Sporadic Lymphangitis. This disease is characterised by fever lymphangitis and swelling of one or both hind legs.

SYMPTOMS

Febrile signs usher in the disease accompanied by rapid pulse and increased respiration. Pain is obvious and palpation of the area is resented. The limb is swollen and hot and may be carried off the ground. The lymphatics on the inside of the leg become thickened and the associated lymph glands become enlarged. The disease may persist for many weeks, producing a fibrous thickening of the limb. It frequently appears in animals fed on nutritious rations with little exercise. It can also be associated with superficial wounds which allow infection to gain access to underlying tissues. The resultant lymphadenitis causes in turn a septic lymphangitis.

TREATMENT

Aconitum napellus 6c   Always give first, in the early febrile stage. Dose: every hour for four doses.

Calcarea fluorica 30c   Early inflammation of the lymphatics and later fibrous stage. Dose: three times daily for four days.

Kali bichromicum 30c   Serum oozes from the inflamed lymphatics. Dose: three times daily for three days.

Apis 6c   Oedema accompanies lymphangitis. Dose: every two hours for four doses.

Rhus toxicodendron 30c   Superficial skin lesions become inflamed and erysipelatous. Dose: three times daily for three days.

Externally, a lotion of *Rhus toxicodendron* and *Arnica* will be helpful.

7.   Anhydrosis.   This condition is characterised by the absence of sweating and occurs mainly in humid climates among horses imported from more temperate zones.

SYMPTOMS

Although excessive sweating occurs in the early stages, this soon disappears and any sweating appearing later is patchy in distribution and confined to the skin under the mane. Skin becomes dry and scaly. Acute pyrexia occurs and dyspnoea becomes severe. The temperature may rise as high as 108°F.

TREATMENT

Aconitum napellus 6c   Early in acute febrile stage. Dose: hourly for four doses.

Arsenicum alb. 1M   Skin dry and scaly. Dose: three times daily for three days.

Arsenicum iodatum 6c   Respiratory signs. Dyspnoea. Dose: every three hours for four doses.

Calcarea carbonica 200c   Patchy sweating. Dose: one dose per day for four days.

Alumina 30c   Excessive dryness of skin, with itching. Tendency to constipation. Dose: night and morning for four days.

Berberis aquifolium 6c   This remedy will promote glandular activity and help promote sweating. Dose: three times daily for ten days.

Petroleum 6c Dry, scaly skin, with pyrexia. Remedy stimulates sweat glands. Dose: three times daily for five days.

Nux moschata 6c Extreme dryness of the skin accompanied by weakness and faltering gait. Dose: three times daily for five days.

XXIII   Metabolic Diseases

1.   Lactation Tetany of Mares – Eclampsia.   This condition is accompanied by hypo-calcaemia, and in cases which have a history of recent transportation, by a hypo-magnesaemia also. It occurs usually about the tenth day after foaling, or again a few days after weaning. It is commonest in mares which are lactating heavily and may be brought on by hard physical work, or prolonged transport. Mares requiring medicinal help at the foaling heat are usually more severely affected than those showing symptoms following transportation.

SYMPTOMS
Profuse sweating occurs and movement becomes difficult because of tetanic spasm of the muscle of the limbs. Respiration becomes difficult and dilation of nostrils is evident. Tremors of the jaw and shoulder muscles occur, but there is no aversion to light (unlike tetanus). The pulse becomes rapid and irregular. Cessation of urination and bowel movements are common sequelae. In the later stages convulsions appear and may become continuous. Recovery is associated with large quantities of urine.

TREATMENT
To supplement the use of normal calcium injections, which normally promote recovery, the following remedies will help to minimise the risk of damage to the central nervous system and prevent relapse.
Calcarea carbonica 200c   This remedy is especially suitable for fat mares which show abundant sweating. Dose: every hour for four doses.
Magnesium phosphoricum 6c This remedy can be used in

alternation with the previous one, for cases associated with hypomagnesaemia. Dose: every hour for four doses.

Cuprum metallicum 6c   This remedy will be useful in controlling muscle cramps, associated with rigidity. Dose: every two hours for four doses.

Belladonna 1M   Indicated in those cases showing convulsions. The patient is excitable prior to the onset of symptoms. The pupils become dilated, there is head shaking and a full bounding pulse. Dose: every hour for four doses.

Agaricus muscarius 6c   When this remedy is called for, the animal tends to fall backwards or sideways. If given early enough it may prevent convulsions. Dose: every two hours for four doses.

2.   Paralytic Myoglobinuria – Azoturia.   This disease occurs during exercise and appears after a period of rest, during which time the animal has been receiving full rations. Muscular degeneration is the main feature of the condition, associated with myoglobinuria – the appearance in the urine of muscle pigment. In the majority of cases there is complete inactivity for two or more days before exercise. A rest of twenty-four hours or more than two weeks is unlikely to produce the condition. Attacks may occur after general anaesthesia and it has been reported in horses grazing good pasture land for a few days and then subjected to hard work. It is thought that a lack of vitamin E may be a contributory cause.

SYMPTOMS

The gluteal muscles are most frequently affected and become hard and painful. The affected muscles liberate myoglobin, which subsequently appears in the urine, colouring it dark reddish brown. Sweating appears as the first sign which comes on about one hour after exercise has started. The animal becomes averse to movement but if made to move, shows stiffness of gait. Recumbency soon sets in, pain and restlessness are evident and there is an increase in respiration. The pulse is hard and wiry and the temperature is raised. Both hind legs are invariably affected, the muscles of the upper region becoming hard and board-like. Less severe cases show slight lameness and tenderness over the sacral region, with restricted movement.

TREATMENT

Aconitum napellus 6c   Should always be given as early as possible in the febrile stage. Dose: hourly for four doses.

Belladonna 1M   Indicated when there are signs of nervousness, dilated pupils, full bounding pulse and a smooth, hot skin. Dose: hourly for four doses.

Thallium 30c   This remedy may be of use in the early paralytic stage, accompanied by sweating. Dose: three times daily for three days.

Berberis vulgaris 30c   When there is pain and tenderness over the kidney region with pronounced stiffness, this remedy is indicated. Dose: three times daily for three days.

Arnica 30c   This is a good, general remedy indicated at the commencement of symptoms in most cases. It may be associated with a fear of being approached or touched. Dose: two doses three hours apart.

Bryonia 30c   Indicated when stiffness or tenseness of muscles is associated with disinclination to move. The animal is better at rest. Dose: three times daily for two days.

Rhus toxicodendron 1M   When this remedy is needed, the symptoms are ameliorated when the animal can be made to move. There is heat and tenderness over the sacral region. Dose: every two hours for four doses.

Bellis perennis 30c   This is a principle remedy. There is congestion of local blood vessels and it is also associated with unduly dark urine. Dose: three times daily for two days.

Cimicifuga 30c   Indicated when there is twitching of muscles, accompanied by stiffness and restlessness. Dose: three times daily for three days.

Helonias 30c   This is a useful remedy in mild cases, especially indicated when mares are affected. Dose: three times daily for three days.

XXIV   Fore Leg Lameness

1. Inflammation of Bicipital Bursa – Bicipital Bursitis. This bursa is found between the tendon of the biceps brachii muscle and the bicipital groove of the humerus. The bursa together with its tendon may become the seat of inflammation which may be either acute or chronic. It frequently arises as a result of a blow to the point of the shoulder. An infective bursitis can arise from streptococcal diseases and from brucellosis.

SYMPTOMS

The horse tries to advance the limb without flexion and this causes lifting of the head. Consequent on poor flexion, the foot is lifted from the ground with difficulty. On moving forward, there is a shortened stride and stumbling occurs. The shoulder joint (scapulo humeral) becomes fixed and is one of the major signs of shoulder lameness. The limb may be moved in an outward circular fashion in an attempt to move forward without advancing the limb. The leg may be carried in acute cases. At rest the affected limb is drawn slightly backwards and the animal rests on the toe.

TREATMENT

Ruta graveolens 6c   Flexor muscles and tendons are injured. There may also be additional periostitis. Dose: three times daily for three days.

Arnica 30c   Always give this remedy as a routine measure. Dose: one dose twelve hours apart for two doses.

Apis 6c   Synovitis of the bursa. Dose: every two hours for four doses.

Benzoic acid 6c   Accompanying nephritis yielding offensive urine. Dose: two hourly for three doses.

Bryonia 6c   Animal is relieved by pressure over the bursa region and symptoms worse on movement. Dose: three times daily for three days.

Kali muriaticum 30c   Joint swelling, involving surrounding areas. Worse in warm condition. Dose: three times daily for three days.

Hypericum 1M   Damage to nerve endings. Dose: once daily for two days.

2. Radial Paralysis.   The radial nerve supplies impulses to the elbow, knee and digital joints, together with the ulnaris lateralis muscle – the lateral flexor of the carpal or knee joint. Paralysis of varying degrees arises usually from some injury at the point where the nerve crosses the musculo-spiral groove of the humerus. This could happen from a kick at this point, or from a fall.

SYMPTOMS
These vary according to the degree of nerve damage. If the extensor tendons of the digit are affected the animal is unable to advance the limb. Dropped elbow is apparent when the branch of the nerve supplying the triceps muscle is involved and this also causes flexion of the digits. This makes the limb appear longer than usual. Mild cases may show little more than stumbling or slight lameness when walking slowly.

TREATMENT
Gelsemium 200c   Stumbling and weakness of leg muscles. Dose: three times daily for three days.

Plumbum metallicum 6c   Extensor tendons show involvement and reflexes are diminished. Dose: three times daily for four days.

Curare 30c   Weakness of muscles is associated with trembling and loss of reflex action. Dose: three times daily for five days.

Ruta graveolens 6c   Tendon injury, with possible periostitis. Dose: night and morning for one week.

Arnica 30c   Paralysis resulting from kick or fall. Dose: every twelve hours for two doses.

3. Hygroma of Carpus or Knee.   This is a synovial swelling affecting the bursa of the knee joint on its anterior surface. The tendon sheaths of the associated extensor muscles may also be involved. It is caused by injury and can exist as a result of the animal repeatedly striking the knee against a manger or stall.

SYMPTOMS

A swelling occurs over the knee joint, the swelling containing synovial fluid. There may be additional swellings in the joint region depending on which tissues are involved. Acute cases show pain on pressure while neglected cases show fibrous thickening.

TREATMENT

Apis 6c Acute cases showing tenderness and oedema of the joint, with synovial effusion. Dose: every two hours for four doses.

Bryonia 6c Joint hard, shiny and tense. Pressure on joint relieves pain. Worse on movement. Dose: three times daily for four days.

Ruta graveolens 30c Associated tendon sheaths are involved. Dose: night and morning for four days.

Silicea 200c Fibrous tissue develops in neglected cases. Dose: once daily for two weeks.

Calcarea fluorica 30c Chronic synovitis with lumpy deposits showing in joint. Dose: once daily for ten days.

Hepar sulphuris 200c Hygroma infected with pyogenic bacteria. Dose: night and morning for one week.

4. Carpitis. This is acute or chronic inflammation of the knee joint and may involve the joint capsule and associated ligaments. Early movement is an arthritis which, if neglected, can lead to more severe osteoarthritis. The main cause is an injury such as concussion to the joint and is frequently seen in animals subjected to hard exercise.

SYMPTOMS

The anterior surface of the knee bones becomes the seat of pathological change, along with the distal end of the radius and may involve bony structures as far down as the third metacarpal bone. Changes bring about the deposition of new bone as a consequence of periostitis. Osteoarthritis develops in those cases which involve bone change. Mild arthritis develops in those cases where no body changes take place. Lameness may not be evident in chronic cases, although enlargements are evident over the area, either fibrous or bony.

TREATMENT

Ruta graveolens 30c   Accompanying periostitis. Dose: three times daily for three days.

Rhus toxicodendron 1M   Mild arthritis, when animal shows improvement on exercise. Dose: once daily for one week.

Calcarea fluorica 30c   Bony exostoses develop. Dose: night and morning for three days, followed by one dose daily for three weeks.

Silicea 200c   Fibrous enlargements in chronic cases. Dose: once daily for ten days.

Hecla lava 12c   A useful remedy for bony exostoses. Dose: one twice daily for one week.

5.   Contraction of Superficial Digital Flexor – The Perforatus Tendon.   Contraction of this tendon may be congenital or acquired. If the former, the condition is usually present in both limbs; if the latter, it is normally unilateral.

SYMPTOMS

Knuckling of fetlocks is one early sign. Severe contraction may lead to the animal walking on the front part of the fetlock.

TREATMENT

In the young animal, if the contraction is not so severe as to warrant surgical correction, the following remedies will be of use:–

Ruta graveolens 6c   Periosteum affected, a likely sequel if the condition is acquired due to an injury. Dose: three times daily for one week.

Rhus toxicodendron 1M   Contraction accompanied by heat and tenderness. Improvement with exercise. Dose: night and morning for four days.

Arnica 30c   Condition associated with injury and shock. Dose: every twelve hours for two doses.

Externally, the application of a lotion of *Arnica* and *Ruta* is beneficial.

6.   Tendinitis – Tenosynovitis.   This is the name given to inflammation of one or both of the flexor tendons, the perforans (deep) and the perforatus (superficial) and their associated tendon sheaths. The injury which produces this condition causes a tearing of the sheath attachments from their insertion on the tendons. This causes inflammation and transient slight haemorrhage. This in turn produces adhesions between the tendons and also between tendons and sheath, leading to formation of fibrous or scar tissue.

SYMPTOMS

The tendons assume a bowed appearance resulting from adhesions developing on the volar (posterior) aspect of the metacarpal region. There are various names for this condition: (a) High Tendo-vaginitis, involving the area immediately below the carpus, (b) Middle Tendovaginitis, involving the middle third of the metacarpus or cannon, and (c) Low Tendovaginitis, the area involving the volar annular ligament and the distal third of the cannon bone.

While the condition may be seen in the high or low areas alone, the middle area involves one of the other two. High and middle involvement is commoner in the fore leg and arises as a result of severe strain of the flexor area. Low area involvement is the rule when the hind limb is affected. Early symptoms include sudden lameness after severe exercise, producing a diffuse swelling of the affected area, with pain on palpation. There is pointing of the toe to ease pressure on the heel area and the animal favours the toe when made to move. When the condition becomes chronic it is evidenced by a firm, fibrous swelling over the flexor area. Such animals may not show lameness unless subjected to severe exercise.

TREATMENT

Arnica 30c Should be given as soon as possible after injury sustained. Dose: every twelve hours for two doses.

Ruta graveolens 30c Severe cases, with haemorrhage and consequent threat of periostitis. Dose: three hourly for four doses.

Rhus toxicodendron 1M Tendon inflammation generally. Pain eased by movement. Dose: night and morning for four days.

Apis 6c Oedematous swellings, especially over fetlock area. Swellings usually hot and puffy. Dose: two hourly for five doses.

Silicea 200c Chronic cases. This remedy will help resorption of fibrous tissue. Dose: once daily for ten days.

Externally, the application of *Arnica* and *Rhus* liniments will be of benefit.

7.   Metacarpal Periostitis – Sore Shins.   This is a periostitis of the anterior surface of the third metacarpal bone. It is of comparatively rare occurrence in the hind limb, but common in the fore limbs of young racing animals. Concussion is the predisposing cause and both fore limbs may be simultaneously involved. Injuries to the periosteum from blows may also account for some cases.

SYMPTOMS
The main sign is a painful swelling on the anterior surface of the metacarpal bone and is warm to the touch. Subcutaneous oedema may be present. Lameness is increased on exercise and the step becomes shortened. Shifting from one limb to the other occurs in bilateral involvement.

TREATMENT
Arnica 30c   Always begin treatment with two doses, twelve hours apart.
Ruta graveolens 6c   This is one of the main remedies. Will prevent formation of exostosis. Dose: three times daily for three days.
Apis 6c   Oedema prominent under the skin. Dose: two hourly for four doses.
Calcarea fluorica 30c   Neglected cases, if deposits have started on the bone. Dose: once daily for ten days.
Externally, the affected area should be bathed with *Ruta* and *Arnica* lotions.

8.   Splints.   The fore limbs are usually affected in this condition of young horses. The lesion to which the name 'splints' has been applied is found on the inner aspect of the limb between the second and third metacarpal bones. The interosseous ligament between these bones is the seat of the trouble, injury to the periosteum causing the formation of new bone growth. The metatarsal bones are less commonly affected. Injuries by blows may cause the condition, but the chief cause is concussion due to hard work or exercise. The condition is most common in the two year age group.

SYMPTOMS
Lameness seen especially when the animal trots is an early sign. Swelling, accompanied by heat and pain are soon evident. The usual site of splits is about three inches below the knee on the inside

of the leg. There may be one large swelling, or two or three small swellings. Once the swelling subsides it becomes firmer due to deposition of new bone.

TREATMENT

Arnica 30c Give as early as possible once the injury has been sustained. Dose: two doses twelve hours apart.

Ruta graveolens 6c Will help control periostitis and prevent exostosis. Dose: three times daily for three days.

Silicea 200c Exostosis develops in neglected cases. Dose: once daily for ten days.

Calcarea fluorica 30c Exostosis in region of small carpal bones. Dose: once daily for ten days.

Externally, an application of *Ruta* and *Arnica* liniments will be of benefit.

9. Sprain of the Suspensory Ligament. This ligament is the main support tendon of the leg below the knee and sprain of this structure is usually confined to the forelimb. It is invariably produced by an injury. Extreme extension of the fetlock joint can put a heavy strain on the ligament at the point of bifurcation in the lower third of the metacarpal area. It is most likely to occur at the end of a period of long exercise or a hard race. Periostitis may arise if the ligament becomes injured at its attachment to the sesamoid bones, causing formation of new growth.

SYMPTOMS

Lameness is acute and usually involves the flexor tendons as well as the ligament. Swelling is the first sign, with the heel resting on the ground. The fetlock joint is held in an extensor fashion. Chronic involvement of the ligament produces fibrous swelling usually at the point of bifurcation. Palpation of the limb in the region of the sesamoid bones will reveal if any injury has occurred. Thickening of the area will indicate this, and also in the distal metacarpal third where bifurcation occurs.

TREATMENT

Arnica 30c Give immediately sprain has occurred. Dose: two doses twelve hours apart.

Rhus toxicodendron 1M   This remedy will help reduce inflammation and extend its action to tendons as well as ligament. Dose: three times daily for two days.

Ruta graveolens 200c   Periostitis in region of sesamoid bones. Dose: twice daily for four days.

Silicea 30c   In chronic sprain will aid resorption of fibrous thickening. Dose: once daily for ten days.

Externally, the application of *Rhus*, *Ruta* and *Arnica* liniment will assist greatly.

10.   Sesamoiditis.   This is an inflammation of the sesamoid bones at the bottom of the metacarpal bone. It produces periostitis and deposition of new bone growth. It is due to abnormally heavy strain on the fetlock area.

SYMPTOMS
Pain and swelling are first noticed on the volar aspect of the fetlock joint and the area is extremely sensitive to pressure. The fetlock is held in an abnormal position to avoid pressure being put on it. Bony changes will appear about three weeks after the initial injury.

TREATMENT
Arnica 30c   Give as soon as possible after injury has been sustained. Dose: every three hours for two doses.

Ruta graveolens 200c   This will hasten resolution of periostitis and help prevent formation of new bone growth. Dose: twice daily for four days.

Calcarea fluorica 30c   Neglected cases where exostosis has already occurred. Dose: once a week for four weeks.

Silicea 30c   This will help remove fibrous tissue in chronic cases. Dose: once daily for ten days.

Externally, the application of *Ruta* and *Arnica* lotions will be beneficial.

11.   Periostitis of the Fetlock Joint.   Inflammation occurring at the distal end of the metacarpal bone and the proximal end of the first phalanx produces this condition. Mild cases show no more than a simple arthritis without formation of new bone. It is commonest in the forelimbs. The two year age group of racing animals is most commonly affected. Concussion is the main cause and bad conformation of the pastern predisposes to it. The lateral digital extensor is frequently implicated and the resulting periostitis produces new growth which may or may not involve the articular surfaces.

SYMPTOMS

The joint capsule of the fetlock joint is distended on the volar (posterior) surface underneath the suspensory ligament. Osteoarthritis supervenes if the joint is implicated in deposition of new growth. Palpation of the limb produces pain in the area and swelling is evident. Fibrous thickening of tissue on the anterior surfaces can be seen. The animal may point the toe and if made to exercise, the lameness gets worse.

TREATMENT

Arnica 30c   Give first for the initial injury. Dose: two doses, three hours apart.

Ruta graveolens 200c   This will aid considerably in overcoming the condition and will help control deposition of new bone. Dose: twice daily for four days.

Apis 30c   Inflammatory fluid gathers in the joint capsule. Dose: every hour for four doses.

Silicea 30c   In chronic cases, this will help resorption of fibrous tissue. Dose: once daily for ten days.

Calcarea fluorica 30c   When exostoses have already occurred. Dose: once a week for four weeks.

Bryonia 200c   Heat and tenderness occur in early stages. A guiding symptom for its use; worse on movement or better by pressure. Dose: every two hours for four doses.

12.   Ringbone – Phalangeal Exostoses.   This term implies new bone growth occurring on one or other of the phalanges resulting from a periostitis. It leads to ankylosis of the pastern or coffin joint, dependent on an osteoarthritis. There are two varieties:–

(i) High Ringbone in which the distal end of the first and the proximal end of the second phalanx become involved in new bone growth.

(ii) Long Ringbone in which new bone growth involves the distal end of the second phalanx and the proximal end of the third.

Ringbone may be articular when new bone growth involves the joint surfaces, or periarticular when confined to the area surrounding them. The latter is common is high ringbone. The primary cause is concussion producing a periostitis resulting from the injury caused by pulling or detachment of associated ligaments. Ringbone is more common in the fore-limb.

SYMPTOMS

Heat and swelling occur initially and lameness is evident. In low ringbone there may be a stiffening of the hair over the coronary band. Periarticular ringbone may show no lameness but the swelling will be obvious.

TREATMENT

Arnica 30c   Give as early as possible after injury. Dose: two doses three hours apart.

Ruta graveolens 200c   Will help control periostitis if given early. Dose: night and morning for four days.

Calcarea fluorica 30c   Tendency to develop exostoses. Dose: once weekly for four weeks.

Silicea 30c   Developing fibrosis. Dose: once daily for two weeks.

Externally, a liniment of *Ruta* and *Arnica* will help in the early stages.

13. Pyramidal Disease.

When the exterior process of the third phalanx is involved in deposition of new bone growth, it is given this name. It is usually due to an underlying periostitis. The digital extensor tendon is frequently involved in the cause of the disease, when it is subjected to excessive strain at its attachment to the extensor process of the third phalanx. Deposition of new bone is the result in the form of a large callus.

SYMPTOMS

The centre area of the hoof shows a swelling at the coronary band. The animal may point the toe of the affected limb. Heat, pain and swelling are early signs and lameness is evident. Osteoarthritis at the coffin joint follows when the condition becomes chronic.

TREATMENT

The same remedies apply here as for Ringbone, but *Calcarea fluorica* is a principal remedy.

14. Quittor. This is a chronic inflammation of the lateral cartilages leading to necrosis and the formation of a purulent sinus. The forelimbs are more commonly affected. Abscess under the coronary band due to injury may cause the condition as may any injury introducing infection to the area of the cartilage.

SYMPTOMS
Either cartilage may be involved and the condition commences as an inflammatory lesion of the coronary band above the cartilage. Sinus formation occurs, discharging purulent material. Lameness is common only in the acute stage.

TREATMENT
Arnica 30c If injury suspected. Dose: two doses three hours apart.
Hypericum 1M Early stages, if ragged or punctured wounds are involved. Dose: two hourly for three doses.
Ledum 6c Symptoms similar to those of *Hypericum*. Dose: two hourly for four doses.
Hepar sulphuris 6x or 200c In the acute, tender, inflammatory stage, this will promote quick healing. Given in high potency at this stage it will prevent suppuration. Once pus has gathered, low potency will hasten its elimination. Dose: 6x – every hour for four doses; 200c – three times daily for two days.
Silicea 30c Once a sinus has developed in an established case this remedy will help removal of necrotic tissue, leading to healthy granulation. Dose: once daily for one week.
Externally, a lotion of *Calendula* will effect quick healing in stubborn cases.

15. Sidebones. This term implies ossification of the lateral cartilages usually in the forefeet. It is probably caused by concussion in the region of the quarter of the wall producing a primary inflammation of the lateral cartilage.

SYMPTOMS
Pain is evident if palpation is exerted during the process of bone deposition. In the established case the cartilage loses it normal resilient feel and bone formation can be felt. Lameness is not always present but when it does occur it is usually related to the inflammatory stage.

TREATMENT
This is essentially the same as for Ringbone and Pyramidal Disease.

16. Laminitis.   This is an inflammation of the sensitive laminae of the foot leading to an acute local congestion. The pressure of this blood on the laminae causes severe pain. Acute and chronic forms of the condition are recognised and may involve two front or two hind feet or all four together. The fore feet are more commonly affected. Predisposing causes may be systemic or may be due to bacterial infection.

SYMPTOMS
(i) The acute form:– When the fore feet are involved, the animal assumes a position where the hind feet are drawn under the body to relieve pressure on the fore feet which are extended, the heels taking the weight of the animal. There is great disinclination to move and the feet can be raised only with difficulty. External signs include heat over the coronary band and the wall. The digital arteries show a bounding pulse and the animal exhibits acute pain, anxious expression, sweating and increased respiration. The conjunctiva become brick-coloured. In parturient laminitis as a result of metritis due to retention of infected placenta, there is usually a rise of temperature sometimes as high as 107°F and a discharge of blood-stained fluid from the uterus.

(ii) The chronic form:– Displacement of the third phalanx takes place due to separation of sensitive and insensitive laminae, resulting in rotation of the phalanx. This displacement is usually permanent. The sole becomes flat and when the animal moves, the heel is put to the ground in an exaggerated manner. The wall of the heel grows more rapidly than usual and shows as rings on the wall surface, dependent on inflammation of the coronary band. Mild or sub-acute attacks may occur during the chronic stage if predisposing conditions such as rich grazing arise.

TREATMENT
Aconitum napellus 30c   This should be given immediately the first symptoms are seen, and will help to allay anxiety and regulate pulse and respiration. Dose: every 30 minutes for six doses.

Belladonna 1M Throbbing arteries, full bounding pulse, pyrexia and sweating. Dose: every 30 minutes for six doses. *Aconite* and *Belladonna* may be given together in the same dosage.

Nux vomica 1M Systemic congestion. Dose: every two hours for four doses.

Calcarea fluorica 30c Tissue involvement in the chronic case. This remedy will help reduce involvement and promote a return to normal structure if not too far advanced. Dose: once a week for four weeks.

17. Seedy Toe. This is a complication of chronic laminitis due to separation of sensitive and insensitive laminae allowing infection to gain entrance to the sensitive laminae. This causes a purulent discharge from the white line.

TREATMENT

Silicea 30c This is the main remedy in controlling septic involvement. Dose: once daily for one week.

Hepar sulphuris 6c This should be used in the early acute stage. Dose: hourly for four doses.

Externally bathing with *Calendula* lotion will assist healing.

18. Navicular Disease This condition consists of a bursitis of the perforans tendon bursa where it joins the navicular bone causing adhesions between the bone and the deep flexor tendon. The inflammation set up may lead to decalcification of the bone itself. The condition is confined to the fore feet.

CAUSES

Deprivation of blood to the navicular bursa is considered to be the main factor in the development of navicular disease, due to blockage or thrombosis of the plantar blood vessels. Concussion is thought to play a contributory part in its development and it is particularly liable to occur in horses put to work on hard ground.

SYMPTOMS

There is frequently a history of intermittent lameness which improves on resting. Both fore feet may be involved but the lameness is usually worse in one than the other. Symptoms may disappear at rest but always reappear on exercise. Pointing of the toe is common and this may be seen alternately if both feet are involved. During movement the toe takes the weight of the animal most noticeably when walking or trotting. The toe may show excessive wear. Pressure over the frog evinces pain and this is increased when the animal is turned in the direction of the affected foot. In prolonged affections the foot changes shape due to lack of pressure on the frog. The heels become contracted and the foot assumes a 'box-like' appearance. The concavity of the sole is accentuated and the foot becomes elongated. Changes occurring in the navicular bone itself include necrosis and osteoporosis while fibrous adhesions develop in the bursa.

TREATMENT

Crotalus horridus   Since research has shown that disturbances in the peripheral circulation are primarily responsible the use of this remedy is indicated. In potency the snake venom remedies have a proven value in the treatment of thrombosis and this particular one has given excellent results. One of the virtues of the homoeopathic approach to the treatment of this condition is that it is confined to the affected area, haemorrhages and other disturbances of the main circulation being unlikely to occur. The suggested potency should be high, viz. 10M or 1M, one dose night and morning for five days.

Secale   This substance in the natural state is ergot, the fungus which grows on rye and in substantial doses causes deprivation of blood to the peripheral arteries, with resultant necrosis and ultimately, in extreme cases, gangrene. In potency it therefore aids the circulation to the feet and should always follow on after administration of the previous remedy. Suggested potency 200c, one dose three times per week for four weeks.

Bryonia alba   This remedy is indicated in conditions which are better at rest and worse on movement. As this occurs in navicular disease the remedy should be considered after the administration of the previous remedies. A potency of 30c should be given daily for fourteen days.

Calcarea fluorica   This is a useful remedy in long-standing or neglected cases where exostoses and bony changes have taken place as illustrated by X-ray examination. Potency 30c three times per week for four weeks.

19.   Corns.   These occur in the angle formed by the wall and the bar of the foot and include the sensitive and insensitive tissues of the foot. Corns usually occur on the fore feet and favour the inner angle. Any pressure on this area may produce a corn. Lack of frog pressure is also a predisposing cause. A history of laminitis may result in the development of a corn. Corns may be dry, moist or suppurating. The first is due to bruising of sensitive tissue causing haemorrhage, showing as a red stain in the corn area. Severe injury can lead to a moist corn with the appearance of serum underneath the injured sole and infection of this type leads to the suppurative form.

SYMPTOMS
Lameness varies according to location of the corn. The animal tends to put weight on the toe to decrease pressure over the affected area.

TREATMENT
Arnica 30c   Give this remedy first, as the corn usually develops from an injury. Dose: two doses three hours apart.
Calcarea fluorica 30c   This remedy will aid absorption of hard tissue and promote growth of healthy horn. Dose: once a week for four weeks.
Silicea 30c   In suppurative corns, this remedy will control infection and prevent necrosis of tissue. Dose: once daily for ten days.

XXV   Lameness of the Hind Limb

1.   Iliac Thrombosis.   Damage by strongyle worms may arise in the posterior aorta and the iliac artery, leading to an arteritis. The resulting thrombosis leads to circulatory interference causing lameness.

SYMPTOMS
Lameness usually supervenes after a short period of exercise and the severity depends on the size of the thrombus. Severe cases may show lameness when walking. Anxiety, pain and sweating accompany the lameness, but sweating is absent over the affected area. The affected limb loses some of its warm feeling. Lameness is intermittent, disappearing on rest and appearing again on exercise.

TREATMENT
Bothrops 30c   Condition accompanied by nervous trembling, with possible bowel haemorrhage. Dose: three hourly for three doses.
Lachesis 30c   Rectal straining, with pain over the sacral region. Dose: two hourly for four doses.
Calcarea fluorica 30c   This remedy will hasten dissolution of the thrombus and resolution of the aneurism. Dose: once a week for four weeks.
Vipera 6c   Associated cramping of muscles of the limb, with possibly an accompanying jaundice. Dose: three times daily for four days.

2.   Bursitis of the Tendon of the Middle Gluteus Muscle.   This inflammation arises when the bursa is affected as the tendon passes over the great trochanter of the femur. Falling on this area or strain of the tendon can bring it about.

SYMPTOMS

Pain becomes evident over the great trochanter if pressure is applied. Flexion of the limb is common at rest while weight is placed on the inside of the foot when the animal moves. This causes the inside wall to wear more than the outside and movement tends to go towards the sound limb.

TREATMENT

Apis 30c Synovitis. Oedema of the bursa. Dose: two hourly for four doses.

Bryonia 30c Relief from pressure. Symptoms worse on movement. Dose: two hourly for four doses.

Ruta graveolens 200c Tendency to periostitis. Dose: night and morning for three days.

Note:– The possibility of infection by *Brucella abortus* as a cause should not be forgotten. The use of the nosode in treatment will help considerably if this is the case.

3. Crural Paralysis. Paralysis of Femoral Nerve. The quadriceps group of muscles is involved in this paralysis being made up of the rectus femoris, the vastus lateralis, the vastus medialis and the vastus intermedius. It covers the area of the front of the femur and both sides. Azoturia has been listed as a cause of this paralysis which also arises from injury.

SYMPTOMS

When standing, all joints become flexed and no weight is put on the leg. There is difficulty in advancing the limb.

TREATMENT

Arnica 30c Always if injury is suspected. Two doses three hours apart.

Gelsemium 200c Accompanying weakness and lassitude. Dose: night and morning for four days.

Conium 30c Tendency for paralysis to ascend, affecting areas further up the limb. Dose: night and morning for one week.

Plumbum metallicum 30c Difficulty in extending the limb. Reflexes are lost and the foot may be swollen. Dose: night and morning for one week.

4.   Gonitis.   This term is used to denote inflammation of the stifle joint and leads to arthritis. It may be caused by injuries to the bones forming the joint and associated cartilages and ligaments. Infective agents can produce arthritis of this joint, e.g. navel-ill, brucellosis and E. coli infection.

SYMPTOMS

Lameness varies according to the severity of the injury. If the joint cartilages are involved, lameness can be severe. The joint capsule becomes swollen and hot and pain is evident when the animal moves the leg forward. Flexion of the limb is usual to avoid putting the foot on the ground as this aggravates the pain.

TREATMENT

Apis 30c   Inflammation is accompanied by oedema of the joint capsule. Dose: two hourly for four doses.

Bryonia 30c   Joint swollen, pressure relieves, symptoms worse on movement. Dose: two hourly for four doses.

Ruta graveolens 200c   Periostitis round the joint. Dose: night and morning for four days.

Rhus toxicodendron 1M   Arthritis of joint developing. Dose: once daily for one week.

Streptococcus nosode 30c   Navel-ill infection suspected to have led to the condition. Dose: once daily for three days.

Brucella abortus nosode 30c   If brucellosis suspected, one dose daily for three days.

5.   Stringhalt.   This is an involuntary flexion of the hock during progression, affecting one or both hind limbs. The lateral digital extensor is usually involved, injury of some kind being considered the cause. Adhesions may form as the tendon crosses the lateral surface of the hock joint.

SYMPTOMS

These vary from mild flexion to a severe involuntary movement which brings the leg up almost to the abdomen. The condition is exaggerated when the animal is made to turn round sharply.

TREATMENT

Strychninum 200c   This remedy will help reduce the spasmodic flexion. Dose: once daily for five days.

Arnica 30c   Give at once if injury suspected. Dose: two doses three
hours apart.

Gelsemium 200c   Tendency to accompanying paralysis. Dose:
once daily for five days.

6. Bone Spavin.   This is a periostitis or osteitis affecting the
inside of the hock joint below the articular surface of the main joint.
It causes osteoarthritis and ankylosis of the tarsal joints. Poor
conformation contributes to the condition and it can be precipitated
by injuries.

SYMPTOMS
Pain is evident on flexion of the joint and there is a shortening of the
forward movement. The animal always puts the toe on the ground
first. Lameness is worse when the animal moves after rest and mild
cases can improve on exercise. Severe flexion of the joint causes
increased lameness when the animal is moved immediately
afterwards.

TREATMENT
Rhus toxicodendron 1M   Cases which improve on exercise. Dose:
once daily for one week.

Ruta graveolens 200c   Early stages, when periostitis first
develops. Dose: three times daily for two days.

Arnica 30c   When injury is suspected as the contributing cause.
Dose: two doses three hours apart.

7. Bog Spavin.   This term implies a swelling of the joint capsule
with fluid seen on the antero-medial aspect of the hock joint. Injury
to the hock joint can predispose to the condition which is
characterised by three fluctuating swellings.

SYMPTOMS
The largest swelling is located at the antero-medial aspect of the
hock joint. Two smaller swellings occur on either side of the
posterior surface of the joint. Pressure on any one swelling causes
an increase in the others. When due to injury there will be local heat
and pain, and lameness occurs, but this is absent when the condition
is due to other causes.

TREATMENT

Arnica 30c   Give at once if injury has occurred. Dose: two doses three hours apart.

Apis 30c   Oedema and synovitis. Give early in the inflammatory stage. It will also reduce fluid in non-inflammatory cases. Dose: once three times daily for three days.

Bryonia 30c   Helpful in inflammatory states where there is tenderness over the joint and pressure relieves. Dose: two hourly for four weeks.

8.   Curb.   This is an enlargement at the posterior aspect of the fibular-tarsal bone. It is dependent on inflammation and thickening of the plantar ligament. Poor conformation puts stress on the plantar ligament and this is a predisposing cause. Violent exertion can also cause curb.

SYMPTOMS

The condition is characterised by an enlargement on the posterior surface of the fibular-tarsal bone. Inflammation and lameness are present in the acute phase. The heel becomes elevated and swelling appears over the area which does not decrease on exercise. In chronic cases, tissues surrounding the area may become infiltrated with scar tissue.

TREATMENT

Arnica 30c   Condition due to violent exercise, concussion or injury. Dose: two doses three hours apart.

Rhus toxicodendron 1M   Acute inflammatory stage, especially if there is improvement on exercise. Dose: two hourly for four doses.

Ruta graveolens 200c   Periostitis. This remedy will help prevent deposition of new bone. Dose: night and morning for three days.

Silicea 200c   In chronic cases, this remedy will hasten absorption of scar tissue. Dose: once daily for five days.

Externally, the application of *Arnica*, *Ruta* and *Rhus* liniment will be very beneficial.

9.   Canker.   This is a chronic hypertrophy of the horn-producing tissues of the foot, especially of the hind limb. Infection by necrotic bacilli takes place in the horn which has been softened by the animal standing for long periods in urine-soaked bedding or mud. The disease frequently runs a long course before signs appear.

SYMPTOMS

Lameness is evident. There is a specific odour associated with the condition and inspection of the foot reveals a ragged appearance of the frog, the tissue of which is easily removed, showing a cheese-like deposit underneath. The lesions are necrotic, slow to heal and bleed easily.

TREATMENT

Natrum muriaticum 200c This will help prevent extension of necrosis and hasten healing. Dose: once daily for one week.

Silicea 200c Useful in helping to harden the horn of the foot. Dose: once daily for five days.

Externally, after removal of dead tissue, the cavities should be packed with cotton-wood soaked in *Calendula* and *Arnica* lotions.

XXVI   Affections of Fore and Hind Limbs

1. Windgalls. This is a distension of a joint capsule, tendon-sheath or bursa with synovial fluid. The fetlock joint capsule is the one usually affected and swellings may be seen above and at the front of the seasmoid bones. When they affect the tendons, they occur between the suspensory ligaments and the flexor tendons.

SYMPTOMS
The swellings are usually tense because of the amount of synovial fluid in them but lameness is absent.

TREATMENT
Apis 30c   Will control the amount of synovial fluid and hasten its absorption. Dose: hourly for four doses,.
Kali bichromicum 30c Will help prevent the expression of synovial fluid through the skin. Dose: once daily for five days.
Externally, an application of *Arnica* and *Rhus tox.* liniments will be of great help in the healing process.

2. Gravel. This is a term used to denote an infection which invades the sensitive structures through a crack in the white line. The lack of a drainage point permits the infection to reach the heel area where drainage may take place.

SYMPTOMS
Lameness varies according to the severity of the infection and the location of the original injury. Black spots appear on the white line and may penetrate to the laminae. Penetration of one or other of the black spots usually yields pus. Heel drainage occurs through time at the coronary band.

TREATMENT

Hepar sulphuris 200c Will present suppuration if given early. Dose: once daily for four days.

Silicea 200c Pyogenic infection will often yield to this remedy, which will also aid healing of necrotic tissue. Dose: once daily for five days.

Calcarea fluorica 30c Will promote hardening and granulation of tissue. Dose: once a week for four weeks.

Externally, any opening of black spots should be bathed with *Calendula* lotion.

3. Thrush. This is a degenerative condition of the frog and is accompanied by the presence of black necrotic material in the grooves. Prolonged involvement may cause spread to the horn and sensitive laminae. Lack of frog pressure may contribute to the condition along with unhygienic stabling, allowing entrance of the necrosis bacillus.

SYMPTOMS

Early signs include an increase of moisture on the frog and a black discharge from the grooves. The discharge has the characteristic odour of necrotic horn. The grooves of the frog become deeper than usual and the structure itself may be destroyed.

TREATMENT

Kreosotum 200c Associated with constitutional upsets along with thrush, e.g. discharge from nose, offensive urine, etc. Dose: once daily for five days.

Silicea 200c Will help healing necrotic tissue and promote healthy granulation. Dose: once daily for five days.

Kali bichromicum 30c Discharge of offensive material. Dose: night and morning for seven days.

Externally, the grooves of the frog should be dressed early with plugs of cotton wool soaked in a lotion of *Calendula*, *Kali bich.* and *Arnica*.

4. Sandcrack. Cracks in the wall of the hoof may commence from the coronary band or from the bearing surface of the wall, and may appear at the toe, quarter or heel. Lameness is not necessarily an accompaniment, but if infection gains entrance to the sensitive laminae through the crack it will result in suppuration and escape of purulent material through the crack or at the white line.

TREATMENT

Silicea 200c Will help promote hardening and growth of new horn. Dose: once daily for five days.

Calcarea fluorica 30c A good tissue remedy which will also promote horn growth. Dose: twice weekly for eight weeks.

Hepar sulphuris 1M Infection in laminae. Dose: once daily for seven days.

Materia Medica

Abies Canadensis. Hemlock Spruce. N.O. Coniferae.
The Ø is made from the fresh bark and young buds.

This plant has an affinity for mucous membranes generally and that of the stomach in particular, producing a catarrhal gastritis. Impairment of liver function occurs leading to flatulence and deficient bile-flow. Appetite is increased and hunger may be ravenous. It is chiefly used as a digestive remedy.

Abrotanum. Southernwood. N.O. Compositae.
Tincture of fresh leaves.

This plant produces wasting of muscles of lower limbs and is used for animals showing this weakness. A prominent guiding symptom in the young animal is umbilical oozing of fluid. It is one of the remedies used to control worm infestation in young animals and also has a reputation in certain forms of acute arthritis where overall symptoms agree.

Absinthum. Wormwood.
Infusions of active principle.

The effect on the system of this substance is to produce a picture of confusion and convulsions preceded by trembling of muscles. There is a marked action on the central nervous system causing the patient to fall backwards. The pupils of the eye may show unequal dilation. It is one of the main remedies used in practice to control epileptiform seizures and fits of varying kinds.

Acidum Salicylicum. Salicylic Acid.
Trituration of powder.

This acid has an action on joints producing swellings and in some cases caries of bone. Gastric symptoms e.g. bleeding are also prominent in its provings. Homoeopathically indicated in the treatment of rheumatic and osteo-arthritic conditions and idiopathic gastric bleeding.

Aconitum Napellus. Monkshood. N.O. Ranunculaceae.
In the preparation of the Ø the entire plant is used as all parts contain aconitine the active principle.

This plant has an affinity for serous membranes and muscular tissues leading to functional disturbances. There is sudden involvement and tension in all parts. This remedy should be used in the early stages of all feverish conditions where there is sudden appearance of symptoms which may also show an aggravation when any extreme of temperature takes place. Predisposing factors which may produce a drug picture calling for aconitum include shock, operation and exposure to cold dry winds, or dry heat. It could be of use in puerperal conditions showing sudden involvement with peritoneal complications.

Actaea Racemosa. Black Snake Root. Also referred to as Cimici-fuga Racemosa. N.O. Ranunculaceae.
Trituration of its resin.

This plant resin has a wide range of action on various body systems, chief among which are the female genital and the articular leading to disturbances of the uterus in particular and small joint arthritis. Muscular pains are evident, affection of cervical vertebrae are evidenced by stiffening of neck muscles.

Adonis Vernalis. N.O. Ranunculaceae.
Infusion of fresh plant.

The main action of the remedy which concerns us in veterinary practice is its cardial action which becomes weak leading to dropsy and scanty output of urine. It is one of the main remedies used in valvular disease and difficult respiration dependent on pulmonary congestion.

Aesculus Hippocastanum. Horse Chestnut. N.O. Sapindaceae.
The Ø is prepared from the fruit with capsule.

The main affinity of this plant is with the lower bowel producing a state of venous congestion. There is a general slowing down of the digestive and circulatory systems, the liver and portal action becoming sluggish. This is associated with a tendency to dry stools. It is a useful remedy in hepatic conditions with venous congestion affecting the general circulation and it also has a place in the treatment of congestive chest conditions.

Agaricus Muscarius. Fly Agaric. N.O. Fungi.
The Ø is prepared from the fresh fungus.

Muscarin is the best known toxic compound of several which are found in this fungus. Symptoms of poisoning are generally delayed from anything up to twelve hours after ingestion. The main sphere of action is on the central nervous system producing a state of vertigo and delirium followed by sleepiness. There are four recognised stages of cerebral excitement. Viz: 1. Slight stimulation. 2. Intoxication with mental excitement accompanied by twitching. 3. Delirium. 4. Depression with soporific tendency. These actions determine its use in certain conditions affecting the central nervous system, e.g. cerebro-cortical necrosis and meningitis, which may accompany severe attacks of hypomagnesaemia. Tympanitic conditions with flatus may respond favourably while it also has a place as a rheumatic remedy and in the treatment of some forms of muscular cramp.

Agnus Castus. Chaste Tree. N.O. Verbenaceae.
Tincture of ripe berries.

One of the principal spheres of action relating to this plant is the sexual system where it produces a lowering or depression of functions with accompanying debility. In the stallion there may be induration and swelling of testicles and in the mare sterility has been reported.

Aletris Farinosa. Star Grass. N.O. Haemodoraceae.
The Ø is prepared from the root.

This plant has an affinity with the genital tract of the mare, especially the uterus and is used mainly as an anti-abortion remedy and in the treatment of uterine discharges and also in silent heat in mares which may show an accompanying loss of appetite.

Allium Cepa. Onion. N.O. Liliaceae.
The Ø is prepared from the whole plant.

A picture of coryza with acrid nasal discharge and symptoms of laryngeal discomfort is associated with this plant. It could be indicated in the early stages of most catarrhal conditions producing the typical coryza.

Alumen. Potash Alum.
Trituration of the pure crystals.

Indicated in conditions affecting mucous membranes of various body systems, producing dryness: affections of the central nervous system are also common, resulting in varying degrees of paralysis.

Ammonium Carbonicum. Ammonium Carbonate.
This salt is used as a solution in distilled water from which the potencies are prepared.

It is primarily used in respiratory affections especially when there is an accompanying swelling of associated lymph glands. Emphysema and pulmonary oedema are thoracic conditions which may be helped by this remedy. It is also useful in digestive upsets and may promote rumenal activity in sluggish states.

Ammonium Causticum. Hydrate of Ammonia.
Potencies are again prepared from a solution in distilled water.

This salt has a similar but more pronounced action on mucous membranes to that of the carbonate producing ulcerations on these surfaces. It is also a powerful cardiac stimulant. Mucosal disease may call for its use; also respiratory conditions showing severe involvement of the lungs. There is usually an excess of mucus with moist cough when this remedy is indicated.

Angustura Vera. N.O. Rutaceae.
Trituration of tree bark.

Bones and muscles come prominently into consideration when this plant is specified. Stiffness and limb pains of varying degree are prominent along with exostosis. Mild paralysis of legs has been noted. The action on bones may lead on to caries with possible fractures developing.

Anthracinum.

The Ø is prepared from affected tissue or culture dissolved in alcohol.

This nosode is indicated in the treatment of eruptive skin diseases which are characterised by boil-like swellings. Cellular tissue becomes indurated and swelling of associated lymph glands takes place. The characteristic lesion assumes the form of a hard swelling with a necrotic centre and surrounded by a blackened rim. It has proved useful in the treatment of septic bites.

Antimonium Arsenicosum. Arsenate of Antimony.

Potencies are prepared from trituration of the dried salt dissolved in distilled water or alcohol.

This salt possesses a selective action on the lungs especially the upper left area and is used mainly in the treatment of emphysema and long-standing pneumonias. Coughing, if present, is worse on eating and the animal prefers to stand rather than lie down.

Antimonium Crudum. Sulphide of Antimony.

Potencies prepared from trituration of the dried salt.

This substance exerts a strong influence on the stomach and skin producing conditions which are aggravated by heat. Any vesicular skin condition should be influenced favourably.

Antimonium Tartaricum. Tartar Emetic.

Trituration of the dried salt is the source of potencies.

Respiratory symptoms predominate with this drug, affections being accompanied by the production of excess mucus, although expectoration is difficult. The main action being on the respiratory system, we should expect this remedy to be beneficial in conditions such as broncho-pneumonia and pulmonary oedema. Ailments requiring this remedy frequently show an accompanying drowsiness and lack of thirst. In pneumonic states the edges of the eyes may be covered with mucus.

Apis Mellifica. Bee Venom.

The Ø is prepared from the entire insect and also from the venom diluted with alcohol.

The poison of the bee acts on cellular tissue causing oedema and swelling. The production of oedema anywhere in the system may lead to a variety of acute and chronic conditions. Considering the well documented evidence of its sphere of action affecting all tissues and mucous membranes, we should consider this remedy in conditions showing oedematous swellings. Synovial swellings of joints may respond to its use. Respiratory conditions showing an excess of pulmonary fluid or oedema, e.g. fog fever, have been treated successfully with this remedy, while it has also been used to good effect in the treatment of cystic ovaries. All ailments are aggravated by heat and are thirstless.

Apocynum Cannabinum. Indian Hemp. N.O Apocynaceae.
Infusions of the fresh plant.

This substance produces disturbance of gastric function along with affection of heart muscle leading to a slowing of its action. There is also a marked action on the uro-genital system producing diuresis and uterine bleeding. The patient requiring this remedy may present symptoms of drowsiness or stupor. Upper respiratory symptoms are common e.g. nasal secretions of yellowish mucus.

Argentum Nitricum. Silver Nitrate.
This remedy is prepared by trituration of the salt and subsequent dissolving in alcohol or distilled water.

It produces incoordination of movement causing trembling in various parts. It has an irritant effect on mucous membranes producing a free-flowing muco-purulent discharge. Red blood cells are affected, anaemia being caused by their destruction. Its sphere of action makes it a useful remedy in eye conditions.

Arnica Montana. Leopard's Bane. N.O. Compositae.
The Ø is prepared from the whole fresh plant.

The action of this plant upon the system is practically synonymous with a state resulting from injuries or blows. It is known as the 'Fall Herb' and is used mainly for wounds and injuries where the skin remains unbroken. It has a marked affinity with blood-vessels leading to dilation, stasis and increased permeability. Thus various types of haemorrhage can occur. It reduces shock when given in potency and should be given routinely before and after surgical interference when it will also help control bleeding. Given after parturition it will hasten recovery of bruised tissue, while given during pregnancy at regular intervals, it will help promote normal easy parturition.

Arsenicum Album. Arsenic Trioxide.
This remedy is prepared by trituration and subsequent dilution.

It is a deep acting remedy and acts on every tissue of the body and its characteristic and definite symptoms make its use certain in many ailments. Discharges are acrid and burning and symptoms are relieved by heat. It is of use in many skin conditions associated with dryness, scaliness and itching. Colibacillosis and coccidiosis are conditions which may call for its use. It could also have a role to play in some forms of pneumonia when the patient may show a desire for small quantities of water and symptoms becoming worse towards midnight.

Arsenicum Iodatum. Iodide of Arsenic.
Potencies are prepared from the triturated salt dissolved in distilled water.

When discharges are persistently irritating and corrosive, this remedy may prove more beneficial than arsen. alb. The mucous membranes become red, swollen and oedematous, especially in the respiratory sphere. This remedy is frequently called for in bronchial and pneumonic conditions which are at the convalescent stage or in those ailments which have not responded satisfactorily to seemingly indicated remedies.

Atropinum. An Alkaloid of Belladonna.
This alkaloid produces some of the effects of Belladonna itself but acts more particularly on the eyes causing dilation of pupils and mucous membranes generally which become extremely dry. It could be indicated where overall symptoms of Belladonna are not well-defined.

Baptisia Tinctoria. Wild Indigo. N.O. Leguminosae.
The Ø is prepared from fresh root and bark.

The symptoms produced by this plant relate mainly to septicaemic conditions producing prostration and weakness. Low grade fevers and great muscular lethargy are present in the symptomatology. All secretions and discharges are very offensive. Profuse salivation occurs together with ulceration of gums which become discoloured. Tonsils and throat are dark red and stools tend to be dysenteric.

Baryta Carbonica. Barium Carbonate.
Potencies are prepared from trituration of the salt dissolved in distilled water.

The action of this salt produces symptoms and conditions more usually seen in old and very young subjects and should be remembered as a useful remedy for certain conditions affecting the respiratory system especially.

Baryta Muriatica. Barium Chloride.
Solution of salt in distilled water.

This salt produces periodic attacks of convulsions with spastic involvement of limbs. Ear discharges appear which are offensive and the parotid salivary glands become swollen. Induration of abdominal glands develop including the pancreas. It is indicated in many instances of ear canker and also in animals which show a tendency to develop glandular swellings along with the characteristic involvement of the nervous system.

Belladonna. Deadly Nightshade. N.O. Solanaceae.
The Ø is prepared from the whole plant at flowering.

This plant produces a profound action on every part of the central nervous system causing a state of excitement and active congestion. The effect also on the skin, glands and vascular system is constant and specific. One of the main guiding symptoms in prescribing is the presence of a full bounding pulse in any feverish condition which may or may not accompany excitable states. Another guiding symptom is dilation of pupils.

Bellis Perennis. Daisy. N.O. Compositae.
The Ø is prepared from the whole fresh plant.

The main action of this little flower is on the muscular tissues of blood vessels producing a state of venous congestion. Systemic muscles become heavy leading to a halting type of gait suggestive of pain. This is a useful remedy to aid recovery of tissues injured during cutting or after operation. Sprains and bruises in general come within its sphere of action and it should be kept in mind as an adjunct remedy along with arnica. Given post-partum it will hasten resolution of bruised tissue and enable the pelvic area to recover tone in a very short time.

Benzoicum Acidum. Benzoic Acid.
Potencies are prepared from gum benzoin which is triturated and dissolved in alcohol.

The most outstanding feature of this remedy relates to the urinary system producing changes in the colour and odour of the urine, which becomes dark red and aromatic with uric acid deposits. It may have a place in the treatment of some kidney and bladder conditions.

Berberis Vulgaris. Barberry. N.O. Berberidaceae.
The Ø is prepared from the bark of the root.

This shrub of wide distribution has an affinity with most tissues. Symptoms which it produces are liable to alternate violently, e.g. feverish conditions with thirst can quickly give way to prostration without any desire for water. It acts forcibly on the venous system producing especially pelvic engorgements. The chief ailments which come within its sphere of action are those connected with liver and kidney leading to catarrhal inflammation of bile ducts and kidney pelvis. Jaundice frequently attends such conditions. Haematuria and cystitis may occur. In all these conditions there is an accompanying sacral weakness and tenderness over the loins.

Beryllium. The Metal.
Trituration and subsequent dissolving in alcohol produces the tincture from which the potencies are prepared.

This remedy is used mainly in respiratory conditions where the leading symptom is difficult breathing on slight exertion and which is out of proportion to clinical findings. Coughing and emphysema are usually present. This is a useful remedy in virus pneumonia, both acute and chronic forms, where symptoms are few while the animal is resting, but become pronounced on movement. It is a deep acting remedy and should not be used below 30c potency.

Borax. Sodium Biborate.
Potencies are prepared from trituration of the salt dissolved in distilled water.

This salt produces gastro-intestinal irritation with mouth symptoms of salivation and ulceration. With most complaints there is fear of downward motion. The specific action of this substance on the epithelium of the mouth, tongue and buccal mucosa determines its use as a remedy which will control such conditions as vesicular stomatitis and allied diseases, e.g. mucosal disease.

Bothrops Lanceolatus. Yellow Viper.
Potencies are prepared from solution of the venom in glycerine.

This poison is associated with haemorrhages and subsequent rapid coagulation of blood. Septic involvement takes place as a rule and this is, therefore, a useful remedy in septic states showing haemorrhagic tendencies. Gangrenous conditions of the skin may respond to it.

Bromium. Bromine. The Element.
Potencies are prepared from solutions in distilled water.

Bromine is found in combinations with iodine in the ash when seaweed is burned, and also in sea water. It acts chiefly on the mucous membrane of the respiratory tract, especially the upper trachea causing laryngeal spasm. This is a useful remedy for croup-like cough accompanied by rattling of mucus. Its indication in respiratory ailments is related to symptoms being aggravated on inspiration. It may be of use also in those conditions which arise from over-exposure to heat.

Bryonia Alba. White Bryony. Wild Hop. N.O. Cucurbitaceae.
The Ø is prepared from the root before flowering takes place.

This important plant produces a glucoside which is capable of bringing on severe purgation. The plant itself exerts its main action on epithelial tissues and serous and synovial membranes. Some mucous surfaces are also affected producing an inflammatory response resulting in a fibrinous or serous exudate. This in turn leads to dryness of the affected tissue with later effusions into synovial cavities. Movement of the parts is interfered with and this leads to one of the main indications for its use, viz. all symptoms are worse from movement, the animal preferring to lie still. Pressure over affected areas relieves symptoms. This remedy may be extremely useful in treating the many respiratory conditions met with, especially pleurisy where the above symptom picture is seen.

Bufo. The Toad. N.O. Buforidae. Solution of Poison.
This remedy is used in states of cerebral excitement sometimes severe enough to precipitate epilepsy. Dropsical states also develop. Has also been used in cases of exaggerated sexual impulses especially in the male.

Cactus Grandiflorus. Night-Blooming Cereus. N.O. Cactaceae.
The Ø is prepared from young stems and flowers.
     The active principle of this plant acts on circular muscle fibres and has a marked affinity for the cardio-vascular system. It is mainly confined to the treatment of valvular disease, but it may also be of service in some conditions showing a haemorrhagic tendency.

Calcarea Carbonica. Carbonate of Lime.
Trituration of the salt in alcohol or weak acid produces the solution from which potencies are prepared. The crude substance is found in the middle layer of the oyster shell.
     This calcareous substance produces a lack of tone and muscular weakness with muscle spasm affecting both voluntary and involuntary muscles. Calcium is excreted quickly from the system and the intake of calcium salts does not ensure against conditions which may need the element prepared in the homoeopathic manner. Calc. carb. is a strong constitutional remedy causing impaired nutrition, and animals which need potentised calcium show a tendency to eat strange objects. It is of value in the treatment of skeletal disorders of young animals and in the older animal suffering from osteomalacia.

Calcarea Fluorica. Fluorspar. Fluoride of Lime.
Potencies are prepared from trituration of the salt with subsequent dilution in distilled water.

Crystals of this substance are found in the Haversian canals of bone. This increases the hardness, but in excess produces brittleness. It also occurs in tooth enamel and in the epidermis of the skin. Affinity with all these tissues may lead to the establishment of exostoses and glandular enlargements. It is in addition a powerful vascular remedy. The special sphere of action of this remedy lies in its relation to bone lesions especially exostoses. Both actinomycosis and actinobacillosis may benefit from its use.

Calcarea Iodata. Iodide of Lime.
Solution of salt in distilled water.

This remedy is used in cases of hardening of tissue, especially glands and tonsils. The thyroid gland is also affected and occasionally the thymus as well.

Calcarea Phosphorica. Phosphate of Lime.
Potencies are prepared from trituration and subsequent dilution, from adding dilute phosphoric acid to lime water.

This salt has an affinity with tissues which are concerned with growth and the repair of cells. Assimilation may be difficult because of impaired nutrition and delayed development. Brittleness of bone is a common feature. This is a remedy of special value in the treatment of musculo-skeletal disorders of foals.

Calc. Renalis Phosph and Calc. Renalis Uric.
These two salts are indicated in cases of lithiasis due to the presence of stones of the respective substances. They aid the action of remedies such as Berberis and Hydrangea and Thlaspi and can be used along with them.

Calendula Officinalis. Marigold. N.O. Compositae.
The Ø is prepared from leaves and flowers.

Applied locally to open wounds and indolent ulcers this remedy will be found to be one of the most reliable healing agents we have. It will rapidly bring about resolution of tissue promoting healthy granulation. It should be used as a 1/10 dilution in warm water. It is helpful in treating contused wounds of the eyes and it can be combined with Hypericum when treating open wounds involving damage to nerves.

Calici Virus.
The potentised virus can be used either by itself or combined with other viruses in the treatment of gingivitis and respiratory conditions where it is thought that the disease is implicated.

Camphora. Camphor. N.O. Lauraceae.
Potencies are prepared from a solution of the gum in rectified spirit.

This substance produces a state of collapse with weakness and failing pulse. There is icy coldness of the entire body. It has a marked relationship to muscles and fasciae. Certain forms of scour will benefit from this remedy, viz. those forms accompanied by collapse and extreme coldness of body surfaces. Any form of enteritis showing exhaustion and collapse may require this remedy. It may be needed in disease caused by salmonella species.

Cannabis Satna. American Hemp. N.O. Cannabinaceae.
The Ø is prepared from the flowering tops of the plant.

This plant affects particularly the urinary, sexual and respiratory systems, conditions being accompanied by great fatigue. There is a tendency to pneumonia, pericarditis and retention of urine: this may lead to cystitis and a mucoid blood-stained urine.

Cantharis. Spanish Fly.
The Ø is prepared by trituration of the insect with subsequent dilution in alcohol.

The poisonous substances contained in this insect attack, particularly the urinary and sexual organs setting up violent inflammation. The skin is also markedly affected, a severe vesicular rash developing with intense itching. This is a valuable remedy in nephritis and cystitis typified by frequent attempts at urination, the urine itself containing blood as a rule. It may be indicated in certain post-partum inflammations and burning vesicular eczemas.

Carbo Vegetabilis. Vegetable Charcoal.
Potencies are prepared by trituration and subsequent dilution in alcohol.

Various tissues of the body have a marked affinity with this substance. The circulatory system is particularly affected leading to lack of oxygenation with a corresponding increase of carbon dioxide in the blood and tissues. This in turn leads to a lack of resistance to infections and to haemorrhages of dark blood which does not readily coagulate. Coldness of the body surface supervenes. When potentised this is a very useful remedy in all cases of collapse. Pulmonary congestions will benefit and it restores warmth and strength in cases of circulatory weakness. It acts more on the venous than on the arterial circulation.

Carduus Marianus. St. Mary's Thistle. N.O. Compositae.
Trituration of seeds dissolved in spirits.

This remedy is indicated in disorders arising from inefficiency of liver function. The action of the liver indicates its main use in veterinary practice. Cirrhotic conditions with accompanying dropsy respond well.

Caulophyllum. Blue Cohosh. N.O. Berberidaceae.
The Ø is prepared from trituration of the root dissolved in alcohol.

This plant produces pathological states related to the mare's genital system. Extraordinary rigidity of the *os uteri* is set up leading to difficulties at parturition. Early abortions may occur due to uterine debility. These may be accompanied by fever and thirst. There is a tendency to retention of afterbirth with possible bleeding from the uterus. In potentised form this remedy will revive labour pains and could be used as an alternative to pituitrin injections once the os is open. It will be found useful in ringwomb and also in cases of uterine twist or displacement. In these cases it should be given frequently for three or four doses, e.g. hourly intervals. In mares which have had previous miscarriages it will help in establishing a normal pregnancy while post-partum it is one of the remedies to be considered for retained afterbirth.

Causticum. Potassium Hydroxide.
This substance is prepared by the distillation of a mixture of equal parts of slaked lime and potassium bisulphate.

The main affinity is with the neuro-muscular system producing weakness and paresis of both types of muscle. Symptoms are aggravated by going from a cold atmosphere to a warm one. It may be of use in bronchitic conditions of older animals and in those which develop small sessile warts. It appears to have an antidotal effect in cases of lead poisoning and could be used in this connection as an adjunct to versenate injections.

Ceonothus Americanus. New Jersey Tea. N.O. Rhamnaceae.
Tincture of fresh leaves.
Splenic conditions in general come within the range of this remedy. Tenderness of the spleen may be evident. In the mare whitish vaginal discharges may arise. Chiefly used for conditions where it is thought that the spleen is involved.

Chelidonium. Greater Celandine. N.O. Papaveraceae.
The Ø is prepared from the whole plant, fresh at the time of flowering.
A specific action on the liver is produced by this plant. There is general lethargy and indisposition. The tongue is usually coated a dirty yellow and signs of jaundice may be seen in other visible mucous membranes. The liver is constantly upset with the production of clay-coloured stools. Because of its marked hepatic action it should be remembered when dealing with disturbances associated with a sluggish liver action. It may be of use in photosensitisation if signs of jaundice occur.

Chimaphilla Umbellata. Ground Holly. N.O. Ericaceae.
The Ø is prepared from the fresh plant.
The active principle of this plant produces a marked action on the kidneys and genital system of both sexes. In the eyes cataracts may develop. The urine is mucoid and blood-stained. Enlargement of prostate gland may develop while in the mare mammary tumours and atrophy have both been recorded.

Chininum Sulphuricum. Sulphate of Quinine.
Trituration of salt dissolved in alcohol.
This salt closely resembles the action of China and should be remembered as a useful remedy in cases of debility due to loss of essential fluids. It affects the ear producing pain over the area and

excessive secretion of wax. Conditions calling for its use tend to recur after apparent or real remissions. Septic conditions following bites or injuries respond well and thereby reduce the likelihood of future tissue involvement of a septic nature.

Chionanthus Virginica. Fringe Tree.
Tincture of bark.

This remedy is indicated in sluggish states of the liver including early cases of cirrhosis, accompanying a generalised loss of condition and in extreme cases emaciation. The stools produced are clay-coloured and there may be jaundice and high-coloured urine.

Cinchona Officinalis. China Officinalis. Peruvian Bark. N.O. Rubiaceae.
The Ø is prepared from the dried bark dissolved in alcohol.

This plant is commonly referred to as 'China' and is the source of quinine. Large doses tend to produce toxic changes, e.g. nervous sensitivity, impaired leucocyte formation, haemorrhages, fever and diarrhoea. Weakness ensues from loss of body fluids. This remedy should be considered when an animal is suffering from debility or exhaustion after fluid loss, e.g. severe diarrhoea or haemorrhage. It is seldom indicated in the earlier stages of acute disease.

Cinnabaris. Mercuric Sulphide.
Trituration of salt dissolved in alcohol.

The action of this substance relates mainly to the genito-urinary sphere where conditions such as albuminuria and balanitis tend to occur. Warts develop in the inguinal area. Eye conditions are also common such as blepharitis and ophthalmia with purulent discharge. Sometimes the ear is affected producing a dry itching condition with scurf around the pinna. Chiefly used in practice where other mercurial remedies have given less than satisfactory results.

Cicuta Virosa. Water Hemlock. N.O. Umbelliferae.
The Ø is prepared from the fresh root at the time of flowering.

The central nervous system is principally affected by this plant, spasmodic affections occurring. A characteristic feature is the head and neck twisted to one side accompanied by violence of one kind or another. Aggravation occurs from jarring or sudden movement.

The general balance becomes upset and there is a tendency to fall to one side while the head and spine bend backwards. Various conditions of the brain and spinal cord may benefit from this remedy showing the typical lateral deviation of neck.

Cineraria Maritima. Dusty Miller. N.O. Compositae.
The Ø is prepared from the whole fresh plant.
  The active principle is used mainly as an external application in eye conditions. The Ø should be diluted 1/10.

Cobaltum. The Metal. Cobaltum Chloridum. The Salt.
Both these remedies are used mainly in the 30c potency in the treatment of cobalt deficiency and give good results over a period of a few weeks.

Cocculus. Indian Cockle. N.O. Menispermacrae.
The Ø is prepared from powdered seeds which contain an alkaloid pectoxin.
  The active principle produces spasmodic and paretic affections deriving from the CNS (cerebrum), not the spinal cord. There is a strong tendency to vomit due to the action on the vomiting centre which appears to be dependent on movement. Mainly used in travel sickness where symptoms agree.

Coccus Cacti. Cochineal.
The Ø is prepared from the dried bodies of the female insects.
  This substance has an affinity for mucous membranes producing catarrhal inflammation. Viscid mucus accumulates in the air passages leading to difficulty in expectoration and spasmodic coughing. Dysuria is common, the urine being scanty and leaving a reddish deposit on standing. It is mainly used in affections of the respiratory and urinary systems.

Colchicum Autumnale. Meadow Saffron. N.O. Liliaceae.
The Ø is prepared from the bulb.
  This plant affects muscular tissues, periosteum and synovial membranes of joints. It possesses also an anti-allergic and anti-inflammatory action which interferes with the natural recuperative powers of the body. Illnesses which may require this remedy are usually acute and severe, accompanied frequently by effusions in

the small joints. Autumnal diarrhoea and dysentery also may be helped, the latter accompanied by tympany and tenesmus. One of its guiding symptoms is aversion to food, while complaints requiring it are generally worse from movement.

Colocynthis. Bitter Cucumber. N.O. Cucurbitaceae.
The Ø is prepared from the fruit and contains a glucoside — colocynthin.

This plant is purgative and causes violent inflammatory lesions of the gastro-intestinal tract. Both onset of and relief from symptoms are abrupt. Diarrhoea is yellowish and forcibly expelled. Relief is obtained by movement while aggravation occurs after eating or drinking.

Condurango. Condor Plant.
The Ø is prepared from bark in tincture.

This plant produces a glucoside-condurangin which affects the nervous system causing an exaggerated gait. It can act constitutionally in promoting the general well-being of the patient. More specifically there is an action on epithelial tissue causing hardening which may lead on to tumour formation. A guiding symptom is said to be cracks at the corners of the mouth. Chiefly used as a remedy to combat incipient cancerous states especially those in the abdomen.

Conium Maculatum. Hemlock. N.O. Umbelliferae.
The Ø is prepared from the fresh plant.

The alkaloid of this plant produces a paralytic action on nerve ganglia, especially the motor nerve endings. This leads to stiffness and a paralysis which tends to travel forward or upward. This remedy is of importance in treating paraplegic conditions and any weakness of hind limbs.

Convallaria Majalis. Lily of the Valley. N.O. Liliaceae.
The Ø is prepared from the fresh plant.

The active principle has the power to increase the quality of the heart's action and this determines its main use as a remedy in congestive heart conditions. It has little action on the heart muscle and is used mainly in valvular disease.

Copaiva. Balsam of Peru. N.O. Leguminosae.
The Ø is prepared from the balsam.

This substance produces a marked action on mucous membranes, especially those of the urinary and respiratory tracts causing a catarrhal inflammation. This action makes the remedy useful in the treatment of urethritis and cystitis. Pyelonephritis is one of the commoner conditions which could be helped.

Cortisone
The potentised steroid is used in practice to combat the effects of the over prescribing of the crude substance where very often a single dose of the 200c potency will suffice along with clearing remedies such as *Nux Vomica* and *Thuja*. In lower potency e.g. 12c–30c it helps in certain skin conditions where dryness and redness predominate along with excessive itching.

Crataegus. Hawthorn. N.O. Rosaceae.
The Ø is prepared from the ripe fruit.

The active principle produces a fall in blood pressure and brings on dyspnoea. It acts on the heart muscle causing an incease in the number and quality of contractions. The specific action on the heart muscle makes this a particularly useful remedy in the treatment of arrhythmic heart conditions.

Crotalus Horridus. Rattlesnake.
The Ø is prepared from trituration of the venom with lactose and subsequent dilution in glycerine.

This venom produces sepsis, haemorrhages and jaundice with decomposition of blood. The marked action of this poison on the vascular system makes it a valuable remedy in the treatment of many low-grade septic states with circulatory involvement, e.g. puerperal fever and wound infections. Septic conditions are accompanied by oozing of blood from any body orifice and are usually attended by jaundice. It should help in conditions such as adder-bite and clover poisoning.

Croton Tiglium. Croton Oil Seeds. N.O. Euphorbiaceae.
The Ø is prepared from the oil obtained from the seeds.

This oil produces violent diarrhoea and skin eruptions causing inflammation with a tendency to vesicle formation. This is one of the many useful remedies for controlling diarrhoea. This is usually accompanied by great urging, the stool being watery.

Cryptococcus
This potentised nosode is used as for chlamaydia and calici and can be combined with them if need be in multiple infections.

Cubeba Officinalis. Cubebs. N.O. Piperaceae.
The Ø is prepared from the dried unripe fruit.

The active principle acts on mucous membranes producing a catarrhal inflammation. Those of the uro-genital tract are particularly affected, the urine becoming cloudy and albuminous.

Cuprum Aceticum. Copper Acetate.
Potencies are prepared from a solution in distilled water.

This salt produces cramping of muscles, spasms and paralytic conditions. It is used chiefly in the treatment of copper deficiency in foals, especially when accompanied by muscle cramping or stiffness. The arsenate of copper and the metal itself are similarly used.

Cuprum Metallicum. Metallic Copper.
The Ø is prepared from trituration of the metal.

The symptoms produced by this metal are characterised by violence including paroxysms of cramping pains which follow no particular pattern. Muscles become contracted and show twitchings. In the central nervous system fits and convulsions occur and may take an epileptiform nature. The head is drawn to one side.

Curare. Woorara. Arrow Poison.
The Ø is prepared from dilutions in alcohol.

This poison produces muscular paralysis without impairing sensation or consciousness. Reflex action is diminished and a state of motor paralysis sets in. It decreases the output of adrenaline and brings about a state of nervous debility.

Damiana
The active principle of this plant has an affinity for the sexual system and is used mainly to promote libido in the stallion where

sexual drive is weak. The action and results are variable but it is a remedy to keep in mind in this connection.

Digitalis Purpurea. Foxglove. N.O. Scrophulariaceae.
The Ø is prepared from the leaves.
The active principle of the foxglove causes marked slowness of the heart's action, the pulse being weak and irregular. This is a commonly used remedy in heart conditions helping to regulate the beat and producing a stable pulse. By increasing the output of the heart when used in low potencies it aids valvular function. This in turn increases the output of urine and helps reduce oedema.

Drosera Rotundifolia. Sundew. N.O. Droseraceae.
The Ø is prepared from the fresh plant.
The lymphatic and pleural systems together with synovial membranes are all affected by this plant. The laryngeal area is also subject to inflammatory processes, any timulus producing a hypersensitive reaction.

Dulcamara. Woody Nightshade. N.O. Solanaceae.
The Ø is prepared from the green stems and leaves before flowering.
This plant belongs to the same family as Belladonna, Hyoscyamus and Stramonium. Tissue affinities are with mucous membranes, glands and kidneys, producing inflammatory changes and interstitial haemorrhages. This remedy may benefit those conditions which arise as a result of exposure to wet and cold, especially when damp evenings follow a warm day. Such conditions commonly occur in autumn and diarrhoea occurring then may benefit. It has proved useful in the treatment of ringworm and could have a beneficial action on large fleshy warts.

Echinacea Angustifolia. Rudbeckia. N.O. Compositae.
The Ø is prepared from the whole plant.
Acute toxaemias with septic involvement of various tissues come within the sphere of action of this plant. It is a valuable remedy in the treatment of post-partum puerperal conditions where sepsis is evident. Generalised septic states having their origin in infected bites or stings will also benefit. This remedy acts best in low decimal potencies.

E. coli
This organism is found in the bowel and plays an essential role in the digestive process. As a remedy the nosode is used in bowel conditions where scouring develops after stress in the young animal or where the balance of the bowel flora has been interfered with.

Eel Serum.
The Ø is prepared from dried serum or solution in distilled water.

The serum of the eel produces an action on the blood equivalent to toxaemia. It affects the kidney particularly with secondary effects on the liver. Renal deposits are found in the urine along with haemoglobin. Threatened anaemic states develop. The cardiac system is also affected, sudden fainting spells being common.

Epigea Repens. Trailing Arbutus. N.O. Ericaceae.
The Ø is prepared from tincture of fresh leaves.

The main action of this remedy is on the urinary system where it produces a state of strangury with the production of renal calculi. It should be remembered in this connection as a useful remedy in cystitis of both male and female and in the treatment of urethral and bladder stones.

Euphrasia Officinalis. Eyebright. N.O. Scrophulariaceae.
The Ø is prepared from the whole plant.

The active principle acts mainly on the conjunctival mucous membrane producing lachrymation. The cornea is also affected, opacities being common. This is one of the most useful remedies in the treatment of a variety of eye conditions, principally conjunctivitis and corneal ulcerations. Internal treatment should be supplemented by its use externally as a lotion diluted 1/10.

Ferrum Iodatum. Iodide of Iron.
Potencies are prepared from trituration of crystals subsequently dissolved in alcohol.

This salt is chiefly of interest as a remedy for iron deficiency associated with respiratory distress, mucous discharges containing blood being present. Metallic iron (Ferrum Metallicum) and chloride of iron (Ferrum Muriaticum) are also used in the treatment of iron deficiency, the former particularly for younger animals and the latter more indicated when heart symptoms such as weak thready pulse are present.

Ferrum Phosphoricum. Ferric Phosphate.
Potencies are prepared from a solution in distilled water.

Febrile conditions in general are associated with this salt. It is frequently used in the early stages of inflammatory conditions which develop less rapidly than those calling for Aconitum. Throat involvement is often the key to its selection. Pulmonary congestions may call for its use if haemorrhages are also present.

Ficus Religiosa. Pakur. N.O. Moraceae.
The Ø is prepared from fresh leaves in alcohol.

Haemorrhages of various kinds are associated with the toxic effects of this plant. Any condition which produces bleeding of a bright red character may indicate the need for this remedy. It could be of value in Coccidiosis, but generally respiratory rather than digestive upsets determine its use.

Fluoricum Acidum. Hydrofluoric Acid.
Potencies are prepared by distilling calcium fluoride with sulphuric acid.

It has an action on most tissues producing deep-seated ulcers and lesions of a destructive nature. It has been used successfully in the treatment of Actinomycosis and in ulcerative conditions of the mouth and throat. Any necrotic condition of bone is likely to benefit.

Folliculinum.
This is one of the ovarian hormones which has a beneficial action on the skin. Used mainly in practice in cases of miliary eczema and alopecia of both sexes. It can also be used in the treatment of eczemas of non-hormonal origin where the typical purply rashes predominate.

Formica. Formic Acid. The Ant. N.O. Hymenoptera.
Tincture made from live ants.

This acid produces rheumatic-like pains along with deposits in the small joints. Occasionally in severe cases the spinal cord may be affected giving rise to a state of temporary paralysis. It is chiefly used in veterinary practice as an anti-arthritis remedy especially affecting carpal and tarsal areas.

Gaertner-Bach.
Marked emaciation or malnutrition is associated with this nosode. Chronic gastro-enteritis occurs and there is a tendency for the animal to become infested with worms. There is an inability to digest fat. Chiefly used in the young animal showing malnutrition associated with other digestive problems.

Gelsemium Sempervirens. Yellow Jasmine. N.O. Loganiaceae.
The Ø is prepared from the bark of the root.

The affinity of this plant is with the nervous system producing varying degrees of motor paralysis. This remedy has proved helpful as a supportive measure in hypomagnesaemia, aiding restoration of normal movement. Single paralysis of different nerves, e.g. the radial may also benefit. Conditions which call for its use are usually attended by weakness and muscle tremors.

Glonoinum. Nitro-Glycerine.
Potencies are prepared from dilutions in alcohol.

This substance has an affinity with the brain and circulatory system causing sudden and violent convulsions and also congestion in the arterial system leading to throbbing and pulsations, seen in superficial vessels. It will be found of use in brain conditions arising from over-exposure to heat or the effects of the sun. It may also help the convulsions associated with hypomagnesaemia and allied conditions.

Graphites. Black Lead.
Potencies are prepared from triturations dissolved in alcohol.

This form of carbon has an affinity with skin and hooves. Eruptions are common and its action on connective tissue tends to produce fibrotic conditions associated with malnutrition. Loss of hair occurs while purply moist eruptions ooze a sticky discharge.

Abrasions develop into ulcers which may suppurate. Favourable sites for eczema are in the bends of joints and behind the ears.

Hamamelis Virginica. Witch Hazel. N.O. Hamamelidaceae.
The Ø is prepared from fresh bark of twigs and roots.
This plant has an affinity with the venous circulation producing congestions and haemorrhages. The action on the veins is one of relaxation, with consequent engorgement. Any condition showing venous engorgement or congestion with passive haemorrhage should show improvement from the use of this remedy.

Hecla Lava. Hecla.
Potencies are prepared from trituration of the volcanic ash. Present in this ash are the substances which accompany lava formation, viz. Alumina, Lime and Silica.
Lymphoid tissue and the skeleton are areas which show the greatest affinity for this substance. The remedy is useful in the treatment of exostoses or tumours of the facial bones and in caries arising from dental disease. It has proved successful in the treatment of actino-mycosis affecting the maxillary and mandibular bones. It should help in the treatment of bony tumours generally.

Helleborus Niger. Christmas Rose. N.O. Ranunculaceae.
The Ø is produced from the juice of the fresh root.
The affinity of this plant is with the central nervous system and the alimentary canal. To a lesser extent the kidneys are involved. Vertigo-like movements arise together with convulsions. Vomiting and purging take place, stools being dysenteric. Heart action is slowed.

Hepar Sulphuris Calcareum. Impure Calcium Sulphide.
This substance is prepared by burning crude calcium carbonate with flowers of sulphur. Potencies are then prepared from the triturated ash.
This remedy is associated with suppurative processes producing conditions which are extremely sensitive to touch. It causes catarrhal and purulent inflammation of the mucous membranes of the respiratory and alimentary tracts with involvement of the skin and lymphatic system. This remedy has a wide range of action and should be considered in any suppurative process showing extreme

sensitivity to touch indicating acute pain. Low potencies of this remedy promote suppuration while high potencies — 200c and upwards — may abort the purulent process and promote resolution.

Hippozaeninum.
This nosode has been known for a long time having been made from glanders, a notifiable equine disease no longer encountered in Britain.

It has a wide range of use in many catarrhal conditions which are characterised by glutinous or honey-coloured discharges, e.g. sinusitis and ozaena with or without ulceration of nasal cartilages. It could be of great benefit in some forms of chronic viral rhinitis.

Hydrangea Arborescons. N.O. Hydrangeaceae.
The Ø is prepared from fresh leaves and young shoots.

This plant exerts a strong influence on the urinary system, especially on the bladder where it helps dissolve gravel. The prostate gland also comes within its range of action.

Hydrastis Canadensis. Golden Seal. N.O. Ranunculaceae.
The Ø is prepared from the fresh root.

Mucous membranes are affected by this plant, a catarrhal inflamma tion being established. Secretions generally are thick and yellow. Any catarrhal condition resulting in a muco-purulent discharge will come within the scope of this remedy, e.g. mild forms of metritis or sinusitis.

Hydrocotyle Asiatica. Indian Pennywort. N.O. Umbelliferae.
The Ø is prepared from the whole plant.

The main difficulty of this plant is with the skin and female genital system. It also has a lesser effect on the action of the liver. Skin conditions showing thickening of epidermis and roughening come within its sphere of action.

Hyoscyamus Niger. Henbane. N.O. Solanaceae.
The Ø is prepared from the fresh plant.

The active principle disturbs the central nervous system producing symptoms of brain excitement and mania. Conditions which call for its use are not accompanied by inflammation (cf. Belladonna).

Hypericum Perforatum. St. John's Wort. N.O. Hyperiaceae.
The Ø is prepared from the whole fresh plant.

The active principle is capable of causing sensitivity to light on some skins in the absence of melanin pigment. The main affinity is with the nervous system causing hypersensitivity. Sloughing and necrosis of skin may take place. This remedy is of prime importance in the treatment of lacerated wounds where nerve endings are damaged. In spinal injuries, especially of the coccygeal area, it gives good results. The specific action on nerves suggests its use in tetanus where, given early after injury, it helps prevent the spread of toxin. It can be used externally for lacerated wounds along with Calendula, both in a strength of 1/10. It has been found useful in the treatment of photosensitisation and similar allergies.

Iodium. Iodine. The Element.
Potencies are prepared from the tincture prepared by dissolving the element in alcohol. A 1% tincture is the strength used in preparation.

In large doses — iodism — sinuses and eyes are at first involved leading to conjunctivitis and bronchitis. Iodine has a special affinity with the thyroid gland. Weakness and atrophy of muscles may follow excessive intake. The skin becomes dry and withered looking and the appetite becomes voracious. Conditions which show a characteristic oppositeness of symptoms, e.g. tissue hyperplasia or atrophy may need this remedy. It may be of use in ovarian dysfunction when the ovaries appear small and shrunken on rectal examination. It is a useful gland remedy and its specific relation to the thyroid should not be forgotten.

Ipecacuanha. N.O. Rubiaceae.
The Ø is prepared from the dried root. Emetine, an alkaloid is its principal constituent.

This plant is associated with haemorrhages and has found a use in the treatment of post-partum bleeding where the blood comes in gushes.

Iris Versicolour. Blue Flag. N.O. Iridaceae.
The Ø is prepared from the fresh root.

This plant produces an action on various glands, principally the salivary, intestinal pancreas and thyroid. It has a reputation also for aiding the secretion of bile. Due to its action on the thyroid gland swelling of the throat may occur. The remedy is chiefly used in veterinary practice in the treatment of disorders of the pancreas where it has given consistently good results.

Kali Arsenicum. Fowler's Solution. Potassium Arsenite.
Dilutions of this salt provide the Ø.

The main action which concerns us in equine practice is exerted on the skin, a dry scaly eczema with itching being established. It is a good general skin remedy.

Kali Bichromicum. Potassium Dichromate.
Potencies are prepared from a solution in distilled water.

This salt acts on the mucous membranes of the stomach, intestines and respiratory tract with lesser involvement of other organs. Feverish states are absent. The action on the mucous membranes produces a catarrhal discharge of a tough stringy character with a yellow colour. This particular type of discharge is a strong guiding symptom for its use. It could be used in broncho-pneumonia, sinusitis and pyelonephritis.

Kali Carbonicum. Potassium Carbonate.
Potencies are prepared from a solution in distilled water.

This salt is found in all plants and in the soil, the colloid material of cells containing potassium.

It produces a generalised weakness which is common to other potassium salts. Feverish states are absent. It could be a useful convalescent remedy.

Kali Chloricum. Potassium Chlorate.
Potencies are prepared from a solution in distilled water.

The urinary organs are chiefly affected, producing a blood-stained and albuminous urine with a high phosphate content.

Kali Hydriodicum. Potassium Iodide.
Potencies are prepared from triturations dissolved in alcohol.

This important drug produces an acrid watery discharge from the eyes and also acts on fibrous and connective tissue. Glandular swellings also appear. This is a widely used remedy in various conditions showing the typical eye and respiratory symptoms.

Kreosotum. Beechwood Kreosote.
The Ø is prepared from solution in rectified spirit.

This substance produces haemorrhages from small wounds with burning discharges and ulcerations. It also causes rapid decomposition of body fluids. Blepharitis occurs with a tendency to gangrene of the skin, while in the mare dark blood appears from the uterus. This substance has been successfully used in threatened gangrenous states showing the typical early stages of spongy bleeding and ulceration.

Lachesis. Bushmaster. Surucucu Snake.
Trituration of venom dissolved in alcohol is the source of the solution which yields the potencies.

This venom produces decomposition of blood rendering it more fluid. There is a strong tendency to haemorrhage and sepsis with profound prostration. This is a useful remedy for adder bites helping to prevent septic complications and reducing swelling. It is particularly valuable if the throat develops inflammation causing left-sided swelling which may involve the parotid gland. Where haemorrhage takes place the blood is dark and does not clot readily while the skin surrounding any lesion assumes a purplish appearance.

Lathyrus Sativus. Chick Pea. N.O. Leguminosae.
The Ø is prepared from the flower and the pods.

This plant affects the anterior columns of the spinal cord producing paralysis of the lower extremities. Nerve power generally is weakened. It should be considered in recumbent conditions associated with mineral deficiencies and in any state involving nerve weakness leading to local paralysis.

Ledum Palustre. Marsh Tea. Wild Rosemary. N.O. Ericaceae.
The Ø is prepared from the whole plant.

The active principle produces tetanus-like symptoms with twitching of muscles. It is one of the main remedies for punctured wounds, especially when the surrounding area becomes cold and discoloured. Insect bites respond well. Also injuries to the eye.

Lemna Minor. Duckweed. N.O. Lemnaceae.
The Ø is prepared from whole fresh plants.

This is a remedy for catarrhal conditions affecting mainly the nasal passages: a muco-purulent nasal discharge develops which is extremely offensive. In the alimentary sphere diarrhoea and flatulence can occur.

Lilium Tigrinum. Tiger Lily. N.O. Liliaceae.
The Ø is prepared from fresh leaves and flowers.

The action is mainly on the pelvic organs producing conditions which arise from uterine or ovarian disturbances. Urine is scanty and frequently passed. An irregular pulse accompanies an increased heart rate. Congestion and blood-stained discharges arise from the uterus and there may be slight prolapse. Indicated in some forms of pyometra where blood is present and also in ovarian disturbances.

Lithium Carbonicum. Lithium Carbonate.
The Ø is prepared from trituration of the dried salt.

This salt produces a chronic arthritic state with a uric acid diathesis. There is difficulty in passing urine which contains mucus and a red sandy deposit. Cystitis develops leading to a dark urine. It is a useful remedy to consider in some forms of arthritis and urinary conditions producing uric acid deposits.

Lobelia Inflata. Indian Tobacco. N.O. Lobeliaceae.
The Ø is prepared from the dried leaves with subsequent dilution in alcohol.

The active principle acts as a vaso-motor stimulant impeding respiration and producing symptoms of inappetance and relaxation of muscles. It is of value in emphysematous conditions and as a general convalescent remedy.

Lycoplus Virginicus. Bugle Weed. N.O. Labiatae.
The Ø is prepared from fresh whole plant.

The active principle of this plant reduces blood pressure and causes passive haemorrhages. The main sphere of action which concerns veterinary practice is on the cardiac system where the pulse becomes weak and irregular. The heart's action is increased and is accompanied by difficult breathing and cyanosis. Breathing assumes a wheezy character and may produce a blood-tinged cough.

Lycopodium Clavatum. Club Moss. N.O. Lycopodiaceae.
The Ø is prepared from trituration of the spores and dilution in alcohol. The spores are inactive until triturated and potentised.

The active principle acts chiefly on the digestive and renal systems. The respiratory system is also affected, pneumonia being a frequent complication. There is general lack of gastric function and very little food will satisfy. The abdomen becomes bloated with tenderness over the liver. The glycogenic function of the liver is interfered with. This is a very useful remedy in various digestive, urinary and respiratory conditions, a guiding symptom being that complaints frequently show an aggravation in the late afternoon or early evening. It is the first remedy of choice in the digestive form of acetonaemia while its action on the skin suggests its use in alopecia.

Magnesia Phosphorica. Phosphate of Magnesium.
Potencies are prepared from trituration of the salt in solution.

This salt acts on muscles producing a cramping effect with spasm. It is a valuable remedy to be remembered as supportive treatment in hypomagnesaemia where its prompt use will limit the tendency to brain damage and help fix the element in the system, as otherwise it may be quickly excreted.

Malandrinum.
This nosode has been developed from the condition known as grease in the horse after trituration of affected material and discharge.

It is used mainly in the treatment of chronic skin eruptions and discharges. In this connection it is worth remembering as a remedy which might help some forms of ear canker.

Melilotus. Sweet Clover. N.O. Leguminosae.
The Ø is prepared from the whole fresh plant.

This plant is associated with profuse haemorrhages. Clover contains a haemolytic agent which prevents clotting of blood after mechanical injuries. This is more likely to happen if animals are fed mouldy hay. It should be remembered as a possibly useful remedy in haematomas and subcutaneous bleeding of unknown origin.

Mercurius. Mercurius Solubilis. Mercury.
Potencies are prepared from triturations and dilutions in alcohol.

This metal affects most organs and tissues producing cellular degeneration with consequent anaemia. Salivation accompanies most complaints and gums become spongy and bleed easily. Diarrhoea is common, stools being slimy and blood-stained. Conditions calling for its use are worse in the period sunset to sunrise.

Mercurius Corrosivus. Mercuric Chloride. Corrosive Sublimate.
Potencies are prepared from triturations and subsequent dilution.

This salt has a somewhat similar action to mercurius sol., but generally the symptoms produced are more severe. It produces severe tenesmus of the lower bowel leading to dysentery and also has a destructive action on kidney tissue. Discharges from mucous surfaces assume a greenish tinge. It could be of value in severe cases of coccidiosis.

Mercurius Cyanatus. Cyanate of Mercury.
Potencies are prepared from triturations and dilutions.

This particular salt produces an action similar to that associated with bacterial toxins. A haemorrhagic tendency with prostration is a common feature. Ulceration of the mucous membranes of the mouth and throat commonly occur which suggests its use in foal diphtheria. A greyish membrane surrounds these ulcerated surfaces. The phyaryngeal area is one of the main regions to be affected, redness of the membrane preceding necrosis in the later stages.

Mercurius Dulcis. Calomel. Mercurous Chloride.
Potencies are prepared from triturations and dilution.

This salt has an affinity with the ear and liver especially. Hepatitis with jaundice may result. It is worth considering as a possibly useful remedy in mild forms of cirrhosis.

Mercurius Iodatus Flavus. Yellow Iodide of Mercury.
Potencies are prepared from triturations in dilution.

Mercurous Iodide produces a tendency to glandular induration with attendant coating of the tongue. Sub-maxillary and parotid glands become swollen, more pronounced on the right side.

Various swellings of glandular tissue come within the sphere of this remedy, e.g. parotitis and lymphadenitis generally. It could be of value in actinobacillosis when lesions attack on the right side.

Mercurius Iodatus Ruber. Red Iodide of Mercury.
Potencies are prepared from trituration of the salt.

Mercuric Iodide also has a tendency to produce glandular swellings, but in this case the left side of the throat is involved. Stiffness of neck mucles may be a prominent symptom.

Millefolium. Yarrow. N.O. Compositae.
The Ø is prepared from the whole plant.

Haemorrhages occur from various parts from the action of this plant. The blood is bright red.

Mineral Extract.
This substance has recently been researched and has been shown to have a beneficial effect on certain forms of joint trouble, e.g. arthritis and stiffness especially of the carpal and tarsal areas.

Mixed Grasses.
Some animals show an allergic response to grasses in early spring and summer when excessive itching and skin lesions develop. A combination of various grasses in potency appear to help these conditions and can be combined with other selected remedies.

Morgan-Bach.
Clinical observation has revealed the symptom picture of the bacillus Morgan to cover in general digestive and respiratory conditions with a secondary action on fibrous tissues and skin used mainly in practice to treat inflammatory conditions especially acute eczema combined with appropriate remedies.

Murex Purpurea. Purple Fish.
The Ø is prepared from the dried secretion of the purple gland of one of the Murex species.

It exerts its action mainly on the female genital system producing irregularities of the oestrus cycle. It has been employed both in anoestrus and for stimulating ovulation, but probably it will give best results in cystic ovary leading to nymphomania.

Muriatic Acid. Hydrochloric Acid.
Potencies are prepared from dilutions, in distilled water.

This acid produces a blood condition analogous to that associated with septic feverish states of a chronic nature. There is a tendency for ulcers to form. The throat becomes dark red and oedematous while ulceration of lips accompanies swollen gums and neck glands.

Naja Tripudians. Cobra.
Potencies are prepared from trituration of the venom and subsequent dilution in alcohol. Alternatively the Ø may be prepared by dilution of the pure venom.

This poison produces a bulbar paralysis. Haemorrhages are scanty but oedema is marked. The underlying tissues appear dark purple after a bite, blood-stained fluid being present in large quantities. Loss of limb control supervenes. The heart is markedly affected. It could be of use in angio-neurotic oedema.

Natrum Muriaticum. Common Salt. Sodium Chloride.
Potencies are prepared from triturations dissolved in distilled water.

Excessive intake of common salt leads to anaemia, evidenced by dropsy or oedema of various parts. White blood cells are increased while mucous membranes are rendered dry. This is a remedy which is of value in unthrifty conditions arising as a result of anaemia or chronic nephritis.

Natrum Sulphoricum. Sodium Sulphate.
The Ø is prepared from trituration of the salt.

Glauber's salts (as it is commonly called) produces a state of weakness where the animal has been exposed to damp. The liver is affected and there is a tendency to wart formation. Hepatitis sometimes occurs with jaundice. Flatulent distension and watery diarrhoea supervene. Experience has shown that this remedy has proved to be of great value where there has been a history of head injury leading to a variety of seemingly unrelated conditions.

Nitricum Acidum. Nitric Acid.
Potencies are prepared from a solution in distilled water.

This acid affects particularly body outlets where skin and mucous membranes meet. It produces ulceration and blisters in the mouth and causes offensive discharges. The ulceration may also affect mucous membranes elsewhere and it has been of benefit in some forms of mucosal disease.

Nux Vomica. Poison Nut. N.O. Loganiaeceae.
The Ø is prepared from the seeds.

Digestive disturbances and congestions are associated with this plant, flatulence and indigestion being commonly encountered. Stools are generally hard.

Ocimum Canum. N.O. Labiatae.
The Ø is prepared from the fresh leaves.

This remedy exerts its action mainly on the urinary system producing a turbid urine of a deep yellow colour. The urine itself is slimy and purulent with a musky sweet smell. Mainly used in urinary disturbances showing the typical symptoms.

Opium. Poppy. N.O. Papaveraceae.
The Ø is prepared from the powder after trituration.

Opium produces an insensibility of the nervous system with stupor and torpor. There is lack of vital reaction. All complaints are characterised by soporific states. Pupils are contracted and the eyes assume a staring look.

Ovarium.
This is also one of the ovarian hormones in potency. It covers a range of action similar to Folliculinum but the results have been shown to be less satisfactory than with the latter remedy.

Palladium. The Metal.
Potencies are prepared from triturations and subsequent dilution in alcohol.

This element produces its main action on the female genital system, especially the ovaries causing an inflammation with a tendency to pelvic peritonitis. The right ovary is more usually affected. Pelvic disorders arising as a result of ovaritis should also benefit.

Pancreas — Pancreatinum.
The Ø is prepared from pancreas extract after trituration.

It is used on various disorders of the pancreas either on its own or combined with selected remedies to suit the individual case. In pancreatitis it can be used along with the digestive enzyme Trypsin.

Pareira. Velvet Leaf. N.O. Menispermaceae.
The Ø is prepared from tincture of fresh root.

The active principle of this plant exerts its action mainly on the urinary system producing catarrhal inflammation of the bladder with a tendency to calculus formation. In the mare there may be vaginal or uterine discharge. It is a useful remedy to consider in cases of vesical calculus where the animal is presented with acute strangury and distress.

Parotidinum.
This is the nosode of mumps and in veterinary practice it is a useful remedy in the treatment of cases of parotid gland swellings and associated structures. It may be used either on its own or combined with indicated remedies.

Pasteurella.
This is a nosode prepared from cultures of the Pasteurella organism in cases of disease. It is usually potentised to 30c and used along with selected remedies in cases of pasteurellosis.

Petroleum. Rock Spirit.
The Ø is prepared from the oil.

This substance produces cutaneous eruptions and catarrhal mucous membranes. Eczematous eruptions develop around ears and eyelids and feet producing fissures which are slow to heal. The skin is usually dry. Complaints are usually worse in cold weather. A useful remedy for some forms of chronic skin conditions where symptoms agree.

Phosphoricum Acidum. Phosphoric Acid.
Potencies are prepared from a dilution of the acid in distilled water.

This acid produces a debilitating state in which flatulence and diarrhoea are common features.

Phosphorus. The Element.
The Ø is prepared from trituration of red phosphorus.

This important substance produces an inflammatory and degenerative effect on mucous membranes and causes bone destruction and necrosis of liver and other parenchymatous organs. It has a profound effect on eye structures especially the retina and iris. There is a marked haemorrhagic diathesis associated with this remedy, and small haemorrhages appear on skin and mucous membranes. Its uses in practice are wide and varied and it is one of the most important remedies in the pharmacopoeia.

Phytolacca Decandra. Pore Root. N.O. Phytolaccaceae.
The Ø is prepared from the whole fresh plant.
A state of restlessness and prostration is associated with this plant, together with glandular swellings. It is chiefly used in veterinary practice to combat swellings of the mammary glands in particular when the glands become hard and painful.

Platina. The Metal Platinum.
The Ø is prepared from trituration of the metal with lactose.
This metal has a specific action on the female genital system, especially the ovaries where inflammation readily develops. Cystic ovaries develop frequently.

Plumbum Metallicum. The Metal Lead.
The Ø is prepared from trituration with sugar of milk.
A state of paralysis preceded by pain is produced by exposure to or ingestion with lead. It affects the central nervous system and also causes liver damage leading to jaundiced states. Blood pictures show anaemia. Paralyses of lower limbs develop and convulsions are common leading to coma. It should be remembered as a useful remedy to consider in degenerative renal states associated with liver involvement.

Podophyllum. May Apple. N.O. Ranuculaceae.
The Ø is prepared from the whole fresh plants.
The active principle of this plant exerts its action mainly on the duodenum and small intestine causing an enteritis. The liver and rectum are also affected. Distension of the abdomen occurs with a

tendency to lie on the abdomen. Colicky pains develop with tenderness over the liver. A watery greenish diarrhoea may alternate with constipation. It is a useful remedy for gastro-intestinal disorders of young animals especially and for liver and perital congestion.

Pseudomonas.
This is the potentised organism used in the treatment of cases of Pseudomonas infection. It can be combined with selected remedies in this event.

Psorinum. Scabies Vesicle.
The Ø is prepared from trituration of the dried vesicle.
   This nosode produces a state of debility, especially after acute illness with skin symptoms predominating. All discharges are unpleasant. Chronic ophthalmia is occasionally seen along with otitis media and externa producing an offensive brownish dis-charge. Skin conditions are accompanied by severe itching. Animals needing this remedy prefer warmth.

Ptelea. Water Ash. N.O. Rutaceae.
The Ø is prepared from the bark or root.
   This plant produces its main action on the stomach and liver. Hepatitis occurs with tenderness over liver and stomach areas. This is a good 'cleansing' remedy in that it will aid elimination of toxins and thereby help clear conditions such as eczema and asthmatic tendencies.

Pulsatilla. Anemone. N.O. Ranunculaceae.
The Ø is prepared from the entire plant when in flower.
   Mucous membranes come within the sphere of action of this plant, thick muco-purulent discharges being produced. It has proved useful in the treatment of ovarian hypofunction and in retained placenta.

Pyrogenium. Artificial Sepsin.
The Ø is prepared from solutions of raw protein in distilled water.
   This nosode has a specific relation to septic inflammations associated with offensive discharges. It is indicated in all septic conditions where the animal presents a clinical picture of raised

temperature alternating with a weak thready pulse, or vice versa. It should be used in potencies of 200c and upwards.

Ranunculus Bulbosus. Buttercup. N.O. Ranunculaceae.
The Ø is prepared from the whole plant.

The action is mainly on muscular tissue and skin producing a hypersensitivity to touch. Skin lesions take the form of papular and vesicular eruptions which may cluster together into over-shaped groups.

Rescue Remedy.
This is one of the many Bach Flower remedies and possibly the one most widely known and used. These remedies are not potentised like homoeopathic remedies but have been shown in practice to exert remarkable curative properties. Rescue remedy is used to benefit the patient after exposure to any traumatic experience e.g. stress, shock and post-operative trauma. A very useful remedy to revive weak foals after birth.

Rhododendron. Snow Rose. N.O. Ericaceae.
The Ø is prepared from the fresh leaves.

This shrub is associated with muscular and joint stiffness. Orchitis is not uncommon with the testicles becoming hard and indurated.

Rhus Toxicodendron. Poison Oak. N.O. Anacardiaceae.
The Ø is prepared from the fresh leaves.

The active principles of this tree affect skin and muscles together with mucous membranes and fibrous tissues producing tearing pains and blistery eruptions. Symptoms of stiffness are relieved by movement. Involvement of the skin leads to a reddish rash with vesicles and produces a cellulitis of neighbouring tissues. It could be a useful remedy in muscle and joint conditions which show a characteristic improvement on exercise.

Rumex Crispus. Yellow Dock. N.O. Polygonaceae.
The Ø is prepared from the fresh root.

The active principle of this plant causes a diminution in the secretions from mucous membranes. Chronic gastritis occurs accompanied by an aversion to food and a watery diarrhoea.

Mucous discharges take place from the trachea and nose. These tend to assume a frothy appearance. It is a useful remedy in some forms of respiratory affections.

Ruta Graveolens. Rue. N.O. Rutaceae.
The Ø is prepared from the whole fresh plant.

Ruta produces its action on the periosteum and cartilages with a secondary effect on eyes and uterus. Deposits form around the carpal joints, particularly. It has also a selective action on the lower bowel and rectum and could prove useful in mild forms of rectal prolapse. It has been known to facilitate labour by increasing the tone of uterine contractions.

Sabina. Savine. N.O. Coniferae.
The Ø is prepared from the oil dissolved in alcohol.

The uterus is the main seat of action producing a tendency to abortion. There is also an action of fibrous tissues and serous membranes. It is associated with haemorrhages of bright red blood which remains fluid. This remedy has its main use in uterine conditions including retained placenta. Persistent post-partum bleeding may also be arrested.

Sanguinaria. Blood Root. N.O. Papaveraceae.
The Ø is prepared from the fresh root.

An alkaloid — sanguinarine — contained in this plant has an affinity with the circulatory system leading to congestion and redness of skin. The female genital system is affected, inflammation of ovaries occurring. Small cutaneous haemorrhages arise in various sites. Stiffness of fore-legs, especially the left shoulder region may be seen.

Secale Cornutum. Ergot of Rye. N.O. Fungi.
The Ø is prepared from the fresh fungus.

Ergot produces marked contraction of smooth muscle causing a diminution of blood supply to various areas. This is particularly seen in peripheral blood vessels, especially of the feet. Stools are dark green alternating with dysentery. Bleeding of dark blood occurs from the uterus with putrid discharges. The skin becomes dry and shrivelled-looking with a tendency for gangrene to form. Because of its circulatory action and its effect on smooth muscle it is useful in some uterine conditions, e.g. post-partum bleeding of dark blood and in any condition with impairment of peripheral circulation.

Sepia Officinalis. Cuttlefish.
Potencies are prepared from trituration of the dried liquid from the ink bag.

Portal congestion and stasis are associated with this substance along with disturbances of function in the female genital system. Prolapse of uterus may occur or a tendency thereto. It will regulate the entire oestrus cycle and should always be given as a routine preliminary remedy in treatment. It has also an action on the skin and has given good results in the treatment of ringworm. Post-partum discharges of various sorts will usually respond. It is also capable of encouraging the natural maternal instinct in those mares which are indifferent or hostile to their offspring.

Silicea. Pure Flint.
Potencies are prepared from triturations dissolved in alcohol.

The main action of this substance is on bone where it is capable of causing caries and necrosis. It also causes abscesses and fistulae of connective tissue with secondary fibrous growths. There is a tendency for all wounds to suppurate. This is a widely used remedy indicated in many suppurative processes of a chronic nature.

Solidago Virga. Golden Rod. N.O. Compositae.
The Ø is prepared from the whole fresh plant.

This plant produces an inflammatory action on parenchymatous organs, particularly the kidney. The urine is scanty, reddish and accompanied by albumen deposits. Prostatic enlargement is frequently encountered. It is a useful remedy to consider in certain cases of renal insufficiency either with or without prostatic enlargement in the stallion.

Spigelia. Pink Root. N.O. Loganacea.
The Ø is prepared from the dried herb.

This plant has an affinity for the nervous system and also exerts an action on the cardiac region and the eye, producing ophthalmia and dilated pupils. A useful remedy for certain eye conditions especially if pain above the eyes can be elicited from the patient.

Spongia Tosta. Roasted Sponge.
Potencies are prepared from dilutions in alcohol.

This substance produces symptoms related to the respiratory and cardiac spheres. The lymphatic system is also affected. The thyroid gland becomes enlarged. The general action on glands suggests its use in lymphadenitis. It is principally used as a heart remedy after respiratory infections.

Squilla Maritima. Sea Onion. N.O. Liliaceae.
The Ø is prepared from the dried bulb.

This substance acts especially on the mucous membranes of the respiratory tract. The digestive and renal systems are also affected. Nasal discharges develop accompanied by a dry cough which later becomes mucoid. There is urging to urinate, the urine being watery and profuse. It is a useful remedy for heart and kidney affections being especially valuable in dropsical conditions.

Staphisagria. Stavesacre. N.O. Ranunculaceae.
The Ø is prepared from the seeds.

The nervous system is mainly involved with this plant but there is also an action on the genito-urinary tract and the skin. A useful remedy in cystitis, but probably its most important indication is as a post-operative remedy where it acts on the mental level reducing psychological trauma and hastening the healing of wounds. It is also of benefit in the treatment of hormonal eczemas and alopecias.

Stramonium. Thorn Apple. N.O. Solanaceae.
The Ø is prepared from the whole fresh plant and fruit.

The active principle of this shrub produces its main action on the central nervous system, especially the cerebrum, producing a staggering gait with a tendency to fall forward on to the left side. Dilation of pupils occurs with a fixed staring look. A useful remedy to consider in brain disturbances where overall symptoms agree.

Streptococcus and Staphylococcus.
Streptococcus nosode is used in conditions associated with infections by this organism, e.g. erythematous rashes, tonsillitis and nephritis with associated pyelitis. It can be combined with other selected remedies. Staphylococcus aurens is the main remedy to

consider in staphylococcal affections, e.g. abscesses. These nosodes are used usually in 30c potency.

Strophanthus. Onage. N.O. Apocynaceae.
The Ø is prepared from the seeds dissolved in alcohol.

This shrub produces an increase in the contractile power of striped muscle. It acts especially on the heart increasing systole. The amount of urine passed is increased and albuminuria may be present. This is a useful heart remedy to help remove oedema. It is a safe and useful diuretic especially for the older animal.

Strychninum. Strychnine. Alkaloid Contained in Nux Vomica.
Potencies are prepared from solutions in distilled water.

This alkaloid stimulates the motor centres of the spinal cord and increases the depth of respirations. All reflexes are rendered more active and pupils become dilated. Rigidity of muscles occurs especially of the neck and back with jerking and twitching of limbs. Muscle tremors and tetanic convulsions set in rapidly. This remedy may prove useful in severe forms of hypomagnesaemia or cerebro-cortical necrosis if the specific symptoms are present.

Sulfonal. A derivative of Coal Tar.
The Ø is prepared from solution in alcohol or trituration with lactose.

This substance affects the central nervous system causing irregular movements, twitchings and incoordination of muscles which become stiff with a paralytic tendency. A useful remedy to consider in cases of cerebro-cortical affections showing the typical neuro-muscular symptoms.

Sulphur. The Element.
Potencies are prepared from trituration and subsequent dilution in alcohol.

This element has a wide range of action, but it is chiefly used in skin conditions such as mange and eczema and also as an inter-current remedy to aid the action of other remedies.

Symphytum. Comfrey. N.O. Boraginaceae.
The Ø is prepared from the fresh plant.

The root of this plant produces a substance which stimulates growth of epithelium on ulcerated surfaces and hastens union of bone in fractures. It should always be given as a routine remedy in fractures as an aid to healing. Together with other vulneraries like arnica it is indicated in the treatment of injuries in general. It is also a prominent eye remedy.

Syzygium. Jumbul. N.O. Myrtaceae.
The Ø is prepared from trituration of seeds and subsequent dilution in alcohol.

This plant exerts an action on the pancreas and this defines its use in practice, especially in diabetes where it reduces the specific gravity of the urine and reduces thirst and controls output of urine.

Tabacum Tobacco.
This substance produces nausea and vomiting with intermittent pulse and weakness. In extreme cases there is a picture of muscular weakness and collapse.

Tarentula Hispanica. Spanish Spider.
The Ø is prepared from trituration of the whole insect.

Hysterical states are associated with this poison, and there is also a stimulatory action on the uro-genital system. A useful remedy to consider in cases of hysteria and epilepsy accompanied or preceded by excitement. Excessive libido (satyriasis) in the stallion may be helped.

Tellurium. The Metal.
The Ø is prepared from trituration with lactose.

This element exerts an influence on skin, eyes and ears. There is also an action on the sacral region. Cataracts and conjunctivitis develop. In the skin herpetic eruptions appear which assume an annular shape. This remedy is a useful one to consider in some forms of ear trouble where eruptions appear on the ear flap.

Terebinthinae. Oil of Turpentine.
Potencies are prepared from a solution in alcohol.

Haemorrhages are produced from various surfaces, urinary symptoms predominating. There is difficulty in urinating and blood commonly occurs in the urine. Bleeding may also take place in the uterus, especially after parturition. It is principally used in acute nephritis associated with haematuria and a sweet-smelling urine.

This odour has been likened to that of violets. It also has a use in the treatment of gaseous bloat when low potencies will help.

Thallium Acetas.
The metallic salt is triturated and dissolved in alcohol.

This metal exerts an action on the endocrine system and also on the skin and neuro-muscular system where it produces paralysis followed by muscular atrophy. The skin conditions frequently result in alopecia. It is used mainly in the treatment of trophic skin conditions e.g. chronic alopecia and myelitis.

Thlaspi Bursa Pastoralis. Shepherd's Purse. N.O. Cruciferae.
The Ø is prepared from the fresh plant.

This plant produces haemorrhages with a uric acid diathesis. It favours expulsion of blood clots from the uterus and is indicated after miscarriage. There is frequency of urination, the urine being heavy and turbid with a reddish sediment. Cystitis is commonly seen with blood-stained urine.

Thuja Occidentalis. Arbor Vitae. N.O. Coniferae.
The Ø is prepared from fresh twigs.

Thuja produces a condition which favours the formation of warty growths and tumours. It acts mainly on the skin and uro-genital system. Warts and herpetic eruptions develop, the neck and abdomen being the favourite sites. This remedy is of great importance in the treatment of skin conditions accompanied by the development of warty growths which bleed easily. Papillomatous warts are especially influenced and this action may be enhanced by the external application of the remedy in Ø form.

Thyroidium. Thyroid Gland.
Potencies are prepared from triturations and dilution in alcohol.

Anaemia, emaciation and muscular weakness are associated with excess of thyroid secretion. There is dilation of pupils with prominence. Heart rate is increased. This remedy may be of use in the treatment of alopecia and allied skin conditions.

Trinitrotoluene.
Potencies are prepared from a solution in distilled water.

This substance exerts a destructive influence on red blood cells causing haemolysis with consequent loss of haemoglobin. This produces anaemia and this is the principle of treatment by this remedy. It could be of use in babesiasis and similar conditions.

Tuberculinum Bovinum.
This nosode should be considered if a case of tuberculosis is encountered, but apart from this it is indicated in the treatment of osteomyelitis and some forms of peritonitis and pleurisy with effusions.

Uranium Nitricum. Uranium Nitrate.
The Ø is prepared from solution in distilled water.

Glycosuria and polyuria are the main objective symptoms associated with the provings of this salt. There is a marked action on the pancreas where it influences digestive function. Large amounts of urine are passed. This is a useful remedy in pancreatitis where it follows well after the remedy Iris versicolor.

Urtica Urens. Stinging Nettle. N.O. Urticaceae.
The Ø is prepared from the fresh plant.

The nettle causes agalactia with a tendency to the formation of calculi. There is a general uric acid diathesis with urticarial swellings being present on the skin. There is diminished secretion of urine. The mammary glands become enlarged with surrounding oedema. This is a very useful remedy in various renal and skin conditions. In the treatment of uric acid tendencies it acts by thickening the urine which contains increased deposits of urates.

Ustillago Maydis. Corn Smut. N.O. Fungi.
The Ø is prepared from trituration of the fungus with lactose.

This substance has an affinity for the genital organs of both sexes, particularly the mare where the uterus is markedly affected. Alopecia of varying degrees develop accompanying a dry coat. Uterine bleeding occurs, the blood being bright red and partly clotted. Haemorrhages occur post-partum. In the stallion satyriasis occurs and this leads to one of its main uses in veterinary practice to control excessive sexual activity. The uterine action should not be overlooked.

Uva Ursi. Bearberry. N.O. Ericaceae.
The Ø is prepared from dried leaves and fruit.

The active principles are associated with disturbances of the urinary system. Cystitis commonly occurs and the urine may contain blood, pus and mucus. Kidney involvement is usually confined to the pelvis causing a purulent inflammation. This is one of the main remedies used in the treatment of cystitis and pyelonephritis.

Veratrum Album. White Hellebore. N.O. Liliaceae.
The Ø is prepared from root stocks.

A picture of collapse is presented by the action of this plant. Extremities become cold and signs of cyanosis appear. Purging occurs, the watery diarrhoea being accompanied by exhaustion. The body surface quickly becomes cold and the stools are greenish. Signs of abdominal pain precede the onset of diarrhoea.

Viburnum Opulis. Water Elder. Cranberry. N.O. Caprifoliaceae.
The Ø is prepared from the fresh bark.

Muscular cramps are associated with the action of this plant. The female genital system is markedly affected, chiefly the uterus producing a tendency to abortion in the first quarter of pregnancy, sterility being a common sequel. It is principally used in the treatment of animals with a history of repeated miscarriages.

Vipera. Common Viper.
Potencies are prepared from diluted venom.

This poison causes paresis of the hind limbs with a tendency to paralysis. Symptoms extend upwards. Skin and subcutaneous tissues become swollen after a bite with livid tongue and swollen lips developing. Disturbances of liver function produce a jaundice of visible mucous membranes. Inflammation of veins occurs with attendant oedema. Oedematous states arising from venous congestion provide conditions suitable for its use and it should be remembered as a possibly useful remedy in liver dysfunction.

Zincum Metallicum. Zinc. The Metal.
Potencies are prepared from trituration with subsequent dilution in alcohol.

This element produces a state of anaemia with a decrease in the number of red cells. There is a tendency to fall towards the left side with weakness and trembling of muscles. It is a useful remedy in suppressed feverish states accompanied by anaemia and may prove useful in brain conditions showing typical symptoms.

Nosodes and Oral Vaccines

Reference to nosodes and oral vaccines has already been made in the preface to this book, and it is only necessary to add that all disease products are rendered innocuous after the third centesimal potency which is equivalent to a strength or dilution of 1/ 1,000,000. They are used in the 30c potency.

Bacillinum.
This remedy is prepared from tuberculous material. It has a limited use in equine practice, but it is extremely useful in the treatment of ringworm and similar skin diseases.

Carcinosin.
The Nosode of Carcinoma.
   This little used remedy in equine practice can be helpful in cases of glandular enlargements accompanied by feverish states.

E. Coli Nosode and Oral Vaccine.
Prepared from various strains of E. Coli. It has been found in practice that the strain which has given the most consistent results is the one which was prepared originally from a human source. Both treatment and prevention of coli-bacillosis come within its range and also the specific form of mastitis associated with E. Coli infection.

Folliculinum.
The nosode prepared from the corpus luteum is used chiefly in the treatment of various ovarian and allied conditions.

Oopherinum.
This is the actual ovarian hormone. Ovarian troubles come within its sphere of action, e.g. sterility dependent on ovarian dysfunction. It also has been used in some forms of skin disorder thought to be associated with hormone imbalance.

Psorinum. Scabies Vesicle.
This is a valuable skin remedy. Ringworm may respond as well as other conditions attended by dry coat and great itching.

Pyrogenium. Pyrogen.
This nosode is prepared from decaying animal protein. Despite its origin it is an extremely valuable remedy in the treatment of septicaemic or toxaemic states where vital reserves are low. One of the main indications for its use is illness attended by a high temperature alternating with a weak thready pulse, or alternatively a low temperature with a firm pulse. All discharges and septic states are extremely offensive. It could have a vital part to play in puerperal feverish conditions, and has been used in retained afterbirth after abortions.

Salmonella Nosode and Oral Vaccine.
Prepared from the common Salmonella organisms associated with this disease and used both prophylactically and therapeutically.

Streptococcus Nosode and Oral Vaccine.
Prepared from strains of haemolytic streptococci. It is used in various infections associated with these bacteria.

Sycotic Co. One of the Bowel Nosodes.
This is one of a group of nosodes prepared from the non-lactose fermenting bacilli found in the large intestine. Each one is related to certain homoeopathic remedies and used mainly in conjunction with them. They are also used by themselves. Sycotic Co. has been used successfully in intestinal conditions producing catarrhal inflammation on mucous membranes.

Tuberculinum Aviare.
Avian sources provide the material for this nosode.
This nosode may prove useful in the treatment of some forms of pneumonia, along with indicated remedies. Chronic conditions are the most likely to benefit.

Index

When using the index, please begin with the specific (e.g. cough) and work back to the general (e.g. resiratory tract). Entries use the words shown in the text and there are consequently several ways of describing a condition (e.g. bloating, distention, swelling etc.): although cross references to similar and related terms are given, if you cannot find the particular word you are looking for, please look up a similar term which should lead you to the information you need.

Major entries are numbered in bold.